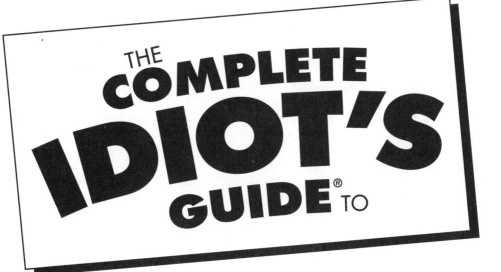

C++

by Paul Snaith

alpha
books

201 W. 103rd Street, Indianapolis, IN 46290

The Complete Idiot's Guide to C++

Copyright © 1999 by *Alpha Books*

International Standard Book Number: 0-7897-1816-2

Library of Congress Catalog Card Number: 98-86974

Printed in the United States of America

First Printing: November 1998

03 02 01   7   6   5

Trademarks

Warning and Disclaimer

Executive Editor
Tracy Dunkelberger

Acquisitions Editor
Holly Allender

Development Editor
Sean Dixon

Managing Editor
Jodi Jensen

Senior Editor
Susan Ross Moore

Copy Editor
Kate Talbot

Illustrator
Judd Winick

Indexer
Erika Millen

Proofreader
Eddie Lushbaugh

Technical Editor
Angela Murdock

Software Development Specialist
Michael Hunter

Team Coordinator
Michelle Newcomb

Cover Design
Michael Freeland

Layout Technicians
Ayanna Lacey
Heather Miller

Contents at a Glance

The following material can be found on the book's companion CD-ROM:

Contents

14 The Parallel Array Is Dead, Long Live the Structure 153

15 The Best of Both Worlds: Structures Meet Functions 163

About the Author

Paul Snaith. As you might have gathered from the book cover, I'm called Paul. I've had a rather varied career, ranging from professional musician and actor to lecturer, to computer programmer and project leader. And, oh yes, I've written a book! I still do all these things, and I love it!

I've been into computers for eons and have played the guitar for just as long. I play a U.S.A. Fender Strat, and, boy, do I love that guitar. I'm currently into MIDI and use the computer to arrange and generate my backing tracks. I'm into several programming languages. Obviously C++, but also C, Java, Visual C++, Visual Basic, and Delphi. I used to know assembly language, but I'm getting a bit rusty on that subject. But there again, you can't do everything.

Anyway, got to go, places to visit, people to meet, things to do, and the telephone's ringing.

Dedication

To Pamela Snaith. This book marks twenty-five years of marriage. Thanks, kidda. Here's to the next twenty-five.

Acknowledgements

I want to thank the guys 'n' gals at Que Publishing who let me have a go at writing this book. It's been great fun working with Americans (by the way, I'm English) and learning a whole new spoken tongue called American English.

I also want to thank my elder son, Stuart Snaith (he's a VB programmer, but that's not his fault, I suppose), for proofreading the work and giving me some alternative ideas when the going got tough. A special thanks to my younger son, Timothy Snaith (he's a chef and cooks a heck of a steak), for lots of cups of coffee to keep me going. Boy, he makes a mean coffee. An apologetic thanks to my wife, Pamela, who spent a lot of time on her own and out of my hair while I hid in the study. She now threatens to spend a lot of my money as revenge.

Tell Us What You Think!

As the reader of this book, *you* are our most important critic and commentator. We value your opinion and want to know what we're doing right, what we could do better, what areas you'd like to see us publish in, and any other words of wisdom you're willing to pass our way.

We welcome your comments. You can fax, email, or write me directly to let me know what you did or didn't like about this book—as well as what we can do to make our books stronger.

Please note that I cannot help you with technical problems related to the topic of this book, and that due to the high volume of mail I receive, I might not be able to reply to every message.

When you write, please be sure to include this book's title and author as well as your name and phone or fax number. I will carefully review your comments and share them with the author and editors who worked on the book.

Fax: 317-817-7070

Email: cigfeedback@pearsoned.com

Mail: Alpha Books
          201 West 103rd Street
          Indianapolis, IN 46290 USA

Introduction

Hi, my name is Paul; consider me to be your spirit guide on your journey through the mysterious world of C++. What makes me qualified to be your guide I hear you ask? The answer is simple. I've done the journey, battled the monsters, and fought the bad guys along the way. I will show you the straight, well-lit paths and avoid the many difficult side roads that abound on the C++ highway.

It's not an easy journey; the ways of C++ are strange and it takes guts and application when the going gets tough. No one will be good at everything but all will be good at something. Now that's a profound statement for a little book, but I think it's true. Why do I say that? Because C++ is arguably the most diverse and flexible programming language around. Once you tame the beast, you can make it do virtually anything; it's down to your imagination after that.

Traditionally, programming books should now tell *you why you need this book* and give a hard sell. I'm not going to do that because I assume the answer is the obvious one. You need to learn C++. If so, this is what the book is about. Good, we're on the right track already.

The next tradition is to explain what C++ actually is. I'm not going to do that either because I assume you know it's a computer programming language. If you didn't know that or you are a technophobe, put the book down now; it's probably not for you.

Still with me? Good! The path to C++ wisdom is actually quite easy. Follow me on the journey one step at a time; don't try to run and don't take short cuts. This journey is the very same journey that I undertook many years ago when I taught myself to speak the language. It's not that books weren't available, the trouble was there were too many but all were of a complex nature. I don't like complicated things; I like to start off very, very simply and build to a crescendo (that's Italian for getting louder). And that is how this book works. I show you the underpinning theory in a simple manner, I explain how a program works, you type it in and play with it, and then we move on. Every step of the way builds on the previous step so you practice every routine many times over. Practice makes perfect, so they say. Do want to take the first step? Okay, turn to Chapter One.

Chapter 1

Things You Always Wanted to Ask About C++ (But You Didn't Want to Look like a Complete Idiot)

In This Chapter

➤ What C++ is and why you use it

➤ The jargon associated with a C++ compiler

➤ The items required to produce a C++ program

➤ An overview of the C++ compilation process

Okay, What Is C++?

C++ is a modern high-level programming language that has evolved from a language called C—logical, I suppose. Incidentally, C and C++ are not the same language. Most C++ compilers support C, but C does not support C++. Although numerous programming statements are the same in C and C++, many new ones are contained only in C++. C++ is therefore a superset of C. C++ is fully modern in that it embraces a modern programming technology called *object-oriented programming* (OOP or OO). OOP topics are gradually introduced as you progress through the chapters. By the time you finish Chapter 19, "An Introduction to Object-Oriented Programming: A Step-by-Step Guide for the Terrified," you will be fully object oriented. OOP is definitely not supported in C; therefore, any C++ program using this technology is incompatible with C. Because C++ is a high-level language, many statements in C++ closely resemble the English language, which makes it relatively easy to learn and understand. These high-level statements are powerful in that it takes very little writing to achieve a lot of computer action.

So Why Do We Use C++?

Object-oriented programming is cool, as well as being highly efficient and, once learned, easy to use. Contrary to popular belief, most programmers do not write new computer programs. Most of their time is spent updating older versions of programs to meet new user requirements, and OOP is ideal for this. A major topic in computer programming is *code reuse*, which simply means that older code is taken from the shelf and used in new programs. OOP has features that make this easy to achieve and thus make C++ a fast and cost-efficient way of programming. In an OOP-style language, data and behavior are modeled into a class. This behavior is copied through a process known as *inheritance* and altered through a process known as *polymorphism*. You will learn all about this from Chapter 19, onwards.

C++ can be used to write virtually any application on any type of computer as long as you have the correct compiler for that machine. A well written C++ program is a complete entity that maximizes the full potential of the computer it runs on. The programmer has real control of the low-level operations of that machine, which results in flexibility and speed of operation. This is not the same for the language known as Java, which relies on a piece of software known as an *interpreter* to make it compatible with a range of computers. Java pays the price through slower speed and lack of true flexibility at machine level. Languages such as Visual Basic are purely for writing Windows applications, and although it is good at this task, the same program can be written with more efficiency in C++.

How Does It Work, Then?

The process of creating a working C++ program falls into three parts, but the eventual aim is to create a set of instructions that the computer's microprocessor can understand. In the case of a PC, you create *exe code*, which is an abbreviation for *executable code*. It is the machine-level code that a PC computer understands. The figure represents the steps involved in the compilation process. This book is based on the two main players (Microsoft and Borland) in the C++ production environment, both of which follow a very similar pattern. Both C++ compilers include a text editor, a compiler, and a linker in their integrated packages. Although I specifically talk about Microsoft and Borland, these are just the biggest; there are other manufacturers. Whatever manufacturer you use, you will need a text editor, a compiler, and a linker. These three items have the following tasks:

1. The *text editor* is used to type in the C++ program very much like a word processor. The resulting text is known as *source code*.

2. The *compiler* is a piece of software that checks the source code for errors and converts it into a piece of code known as *object code*.

3. The *linker* is another piece of software that takes the object code and uses it to join together ready-made low-level routines to produce the executable code that will run on the computer. It might not be obvious at this point, but the linker is what determines whether your C++ program runs in DOS or Windows or even another environment such as UNIX.

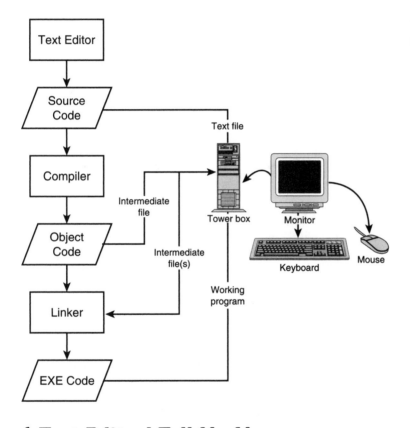

The compilation process of a C++ program.

A Text Editor! Tell Me More

This is what you see on the user screen of the C++ compiler. It is really just a word processor that enables you to enter the text that is your C++ program. This text is known as *source code*. You can manipulate, save, and load the text just as you would with a word processor. (C++ geeks call the text editor *the editor*.)

Compiler—That Sounds Very Complicated

The compiler is really just a spell checker that understands C++ code rather than, say, English or German. After you have typed in and saved your C++ program, you click on the compile option. Without your knowledge, the compiler software is invoked and checks your work. If it finds mistakes, it will down tools (go on strike) and give you a list of errors. In your early days as a C++ programmer, be prepared for lots of errors.

Errors found in the compilation stage are referred to as compilation errors and are caused by the code containing the C++ equivalent of spelling mistakes, which are technically known as syntax errors.

Object Code—Phew, This Is Getting Heavy

If everything is okay, meaning that the compiler finds no syntax errors, the compiler generates an intermediate piece of code, called *object code*, that is used by the next stage of the process. This object code is a translation of the source code and contains information about how the final program will be put together in the next process. (C++ geeks call object code *obj* or *objy* code.)

A Linker—Now I'm Really Getting Into the Jargon

When you have no compilation errors, you can create a working program by converting the object code (or perhaps several object codes, as you will discover much later in Bonus Chapter 3, "Reusable Code, or How to Let someone Else Do the Work,") into a working program. The linker scans the object code(s) and pieces together a working program from libraries that come free with the C++ package. Errors can be reported here if something is wrong. They are called *linker errors* and tend to be quite difficult to find, so be warned and be prepared. It will happen, I promise!

Exe Code—I Can Speak like a Geek...WOW

If your program links correctly and you get the message 0 errors, give a cheer. When you run your program, it will spring to life, and you can sell it to those lovely cash-paying customers. The exe code is the actual bit that you sell and run. (C++ geeks for some strange reason call an *exe* an *exe*. However, they do pronounce it *exee*.) You don't normally release your source code or object code; this is your private work.

The Least You Need to Know

> ➤ C++ is a modern, high-level, object-oriented programming language that evolved from, and is a superset of, another programming language called C.

> ➤ A well-written C++ program is a complete entity that maximizes the full potential of the computer it runs on and that runs more efficiently than equivalent programs written in other languages, such as Visual Basic or Java.

➤ A text editor is like a word processor that enables you to type the text of your C++ program (the source code) into the compiler.

➤ Source code is the basic code of a C++ program, which must be compiled into object code, which in turn is linked to produce exe, or executable, code, which is the final, working version of the program.

➤ A compiler is a piece of software, sort of like a spell checker in a word processor, that checks the source code for errors and converts it into a piece of code known as object code.

➤ The linker is another piece of software that takes the object code from the compiler and uses it to join together ready-made, low-level routines to produce the executable code, which is the working version of your program.

Chapter 2

From Absolutely Nothing to Screen a Display

In This Chapter

➤ How to lay out the code of a C++ program

➤ How to write a simple C++ program, using the `cout` and `endl` commands

➤ The difference between a variable and a constant

A Morale Booster to Get You Started

I know you're dying to start, so I shall grant you your wish. You will look at the basic outline of a C++ program, learn some of the jargon, and then write your first program. After you have the hang of it, I will then cut you loose and let you experiment to your heart's content. In addition to this, you will be able to talk the jargon and impress the folks who know absolutely nothing whatsoever about C++. However, in the immediate future do not attempt the jargon bluff with a C++ expert—wait for several more years.

Laying Down the Rules of the Game

Here is the general basic layout of a C++ program:

```
#include <iostream.h>          // input/output commands
#include <conio.h>             // extra commands

#define constants              // constants for program
```

```
main()                          // start of the program
{
declaration of variables        // list all variables

        statement;              // Statements
        statement;              // More statements
        statement;              // as many as you want

}
```

NOTE

Do not type this into the computer—it is only an outline to be used as a guide.

The C++ language has relatively few keywords but has at its disposal a vast array of external libraries. The #include statements list the libraries used by the program. They allow extra commands such as input/output, string handling, graphics, and so on, to be incorporated.

You use mainly the iostream.h and string.h libraries, which provide control over the screen and keyboard; others are available for virtually any task you can think of.

In a library, parcels of knowledge are contained in books, the books are placed on the shelves, and you can pick out any parcel you want to use. The same can be applied to a C++ library. Books called iostream.h and string.h, to name but two, live in the library that comes with the C++ compiler. If you want to do input/output operations, you use the iostream.h from the library by including it in your program. If you want to do string operations, you choose the string.h book, and so forth. There are scores of books in the C++ library, of which you will borrow but a few. In your life as a programmer, you will discover the ones that meet your needs and become expert in their contents. I don't know of any programmer who uses them all. Constants are defined with the #define directive before the main program and can be used anywhere at any time because they normally remain unchanged. A *constant* is information that does not change throughout the program.

The following few paragraphs are an overview of what constitutes a C++ program, as shown in the preceding code section. Specific C++ programs are introduced later in this chapter where you shall see and use real C++ code.

All C++ programs are made up of blocks of code known as *functions* (you will learn more of this in Chapter 12, "Divide and Conquer: Functions Rule Okay"), but every executable C++ program must contain a function called main() from which all actions are orchestrated.

Next comes a brace, which marks the start of the program section that actually does something useful.

A *variable* is information that can change during the program.Variables are normally typed in (known as *declaring* a variable) immediately after the brace in function main. Their purpose is to permit the programmer to specify the name (known as an *identifier*) of the variable and hence allocate computer memory when the program is compiled. This sounds incredibly technical, but don't worry about it. All will be revealed in the next episode (Chapter 3, "The Old Box of Variables Tricks," and beyond).

Next comes a list of statements to be executed by the program. These are the action lines that actually make the program do something. You will have plenty of practice at this as you progress through the book.

Finally, another brace marks the end of function main.

Down the side of the program is a list of English words prefixed by the symbol //. These are called *comments*, which aid the readability of the program. They play no part in execution of the program but are great assets to anyone attempting to understand how the program works. This includes you when you look back at the code a few weeks from now and think to yourself, "What the heck is this all about?" I wish I had a dollar for every student who said, "I don't need comments. I can remember how my code works!" You are encouraged to use comments liberally in key sections of your program when its operation is not obvious. Don't comment every line or sections of code that perform obvious operations.

In C++ there are two ways to add a comment:

1. // is used to comment a single line—for example,

   ```
   // This is a single line comment!
   ```

2. /* and */ are used for multiple-line comments—for example,

   ```
   /* This is
   a multiple
   line comment! */
   ```

The First Glimpse of a Screen Display

Okay, now I've discussed the theory, so let's do something and write the first program. Wouldn't it be nice if you could have the computer display a message onscreen? Well, you can do that, using the C++ command known as cout. Cout is pronounced *see out*.

A sample program looks like this.

Listing 2.1   Using the cout Command

```
#include <iostream.h>

main()
{
        cout << "Hello everyone...this is easy ";
        return(0);
}
```

The cout Command Explained

The actions part of the program simply prints a line of text onscreen. This figure shows the line that does this.

The format of the cout command.

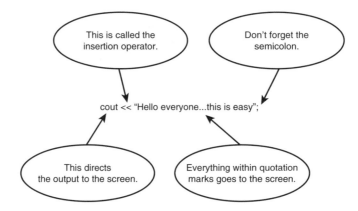

The concept is dead simple. There are four parts to this command:

➤ cout sends data to the screen.

➤ << is known as the insertion operator and inserts anything that follows it into the output stream, in this case the screen.

➤ Anything inside quotation marks is known as a *string* and is literally printed to the screen.

➤ Don't forget the semicolon.

To make this program work, follow the next five steps.

1. Type in the program code shown in Listing 2.1.
2. Save the code to disk. You should always do this.
3. Compile the program.
4. Build the program.
5. Run the program.

Techno Talk

The most common mistake made when learning C++ is to forget to put the semi-colon at the end of the line of code when required. Unfortunately, not all lines of code require the semicolon, and it's a question of laboriously learning which sections of code need one. The compiler will spot the error but report it on the next line. This really confuses students of the language (as well as experienced programmers), so be very careful. To see the way this error is reported, try omitting the semicolon, compile the program, and then view the results. Go on, I dare you!

All being well, you will see some results onscreen that look something like this.

A screen shot of your first program.

This is a screen shot using Microsoft Visual C++. It will probably look slightly different if you use other versions of C++. Microsoft Visual C++ magically adds the line, Press any key, to continue to the end of all development programs. It cunningly omits that line in the release version that you would sell to a customer. Now it's time to get a bit more adventurous, so let's learn another C++ word. This word is endl and is shown in the following program code. This program is very similar to the first one but contains a subtle yet cunning difference.

13

Listing 2.2   A Program with Several Lines of Text and endl

```
#include <iostream.h>

main()
{
    cout << "Hello everyone...this is easy " << endl;
    cout << "Look a new line!" << endl;
    cout << "Get the idea!!" << endl << endl;
    cout << "Dead easy...isn't it?" << endl;
    return(0);
}
```

Note the line shown in the figure; it contains two new variations to the data processed by cout.

➤ endl is used to give a carriage return, which makes the next piece of text appear on the line below.

➤ cout can handle as many insertion operators followed by data as you want. The data can be of any C++ data type. This is a technique called *overloading*, and you will investigate this further in Chapter 16, "Feel You Can't Cope Anymore? Then Take Pity on the Overloaded Operator."

The cout command using several inserted outputs.

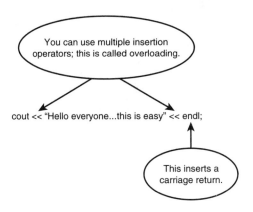

Type in the program; save, compile, and build the program. When you run it, the screen will look something like this.

Your program using endl.

Constants Don't Change! That's Why They Are Constant

Very often in computer programming, things are repeated many times. For example, rather than type out a long piece of text every time you need it, in C++ you define it at the start by giving it a short reference name called an *identifier*. You can then simply refer to the identifier, and C++ substitutes the long piece of text that the identifier represents, thus saving wear and tear on those two tired little typing fingers. The other bonus of this technique is that if you want to change that repetitive piece of text, you need to change it only once at the start where it is set up and not every time it is used.

Here is a sample program that demonstrates the technique.

Listing 2.3   Using Defined Messages

```
#include <iostream.h>

#define message1 "Hello everyone...this is easy "
#define message2 "Look another line!"

main()
{
        cout << message1 << endl;
        cout << message2;
        cout << endl << endl << message1 << endl << endl;
        cout << message2 << endl;
        return(0);
}
```

15

In the code shown in Listing 2.3, the following points are worthy of note:

➤ A string has been defined at the start of Listing 2.3. It can now be referred to anywhere in the program by the word `message1`.

➤ That same definition can be used several times in the program.

➤ `message2` contains another string definition. You can have as many definitions as you want, as long as each one has a unique identifier name.

➤ Note that `endl` can be used in any position in the cout insertion operation.

Check This Out

Listing 2.3 states that multiple `endl` commands may be used in any order. It also states that multiple string definitions may be used. Try experimenting with them and experience the effect.

Mixing Your Text with Numbers

So far, I have demonstrated how to send only text to the screen. You can send numbers to the screen in virtually the same manner. The main point to note is that you DO NOT enclose numbers within quotation marks. Enclosing something in quotation marks tells C++ that it is a string; the absence of quotation marks tells C++ that it is a number. If you put quotation marks around a number, the computer will treat that number as a string. Believe me, computers really are stupid! Be very careful to tell the computer exactly what you want.

Take a look at the next program, which demonstrates the art of mixing strings and numbers.

Listing 2.4   Mixed Data Types

```
#include <iostream.h>

main()
{
        cout << "The answer to" << endl;
        cout << "LIFE THE UNIVERSE AND EVERYTHING is : ";
        cout << 42;
        cout << endl << endl;
        cout << "But what was the question?";
        cout << endl << endl;
        return(0);
}
```

When you run this program, you will see the following output onscreen:

```
The answer to
LIFE THE UNIVERSE AND EVERYTHING is: 42;


But what was the question?
```

The Least You Need to Know

➤ The house rules of how to lay out a C++ program are as follows: The library headers use #include, followed by all definitions, which use #define. Next comes the word main(), which marks the start of the main C++ program. After main() comes a brace followed by the declaration of any variables. Then come the statements of code that achieve the required actions. Your main() C++ code always ends with the word return(0); followed by another brace.

➤ To deliver a simple output to the screen, you use the statement cout followed by the insertion operator << followed by the data that you want to output.

➤ To move the text output to the next line, you add the command endl to the cout statement line.

➤ You can achieve multiple data insertions by using cout followed by as many occurrences of << data as required.

➤ A constant is a data item that never changes during the course of a program.

➤ A variable is a data item that may change during the course of a program.

Chapter 3

The Old Box of Variables Tricks

In This Chapter

➤ The four most useful data types in C++

➤ How to create a variable C++ program

➤ How to use a variable C++ program

Knowing Your `ints` from Your `floats`

All computer languages use the concept of data types. This jargon simply refers to the numeric or text category that an item of information belongs to. In other words, "This number is a whole number," or "This number has a decimal point," and so on. In C++ there are many different data types, but you will initially concern yourself with only the four common ones. They are as follows:

➤ *Integer*—Any whole number, such as 3, 72, –96, 2001, and 0. In C++ it is described as `int`.

➤ *Floating-point number*—Any number with a decimal point, such as 6.75, 95.76, –22.1, and 9.0. In C++ it is described as `float`.

➤ *Character*—Any letter or symbol that can be typed in at the keyboard, such as `'a'`, `'b'`, `'A'`, `'?'`, `'8'`, and `'&'`. In C++ this is described as `char`. Notice that characters have single quotation marks around them.

➤ *String*—Strings are several characters in a row, such as `"Hello"`, "???", `"12345"`, and "a". In C++ this is technically an array of characters; you will learn about arrays in Chapters 9–11. For the moment trust me, and I will guide you through this particular minefield. Notice that strings have double quotation marks around them.

It's All in the Size of the Box

Okay, I've covered a rather academically boring subject, and at this point you should be saying, "What the heck is he talking about?" You were? Good. Now, on with the show. To progress, I must now discuss *variables*. Variables can be thought of as boxes in which you can put information or data. "But how big is the box?" I hear you ask. Well, that depends on what you are trying to put into it; the size of a variable depends on the data type of the information you intend for the variable to hold. In other words, a box that holds integers is a different size from a box that holds `floats` and yet a different size from a box that holds characters, and so on. In C++ you set up the size of the box by stating the data type and then inventing a name for the box. This process is known as *declaring a variable*, and you will have lots of practice at this. Just so you can trade jargon with the professionals, the name of the box is known as the *identifier*, whereas the box itself is known as the *variable*. The figure has a sequence of diagrams to show you what I mean.

The box of variables trick.

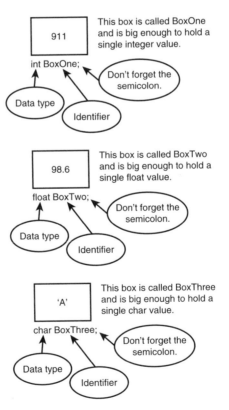

911

int BoxOne;

This box is called BoxOne and is big enough to hold a single integer value.

Data type

Identifier

Don't forget the semicolon.

98.6

float BoxTwo;

This box is called BoxTwo and is big enough to hold a single float value.

Data type

Identifier

Don't forget the semicolon.

'A'

char BoxThree;

This box is called BoxThree and is big enough to hold a single char value.

Data type

Identifier

Don't forget the semicolon.

When you declare a variable, it is good programming practice to invent sensible identifiers that loosely describe the purpose of the variable. A variable that holds someone's age conveys meaning if you name it *age* but is ambiguous if you just name it *x*. There is no technical reason for doing this; it just makes life easier.

Note for the Sheepish

I have talked about boxes and their sizes. For the technically minded or those who seek jargon, you are actually reserving computer RAM for use by the program.

Let's Fill the Box and Call It a Variable

Having shown how to make a variable, I will now show how to put something into the box (or variable, as it is correctly known). Recall that I said that BoxOne is capable of storing a single integer value. Well, this has implications, so hold on and follow the diagram shown in the figure. You will create an integer variable called number and give it a value of 42. This process of assigning a value to the variable is known as *initializing the variable*.

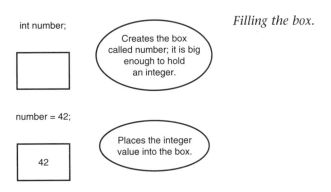

Filling the box.

In the last chapter, you learned how to use the command cout; in the following figure, you shall use it again to send the contents of the box called number to the screen.

How cout looks when using a variable instead of a value.

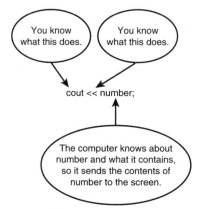

You've seen some pretty pictures and learned some more jargon, so let's do some programming. Here is a simple program to demonstrate the use of variables and data types based on the preceding sequence of diagrams.

Listing 3.1   How to Show the Contents of an Integer Variable Onscreen

```
#include <iostream.h>

main()
{
        int number;        //set up an integer variable

        number = 42;       //give it a value
        cout << number;    //display to screen
        return(0);
}
```

That cout Command Again

Type in the program and save, compile, and build it. When you run it, the screen will display 42. The sequence of events is the same as in the diagrams. Here are the bullet points to remember:

➤ int number;—Sets up the variable as an integer

➤ number = 42;—Puts a value into the variable

➤ cout << number;—Displays the value to the screen

Having dealt with integers, let's take a look at characters. You'll be delighted to know that characters are dealt with in virtually the same way as integers.

Listing 3.2   How to Show the Contents of a `char` Variable Onscreen

```
#include <iostream.h>

main()
{
        char letter;          // set up a character variable

        letter = 'C';         // give it a value
        cout << letter;       // display to screen
        return(0);
}
```

Type in the program; save, compile, and build the program. When you run it, the screen will display the letter `C`.

Having dealt with integers and characters, let's get really smart and take a look at `floats`. It shouldn't surprise you to find that `floats` are dealt with in virtually the same way as integers and characters. Isn't C++ easy?

Listing 3.3   How to Show the Contents of a `float` Variable Onscreen

```
#include <iostream.h>

main()
{
        float number2;          // set up a float variable

        number2 = 98.6;         // give it a value
        cout << number2;          // display to screen
        return(0);
}
```

Type in the program; save, compile, and build the program. When you run it, the screen will display the value `98.6`.

Coming back down to Earth, you probably realize that you are writing simple programs that demonstrate only the basics of C++. Don't worry, this is only the third chapter, and things do get progressively more advanced. Note that I said *advanced* and not *difficult*. Would you like to know a shortcut that professionals use? In C++ you can create a variable and put in a value all in a single line, as shown in the next diagram. It doesn't look like much of a saving in a simple program, but scale this up to a huge program, and you're up there with the professionals.

Declare and initialize all in one fell swoop. This is what the professionals do.

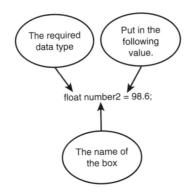

Check This Out

Try changing the values in the previous programs and see the results.

The following program is the shorthand version of Listing 3.3. Give it a try.

Listing 3.4 How to Declare and Initialize in One Line—A Crafty Piece of C++ Shorthand

```
#include <iostream.h>

main()
{
        float number2 = 98.6;  // set up float & initialize

        cout << number2;       // display to screen
        return(0);
}
```

You might have noticed that I haven't mentioned strings in association with variables. They are dealt with in a different way, which I will show you later.

To demonstrate that the boxes really do have a physical size, let's quickly try a program that interrogates computer memory. There's a nifty little C++ utility called sizeof that looks into memory and tells you how many bytes are being used by a variable. This can be very useful in some applications. All the program does is declare and initialize an integer, a float, and a char. It finds the size of the respective variables, then outputs their size and contents to the screen. Just type in the program, run it, and sit back and admire your computer memory.

Know Your Bits and Bytes

Computer people refer to a single memory location as a *byte*. A byte is made up of eight bits. Half a byte is therefore four bits. Would you believe that these crazy computer people refer to half a byte as a *nybble*. Makes you hungry, doesn't it?

Listing 3.5   An Example to Show the Size of the Box

```cpp
#include <iostream.h>

main()
{
    int box1   = 52;
    float box2 = 98.6;
    char box3  = 'Z';
    int size;

    size = sizeof(box1);
    cout << "The integer box is    : " << size
         << " bytes" << endl;
    cout << "This variable contains : " << box1 << endl;
    cout << endl;
    size = sizeof(box2);
    cout << "The float box is       : " << size
         << " bytes" << endl;
    cout << "This variable contains : " << box2 << endl;
    size = sizeof(box3);
    cout << endl;
    cout << "The char box is        : " << size
         << " bytes" << endl;
    cout << "This variable contains : " << box3 << endl;
```

continues

Listing 3.5   An Example to Show the Size of the Box CONTINUED

```
        cout << endl;
        cout << endl;
        return(0);
}
```

The Least You Need to Know

➤ The four most commonly used data types in C++ are integer, float, char, and string.

➤ An integer is in theory any positive or negative whole number. In modern C++ compilers, it is limited by the fact that any integer occupies 4 bytes of memory.

➤ A char is a character. In C++ a char is enclosed in single quotes: 'Y' or '?'. Any symbol visible on the keyboard is a character.

➤ A string is several characters combined as one item. In C++ it is enclosed in double quotes: "This is a string".

➤ A float is in theory any positive or negative number containing a decimal point. In modern C++ compilers, it is limited by the fact that any float occupies 4 bytes of memory.

➤ A variable in C++ is set up by declaring its data type, followed by an identifier name and terminated by a semicolon. A variable can be set up and initialized by declaring its data type, followed by an identifier name followed by = and then a value and terminated by a semicolon.

➤ A variable is a physical memory location that can hold data while an identifier is the name of the variable.

Add, Take Away, and All That Schoolroom Stuff

Back to School for Basic Sums

All programming languages allow some form of number manipulation, and C++ is no exception. In fact, C++ is an engineer's dream and enables all sorts of wonderful mathematical acrobatics to be performed. You will satisfy yourself with some relatively easy calculations and leave the difficult stuff to those who can cope with it.

Let's Review Some Basic Math

C++, like all other high-level programming languages, enables arithmetic operations to be performed on data. To get underway, you need to consider four simple operators: add, subtract, multiply, and divide. The formats for each of these standard arithmetic operators are shown in Table 4.1.

Table 4.1 The Basic Mathematical Operations Available in C++

Operators	Example
+ (add)	C = A + B
- (subtract)	C = A - B
* (multiply)	C = A * B
/ (divide)	C = A / B

The operators are quite straightforward and behave just as you would expect, based on your experience in school. The only one to be careful of is divide. If you divide an integer by an integer, you cannot guarantee that the result will be a whole number—for example,

    4 / 2 = 2   an integer

    3 / 2 = 1.5   a float

Which data type is correct?

Usually, you would anticipate this problem and expect the result to be a float. Unfortunately, this is not necessarily the case with C++, and there are two solutions to the problem. These will be dealt with later in this chapter, so put away your calculators and stop worrying.

The Greeks Had It Cracked

If you are feeling a little apprehensive about all this math stuff, don't be alarmed. About 4000 years ago the ancient Greeks had the same problem (and you know how good they were at math), so they set up some arithmetic rules, called *operator precedence*, that are still used today. For math to work properly, the order of operations must follow a predefined sequence. High-precedence operations are evaluated before low-precedence operations. Unless care is taken, the expression that you want to evaluate might not give the answer that you expect. The pecking order is as follows:

    TOP   multiply (*) and divide (/)

    NEXT   add (+) and subtract (-)

This means that multiply and divide will be done before add and subtract. Multiply and divide have the same precedence, so if you have an operation containing a mixture of the two, it makes no difference in the order of evaluation. The same is true for mixed addition and subtraction. Take the following expression:

    A + B * C

Suppose the letters (variables) have the following values:

A = 3

B = 2

C = 4

Then	A + B * C
becomes	3 + 2 * 4
which is	11

B must be multiplied by C before the result of this operation is added to A. Using my trusty calculator, I find the answer to be 11. If you did it the other way around, the answer would be different. In fact, the (wrong) answer would be 20.

Parentheses Are Just Brackets in Disguise

Parentheses is not just a fancy word for rounded brackets; they actually do something. You can speak the word and sound incredibly cool, or you can use it in C++ to change the order of evaluation.

Using the earlier example, if you include parentheses (now didn't that sound cool), you change the meaning of the mathematical statement.

(A + B) * C

Calculator Time

If you don't believe me, get out your calculator and try it. You'll be amazed at the difference.

This now means that A is added to B before C multiplies the result of the operation. The correct answer is now 20 and the wrong answer is 11. That's clever stuff, isn't it, and weren't those Greeks clever to discover and then solve the problem. Parentheses should be liberally used in your programs, not only to achieve the correct evaluation sequence but also to avoid any chance of ambiguity. This also makes your program easier to read.

Note that

$$A + B * C$$

and

$$A + (B * C)$$

give exactly the same answer, but I think the second expression is much clearer to the reader because B and C are grouped together with brackets. Whoops, I mean parentheses.

Let C++ Do the Hard Math

Try the sample program in Listing 4.1. Before you run it, try to predict what the three answers will be and then see whether you are correct. If you are correct, you may celebrate with an espresso. If you are wrong, have three espressos because you have some revision to do.

Listing 4.1   Demonstrating Add, Subtract, and Multiply

```
#include <iostream.h>

main()
{
    int A = 12;
    int B = 22;
    int C;
    int D;
    int E;

    C = A + B;                      // ADD
    D = A - B;                      // SUBTRACT
    E = A * B;                      // MULTIPLY
    cout << "ADD  : " << C << endl;
    cout << "SUB  : " << D << endl;
    cout << "MULT : " << E << endl;
    return(0);
}
```

Division Isn't Straightforward in C++

As I mentioned earlier, division isn't quite as straightforward. In C++ if you divide an integer by an integer, you end up with a result that is a whole number, which probably is incorrect. Two quick methods overcome this problem. The first is the obvious answer: Don't divide integers by integers; declare the variables as floats instead. Take a look at the following program. It contains three key points to note:

➤ 3 divided by 2 is 1.5, so the variable C should be a float.

➤ However, C++ gives the result as 1(???). Strange!

➤ C++ returns only the *quotient* (the whole bit) of the division and ignores the *mantissa* (the decimal bit).

Run the sample program in Listing 4.2 and verify the preceding comments.

Listing 4.2   Demonstrating a Quirky C++ Division

```
#include <iostream.h>

main()
{
    int A = 3;
    int B = 2;
    float C;

    C = A / B;                        // DIVIDE
    cout << "DIVIDE  : " << C << endl;
    return(0);
}
```

How Do You Fix This Problem?

In Listing 4.3, the data types of A and B have been changed from integer to float. This will give the correct result. Go on, try it.

Listing 4.3   Demonstrating a Nonquirky C++ Division

```
#include <iostream.h>

main()
{
    float A = 3;
    float B = 2;
    float C;

    C = A / B;                        // DIVIDE
    cout << "DIVIDE  : " << C << endl;
    return(0);
}
```

But I Must Have Integers!

The method just described guarantees the correct result, but it might be the case that your original variables A and B have to be of data type integer for some reason. C++ possesses an operation known as a *cast*, which temporarily changes a variable from one data type to another. In this case, you want to cast an integer to a `float`. The variable to be cast is prefixed by the required data type enclosed in parentheses, and now, for the duration of the statement, the variables behave like `float`s. Our integer variables take on the format shown in the figure.

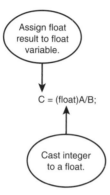

An integer is cast and becomes a `float`.

Assign float result to float variable.

C = (float)A/B;

Cast integer to a float.

Listing 4.4 is the preceding program translated to use casts instead of `float` variables. When you run it, you will get exactly the same answer as Listing 4.3.

Listing 4.4   Demonstrating the Cast Operation

```
#include <iostream.h>

main()
{
    int A = 3;
    int B = 2;
    float C;

    C = (float)A / B;          // CAST AND DIVIDE
    cout << "DIVIDE  : " << C << endl;
    return(0);
}
```

How Do You Get the Decimal Bit?

Now that you know all about simple math, you can show off and do something complicated. It might be that you are concerned only about the decimal part of the number, so apply your recently acquired skills and write a computer program. This requires only the following steps:

1. Find the whole number bit. You know how to do that.

```
C = A / B;
```

32

2. Find the full decimal number. Oh yes, you can do that as well.

```
D = (float)A / B;
```

3. Remove the whole number bit, leaving the decimal bit. That's simple.

```
E = D - C;
```

Hey, I can do math!

Listing 4.5 is the full computer program to verify your newfound mathematical prowess. Note that I have used easy values for A and B. When you are convinced that the program really does work, try changing these values to something more adventurous. Incidentally, that's how professionals work. They never start off by trying to solve the problems of interdimensional travel or warp drive. They kick off with something that they can solve in their head, and then they begin to scale up.

Listing 4.5   Demonstrating Divide and Subtract to Find the Decimal Part of the Calculation

```
#include <iostream.h>

main()
{
    int A = 3;
    int B = 2;
    float C;
    float D;
    float E;

    C = A / B;                          // DIVIDE
    D = (float)A / B;                   // CAST
    E = D - C;                          // DECIMAL BIT
    cout << "DECIMAL   : " << E << endl;
    return(0);
}
```

Introducing `cin`, the Antimatter Version of `cout`

So far, all information contained in variables has been set up at *compile time*. That is, you have typed the values into your source code and then compiled the code. This means that the values are fixed for that run of the program, and if you want different values, you must edit the source accordingly. It is therefore better to invite the user to enter values while the program is running (known as *runtime*). Using this technique, you don't need to edit the code to change the values.

This action is achieved through the C++ command cin, which has the syntax shown in the figure, assuming that you have set up a variable called x.

The cin operation in action.

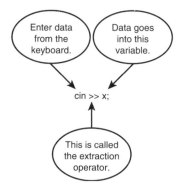

Enter data from the keyboard.

Data goes into this variable.

cin >> x;

This is called the extraction operator.

Enter the Keyboard

Listing 4.6 is Listing 4.1 modified to enable the user to enter values via the keyboard at runtime. It shows how cin is used to collect information. In this program, you invite the user to enter the values for A and B, using the familiar cout command. You then gather the user input via cin and store it in the appropriate variable. This technique is much more flexible than using static values for the variables. Try the program several times, using progressively more complex numbers when you are convinced that it works.

What Is iostream.h Used For?

So far, you have learned how to use cin and cout. These C++ commands are collectively known as *input/output commands* and are contained in the iostream.h library. To use them, you must include iostream.h at the start of your program.

Listing 4.6   Demonstrating cin and a Further Demo of Add, Subtract, and Multiply

```
#include <iostream.h>

main()
{
    int A;
```

```
    int B;
    int C;
    int D;
    int E;

    cout << "Enter the value for A : ";
    cin >> A;
    cout << "Enter the value for B : ";
    cin >> B;
    C = A + B;                          // ADD
    D = A - B;                          // SUBTRACT
    E = A * B;                          // MULTIPLY
    cout << "ADD  : " << C << endl;
    cout << "SUB  : "  << D << endl;
    cout << "MULT : " << E << endl;
    return(0);
}
```

The Least You Need to Know

➤ The underlying mathematical theory behind operator precedence is that multiply and divide are always performed before add and subtract.

➤ Addition in a C++ program uses the symbol +, and the result can be assigned to a variable—for example,

```
answer = first + second;
```

➤ Subtraction in a C++ program uses the symbol -, and the result can be assigned to a variable—for example,

```
answer = first - second;
```

➤ Multiplication in a C++ program uses the symbol *, and the result can be assigned to a variable—for example,

```
answer = first * second;
```

➤ Division in a C++ program uses the symbol /, and the result can be assigned to a variable—for example,

```
answer = first / second;
```

➤ Parentheses are rounded brackets and are used to change the order of precedence of mathematical operations. They can be used also to aid the readability of mathematical statements.

➤ A cast is used to temporarily change one data type into another for the duration of that line of code.

35

➤ The cast operation in a C++ program is used in the following manner:

```
answer = (float)first/second;.
```

➤ The purpose of the `cin` operation in a C++ program is to read a value into a variable. The syntax is

```
cin >> first;
```

Chapter 5

One More Time with the for Loop (or *Noch einmal,* as They Say in Germany)

In This Chapter

➤ What a loop is and why you use it

➤ How to increment and decrement a variable in C++

➤ Some more professional shorthand

➤ How to convert text from one case to another

Learn the Concept of the for Loop

Many operations in computing require statements to be repeated several times, a process known as *iteration*. C++ offers three ways of performing iteration, the first being the for loop. The for loop follows the path shown in the figure. You enter the diamond-shaped box labeled *for loop* from the top; this box would typically tell how many repeats will occur. You then drop down into the box labeled *process* and follow the far left path for the required number of times. Each time you pass through the process box, you perform some useful action. Finally, you drop out of the bottom, and that's the end of the loop.

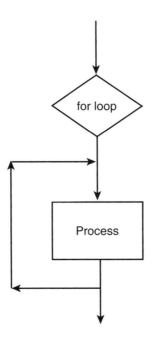

The flow chart of a `for` *loop.*

Increment and Decrement Variables

Before you can make any further progress, I must describe techniques used to permanently alter the contents of a variable. The processes are known as *incrementing* and *decrementing a variable*. All programming languages include such a notion. As an example, I will pick a variable of type integer and call it x. In C++ the following statements can be applied to that variable.

Supposing x assumes the value of 10 by the use of the following statement:

```
x = 10;
```

If the next statement is then applied,

```
x = x + 1;
```

the contents of x will be 11; the variable has been incremented. You can freely use this syntax, but C++ programmers tend to use a shorthand version to achieve the same outcome. You want to be up there with the best, so get used to using C++ shorthand. It has the following syntax:

```
x++;
```

Alternatively, if you want to reduce the contents of a variable by one, which is known as decrementing a variable, you could use the following statement:

```
x = x - 1;
```

or, to use more shorthand, the following:

```
x--;
```

If x initially held a value of 10, it would hold 9 after the decrement command is applied.

The shorthand versions shown here have more power than I have described, but further discussion of those powers will be deferred until later and introduced as necessary throughout the book.

Learn the Syntax of the for Loop

In C++ the for loop has the format shown in the following figure, in which the variable x is declared in the normal manner at the start of the program. The variable x takes on values from 0 to less than 10 (which is actually 9) and is incremented using the command x++. The meaning is that this particular loop will repeat everything within the braces 10 times (0–9 inclusive). If you don't believe me, count them on your fingers, starting with 0 and counting up to 9. I'll bet you that you end up with 10 fingers in the air.

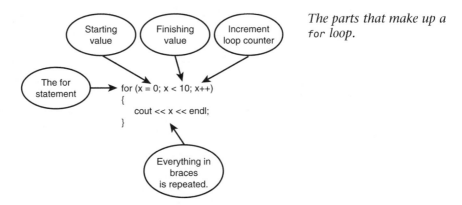

The parts that make up a for *loop.*

Consider the following example, the description of which was given in the preceding dialog. When you run the program, you will see the numbers 0–9 appear in a column down the left side of the screen.

Listing 5.1   Demonstrating a Simple for Loop That Counts from 0 to 9

```
#include <iostream.h>

main()
{
        int x;
```

continues

Listing 5.1 Demonstrating a Simple for Loop That Counts from 0 to 9 Continued

```
for (x = 0; x < 10; x++)
{
    cout << x  << endl;
}
return(0);
}
```

Check This Out

Remember that the number of times the loop happens is controlled by the start and end values of x. Try using the following values by substituting them in the sample program in Listing 5.1 and see the results.

```
for (x = 0;  x < 15;  x++)
for (x = -10; x < 10;  x++)
for (x = 0;  x < 1;  x++)
```

Warning! Warning! Warning!

Now that you are fully conversant with the for loop, I will give you a warning. *NEVER*, I repeat, *NEVER* place a semicolon at the end of the for loop line in the following fashion:

```
for (x = 0; x < 10; x++);
```

THIS IS INCORRECT!

If you put this into a program, it will compile and run, but the bits you want to repeat will not happen. The program will simply skip everything within the parentheses. This is because the semicolon tells the computer, "That's all folks...end of loop." This is another one of those common mistakes made by students (and professionals, if they dare to admit it).

Increase Your Vocabulary with Some Professional C++ Shorthand

Listing 5.2 is designed to invite the user to enter five numbers (of type integer) and return the total of these numbers. This is called *finding a running total*. Several points in this program are worth noting, so read through the code now before I describe it. I appreciate that you cannot wait to type it in and run the thing, but patience, my friend, patience; your day will come.

Listing 5.2   The Running Total Program Finding the Total of a Number of Values Entered at Runtime

```
#include <iostream.h>

main()
{
        int loop;
        int total = 0;         // declare and initialize variables
        int number = 0;

        for (loop = 1; loop <= 5; loop++)
        {
            cout << "Enter a number : ";
            cin >> number;
            total += number;              // keep running total
        }
        cout << endl << "The total is " << total;
        return(0);
}
```

The number to be entered is held in the variable (the box) called number; the answer is held in the variable called total. At the start of the main program, their values are set to zero, a technique known as *initialization of variables*. All good programmers do this as a matter of course, and it avoids introducing many program bugs. So repeat after me, "We are good programmers," and what do we do? Yes, we initialize our variables.

As you enter the loop, the user is asked to enter a number, and the computer responds via the cin statement. Now comes a trick often used by programmers—the variable total is used as a box to hold a running total. The first time around the loop, it holds zero (remember, you put it there). You have just read a value into number; total and number are added together and the result placed back into total. This overwrites the preceding value. Next time around the loop, the same thing occurs, and because total holds the preceding total, it can be added to the new value of number to find the new running total. This is repeated five times to find the value of the sum of five numbers. Clever things these computers!

41

But a Bug Is a Fly, Isn't It?

Correct. And in the good old days of computing, when men were men and dinosaurs were dumb lumbering things and huge electronic machines used valves, things used to get hot. The bugs used to fly in for the warmth and were promptly crushed in the moving relay contacts of these ancient computers. This stopped the ancient computers working, so every now and then you had to take a brush and clean the machine. Hence the term *debug*. The term still lives on, and this is why you call an error in a computer program a *bug*.

Another piece of shorthand preferred by C++ programmers concerns the statement that keeps the running total:

```
total += number;
```

This, for mathematicians among you, is the shorthand version of

```
total = total + number;
```

which means that the contents of total are added to the contents of number and the result placed in total. Both versions produce identical effects.

Okay, I know your fingers are just itching to get at that keyboard, so off you go. Enter and run the program. Don't forget that programmers, being incredibly lazy animals, start off with easy numbers. Don't use big complicated numbers to prove that your program works. Use things such as 1, 2, or 3. When you know this works, try out the big numbers and have confidence that the computer is capable of adding them.

Techno Talk

The following are available with a syntax similar to what I just showed you:

```
total -= number;
```

The contents of number are subtracted from the contents of total and the result placed in total.

```
total *= number;
```

The contents of total are multiplied by the contents of number and the result placed in total.

```
total /= number;
```

The contents of total are divided by the contents of number and the result placed in total.

Don't Mix Your Cases! Converting Lowercase to Uppercase and Vice Versa

In Chapter 14, "The Parallel Array Is Dead, Long Live the Structure," you will investigate some simple database technology. You will encounter a major problem, so I will now give you a hint as to the solution. Computers are not very clever, and they make assumptions. Assuming that you live on the same planet as I do, read the following planet names and see whether you have a vague idea as to where they are in the solar system:

VENUS

Venus

venus

VeNuS

I know what I mean and *you* know what I mean, but a computer would treat these names as different planets. There would now be 12 planets in the solar system (Goodnight NASA, we don't need you anymore).

The computer solution is to decide on a format and store all such names in that format. The fourth name in the list is obviously a bad choice (unless you come from VeNuS). The second name is bad programming practice and should be avoided. That leaves a choice of uppercase or lowercase, because you should never mix cases. Both are valid, and a design choice needs to be made when the program is initially constructed. For the purposes of this example, I have decided to choose uppercase as my design standard. Now wasn't that decisive.

The Case for the Case

I have explained how the computer interprets mixed cases and recommended that you should never do this. The only reason for this is that you would need lots of code to verify all possible inputs against a database entry. In the world of the computer professional, this costs money and is prone to error. The simpler you can make a solution the better, and keeping all letters in the same format is a good starting point.

If the user were to type in a name, the program would force that input to be stored in the correct format, irrespective of what was actually entered. This can easily be done with a `for` loop that examines each letter in the name. Listing 5.3 introduces some new techniques, so read through the program now, and then I shall explain the key points.

Listing 5.3   Converting All Character Inputs to Uppercase

```
#include <iostream.h>
#include <string.h>
#include <ctype.h>
#define MAX 20

main()
{
    char name[MAX];
    int x;

    cout << "Enter a name : ";
    cin >> name;
    for (x = 0; x < strlen(name); x++)
```

```
        {
            name[x] = toupper(name[x]);
        }
        cout << endl << name << endl;
        return(0);
    }
```

Are you ready? Here we go.

a. Note the two new libraries in the program: `string.h`, which deals with strings (would you believe), and `ctype.h`, which deals with C++ data types and their manipulation.

b. For the time being, ignore the data statement `char name[MAX];` and just type it in. All will be revealed in due course, and we need to keep some mystery. I won't tell you that the butler did it—whoops.

c. You encounter the command `strlen(name)`, which is contained in the `string.h` library. Now this is a clever little trick. At this point, you don't know how long the name actually is; `strlen` calculates it for you. It then substitutes that value to complete the `for` loop. Who said that computers were stupid?

d. Again, don't concern yourself about the line `name[x] = toupper(name[x]);`. All will be revealed in, Bonus Chapter, 1, "Advanced File Handling for Masochists." Trust me for now, and all will be well.

Enter the program and test it by entering different combinations of uppercase and lowercase letters; the outcome should always be uppercase letters. You can also try entering a few numbers and see the result.

What If I Want Lowercase Format?

No problem. All you do is replace `toupper` with `tolower` in the sample program, and this will do the hard work. Give it a try if you dare.

What Goes Up Must Come Down: The for Loop in Reverse

Until now, you have seen loops that count upwards, that is, 1 2 3 4...and so on. Within C++ there is a means to count downwards, that is, 4 3 2 1...and so on. It has the format shown in the figure.

The parts that make up a for *loop that counts backwards.*

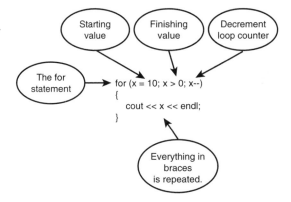

It is nearly identical to the original for loop, except that x starts at a greater value than its finishing value and you decrement rather than increment. Easy!

Try Listing 5.4 to see the effect.

Listing 5.4   Counting in Reverse

```cpp
#include <iostream.h>

main()
{
      int x;

      for (x = 10; x > 0; x--)
      {
        cout << x  << endl;
      }
      return(0);
}
```

The Least You Need to Know

➤ The for loop in a computer program is used to make operations repeat many times.

➤ In a C++ program, the for loop has the following syntax:

```cpp
for (x = 0; x < 6; x++)
```

followed by the statements that you want to repeat.

➤ *Iteration* is a generic term for making operations repeat many times. The for loop is an example of iteration.

➤ To increment a variable, you can use the following syntax:

```
x = x + 1.
```

To decrement a variable, you can use the following syntax:

```
x = x - 1.
```

➤ The shorthand version of increment is x++.

➤ The shorthand version of decrement is x--.

➤ The purpose of the running total program is to find the total of a number of values entered at runtime.

➤ The shorthand addition notation used in the running total program is total += number;.

➤ The shorthand version of subtraction is

```
total -= number;
```

➤ The shorthand version of multiplication is

```
total *= number;
```

➤ The shorthand version of division is

```
total /= number;
```

➤ The reason why you agree to a standard format for stored information is that the computer treats uppercase letters as different values than lowercase letters. This would cause great difficulties in writing code to deal with all eventualities.

➤ The reason why you include the string.h and ctype.h library headers in Listing 5.3 is to use the extra commands necessary to deal with strings and conversion of letters.

➤ The toupper function is used to convert text from lowercase to uppercase.

➤ The strlen function in Listing 5.3 is used to find the number of letters in the string.

➤ The for loop can be made to decrement rather than increment by using the following syntax:

```
for (x = 10; x > 0; x--)
```

Chapter 6

A Case of Déjà Vu: It's the while Loop

In This Chapter

➤ The syntax and use of the while loop

➤ How to determine the truth of an operation

➤ The difference between postfix and prefix notation

➤ Some more professional shorthand

➤ The syntax and use of the do while loop

Go with the Flow: The while Loop

The while statement is used to execute other statements while a condition holds true. This is shown in the flow chart in the figure. You drop in from the top and test for a condition being either true or false within the diamond shape. If the condition is true, you drop through to the process box before returning to the diamond box. You keep on testing until the condition proves to be false, at which point you take the alternative route; you bypass the process box and carry on with whatever comes next.

A Non-Event

It is worth noting that in some cases the test might prove false at the onset, which means that you might not need to do the process. This sounds weird, but there are instances when this process might still be necessary. In a submarine, it isn't wise to open the hatch when you are still under water.

This is the flow diagram of the while *loop.*

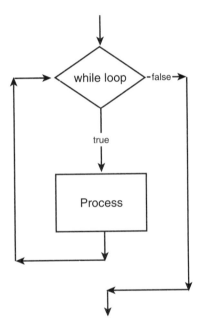

How Do You Know the Truth?

Comparison operators are used to compare two values known as *operands*. The result of the comparison can have only two logical outcomes, true or false. Table 6.1 shows the comparisons that C++ offers.

Table 6.1 The Tests to Establish Whether a Condition Is True or False

Operator	Meaning	Example
==	Equal to	a == b
!=	Not equal to	a != b
<	Less than	a < b
>	Greater than	a > b
<=	Less than or equal to	a <= b
>=	Greater than or equal to	a >= b

The Truth and Nothing But the Truth

If the variable called a is set to 6 and the variable called b is set to 7, you could apply the comparison a==b, and the outcome would be false because 6 is clearly not equal to 7. On the other hand, if you were to apply the comparison a < b, the outcome would be true because 6 is less than 7. By using these comparisons in a C++ program, it becomes possible to dictate the flow of actions.

The Structure of the while Loop

The structure of the while statement is shown in the figure.

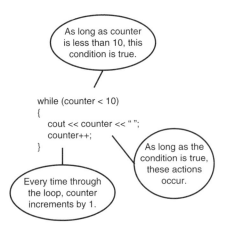

This diagram shows the structure of the while *loop.*

51

Looks Pretty, but How Does It Work?

The program initializes counter as 0. The while statement then performs a comparison to establish whether the condition evaluates to true or false.

```
while (counter < 10)
```

As long as counter is less than 10, the condition is true and the loop will execute. When 10 is reached, the condition is false and the loop will terminate.

At every pass through the body of the while loop, counter is incremented and then tested again to see whether it is still less than 10. The first time around, this test will prove true because counter holds a value of 0, and 0 is less than 10. The loop is entered, and the current value of counter is printed to the screen. The variable counter is increased by 1 every time a comparison is made. The loop will continue to execute as long as counter is less than 10. Eventually counter will reach 10, the condition will evaluate to false, and the loop will terminate. Now try the sample program in Listing 6.1.

The Dreaded Lock Out

What ever you do, make sure that the condition you are testing is updated in the action part of the loop. Failure to do so means that the condition will never change and the program will run forever.

Listing 6.1   Demonstrating a while Loop That Counts from 0 to 9

```cpp
#include <iostream.h>

main()
{
        int counter = 0;                    //set initial value

        while ( counter < 10)               //test condition
        {
            cout << counter << " ";         //display
            counter++;                      //increment
        }
```

```
        return(0);
   }
```

A Warning That's Better Late Than Never

When you are working with loops, it's always a good idea to save your work at regular intervals. You have? Well done. When loops go into dreaded lock-out mode, you might have to switch off the computer and start again, at which point you've lost your precious work.

Prefix, Postfix, What's the Difference? All Is Explained

The dictionary definition of prefix is "to put before or at the beginning." Similarly, postfix is defined as "to put after or at the end." All should now be clear, but translating this into a programming language such as C++ still poses questions. I will try to clarify the situation in the next few pages.

Postfix Notation

Earlier I stated that the increment and decrement commands are more powerful than I had described, so I will tell you more at this juncture. Take a look at the following statement, which is a variation of an earlier program.

```
while (counter++ < 10)
```

Note that an increment ++ comes after the variable counter. This is known as postfix notation, and the actions in a program are very concise. When you use postfix notation, the following chain of events occurs:

➤ The truth of counter, being less than 10, is tested.

➤ counter is incremented.

➤ If the truth test proves true, the actions associated with the loop are executed.

➤ Note that counter has been incremented before any actions such as cout are performed on it.

This is a very powerful statement, and not to be outdone, a prefix notation version is available.

Prefix Notation

The following line of code is another variation on the theme; this time the ++ comes first and is known as *prefix notation*.

```
while (++counter < 10)
```

The following chain of events occurs:

➤ counter is incremented.

➤ The truth of counter, being less than 10, is tested.

➤ If the truth test proves true, the actions associated with the loop are executed.

➤ Again, note that counter has been incremented before any actions such as cout are performed on it.

Again, this is a very powerful statement and is subtly different from the preceding version.

Loopy Program Time (Don't Forget to Save)

At the start of this chapter, you saw and (I hope) ran a program that counted from 0 to 9—not exactly advanced mathematics, but it was only to prove a concept. Now you incorporate your newfound knowledge of postfix and prefix notation and see the difference.

In the Postfix

Enter and run the sample program in Listing 6.2. What do you notice about the numbers in the screen output shown in the figure?

Listing 6.2   Using Postfix Notation to Print Numbers Between 1 and 10

```
#include <iostream.h>

main()
{
        int counter = 0;                //set initial value

        while ( counter++ < 10)         //test condition and increment
        {
            cout << counter << " ";     //display
        }
        return(0);
}
```

This is the output, using postfix notation.

In the Prefix

You now repeat the exercise, using prefix notation. Enter and run the sample program in Listing 6.3 and observe the results shown in the figure.

Listing 6.3   Using Prefix Notation to Print Numbers Between 1 and 9

```
#include <iostream.h>

main()
{
        int counter = 0;                //set initial value

        while ( ++counter < 10)         //test condition and increment
        {
            cout << counter << " ";     //display
        }
        return(0);
}
```

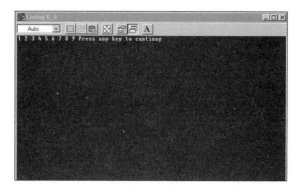

This is the output, using prefix notation.

The Test Comes Last with the do while Loop

The do while statement is similar to the while loop in that statements are executed until a condition becomes true or false. To achieve this, though, the test is done after the loop has been executed, unlike the while loop, in which the test is applied before the loop is executed.

Flow Again: The do while Loop

Like the while statement, the do while is used to execute other statements while a condition holds true. This is shown in the flow chart in the figure. You drop in from the top and immediately do the process; then you check whether a condition is true or false. If the condition is true, you return to the process box before returning to the diamond box for a re-test. You keep on testing until the condition proves to be false, at which point you drop out of the loop and carry on with whatever comes next. The key point with this variation is that the process always occurs at least once.

This is the flow diagram of the do while loop.

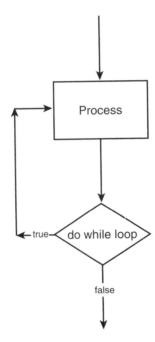

A Definite Event

It is worth noting that the process will always happen at least once because the test comes after the process. In the submarine saga, it isn't a good idea to dive before the hatch has been closed.

The Structure of the do while *Loop*

The structure of the do while statement is shown in the figure.

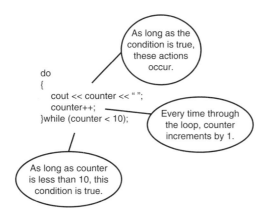

This diagram shows the structure of the do while *loop.*

The do while *Program*

To put the final touches on our tour of iteration...iteration? What was that? The for loop, the while loop, and the do while loop! Let's try a final program to demonstrate a real do while program. Once again, this just counts numbers, but it's still early. Very soon you will move into much more complex things, and you'll be begging me to count numbers again. Try the sample program in Listing 6.4.

Listing 6.4   Printing Numbers Between 0 and 9

```
#include <iostream.h>

main()
```

continues

Listing 6.4   Printing Numbers Between 0 and 9 CONTINUED

```
{
        int counter = 0;                        //set initial value

        do
        {
                cout << counter << " ";    //display
                counter++;                          //increment
        }while ( counter < 10);           //test condition
        return(0);
}
```

The Least You Need to Know

➤ The purpose of the while loop is to perform another form of iteration. The actions within the while loop are executed as long as the condition holds true. The actions within the loop in some circumstances might never occur.

➤ The syntax of the while loop in C++ is as follows:

```
while ( counter < 10)
```

➤ To avoid the dreaded lock out, make sure that the condition you are testing is updated in the action part of the loop.

➤ In postfix notation, the rule is test, then increment.

➤ In prefix notation. the rule is increment, then test.

➤ The purpose of the do while loop is to perform another form of iteration. The actions within the do while loop are executed as long as the condition holds true. The actions within the loop always occur at least once.

➤ The syntax of the equality operator in C++ is a double equals sign (==).

➤ The syntax of the less-than operator in C++ is <.

➤ The syntax of the greater-than operator in C++ is >.

➤ The syntax of the less-than-or-equal-to operator in C++ is <=.

➤ The syntax of the greater-than-or-equal-to operator in C++ is >=.

➤ The syntax of the not-equal-to operator in C++ is !=.

Chapter 7

The Choice Is Logical, Captain, with if else

> **In This Chapter**
>
> ➤ The logic involved in making a program appear intelligent
>
> ➤ The syntax and use of the simple if else statement
>
> ➤ The meaning of the term *nesting*
>
> ➤ The logic, syntax, and use of nested if else statements
>
> ➤ The meaning of the term *program fragment*

The Logic Path to Follow: You Make a Choice

In this chapter, you take a look at the if else statement and the way it is used to pick what appears to be an intelligent route through a program. You will see the flow chart, learn the syntax, and write some programs. Here we go.

The Path Divides

The if else statement is available in C++ to enable choices to be made and hence make the program appear intelligent. The flow chart shown in the figure demonstrates the choice of paths that occur. A comparison that evaluates to true or false, as in Chapter 6, "A Case of Déjà Vu: It's the while Loop," is used to determine which path is to be followed. If the comparison proves true, the Yes path is followed, and the box below Yes is processed. Alternatively, if the comparison proves false, the No route is followed, and the other box is processed. Yes is the if part; No is the else part.

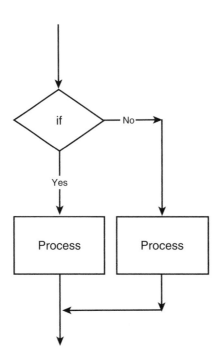

The Structure of *if* *else* in a Picture

The next figure shows the structure (syntax) of the `if else` statement. It operates just the way it sounds and has the following format: If the condition is true, the statements within the first set of braces are executed; the `else` part is ignored. If the condition is false, the statements in the braces following `else` are executed and the first set of statements ignored. With this statement, only one process is carried out, never both, making the computer program appear intelligent.

The structure of the
if else statement.

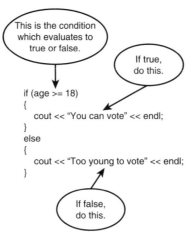

A Conversation with the Senator: Your Age, Please

In Listing 7.1, the person is invited to enter his or her age. If old enough (18 or over is assumed to be correct), he or she can vote; if not, he or she cannot. Try this simple program and see whether you are old enough to vote. For test purposes, you are allowed to lie about your age.

Listing 7.1 A Simple Example of the `if else` Statement

```cpp
#include <iostream.h>

main()
{
      int age;

      cout << "Enter your age : ";
      cin >> age;

      if (age >= 18)
      {
            cout << "You can vote " << endl;
      }
      else
      {
            cout << "Too young to vote" << endl;
      }
      return(0);
}
```

A Message in Reply

The preceding program uses only single-line statements as the two alternative actions. A single-line action is known as a *simple statement*.

```cpp
cout << "You can vote " << endl;
```

is a simple action because only a single line of code forms the action.

Often, more than a single action is required, and several lines of code are involved. This is known as a *compound statement*. All such statements in C++ are enclosed inside braces to show that they are grouped together and jointly constitute a single action, as in the following code:

```cpp
{
            cout << "Hello I am your local senator" << endl;
            cout << "You are over 18" << endl;
```

```
        cout << "That means you can vote" << endl;
        cout << "I will crawl to you" << endl;
    }
```

What! No Braces?

You don't actually need to put braces around a simple statement. I do it out of habit. Including braces makes your code more consistent and easier to read. Try it out if you like.

Take a look at Listing 7.2 and note how the response of our vote-hungry senator is grouped as two alternative compound statements, only one of which will be used, depending on the age of the punter.

Listing 7.2   An Example of Compound Statements Used with the `if else` Statement

```
#include <iostream.h>

main()
{
    int age;

    cout << "Enter your age : ";
    cin >> age;

    if (age >= 18)
    {
        cout << "Hello I am your local senator" << endl;
        cout << "You are over 18" << endl;
        cout << "That means you can vote" << endl;
        cout << "I will crawl to you" << endl;
    }
    else
    {
        cout << "Too young to vote" << endl;
        cout << "Do not waste my time" << endl;
    }
    return(0);
}
```

A Fatal Blunder Revealed

Be careful where you place your braces. If you put them in the wrong place, the logic of your program might appear to be flawed. This is a very common mistake to make when learning C++, so be sure that you understand the concept of compound statements.

The Senator Plays Dumb

Sometimes there are no actions to take if the condition is false. In other words, you don't need the else part. This is shown in the next figure. If the condition proves true, you perform the process just as before. However, in the case of the condition proving false, notice that the line goes directly from the decision box to the end of the flow chart; hence, there is nothing to process. The flow line simply bypasses the true process.

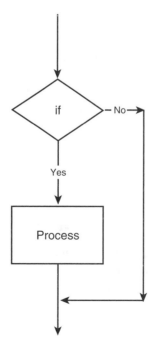

The flow chart of the if else *with the* else *part missing.*

In such an instance, you simply bypass the process, just like the senator's response in Listing 7.3. After all, a negative remark could cost votes.

Listing 7.3   An Example of a Program with No Required Actions If the Condition Proves False

```
#include <iostream.h>

main()
{
        int age;

        cout <<"Enter your age : ";
        cin >> age;
        if (age >= 18)
        {
                cout << "Hello I am your local Senator" << endl;
                cout << "You are over 18" << endl;
                cout << "That means you can vote" << endl;
                cout << "I will crawl to you" << endl;
        }
        return(0);
}
```

A Choice Within a Choice: It's Nesting Time

In the crazy world of computing, you often need to make more than a single choice, and things are rarely as simple as true and false. When multiple choices are required, you can employ a technique known as nested if else statements.

Nested if else

Nesting—or in this specific case, *nested if else*—means that an if else statement is contained inside another if else statement. The same principle can be applied to a loop. You can place a loop within a loop.

A Right-Hand Choice

The `if else` statement can be used to make multiple choices by a technique known as *nesting*. It is used in exactly the same manner as previously described. Keeping a close eye on the next figure, note the following points:

➤ Should the conditional test prove true, the process in the Yes line is executed just as before.

➤ Should the test prove false, you follow the No line, where you find a second `if else` statement nested within the `else` part of the first `if else` statement.

The compound `if else`.

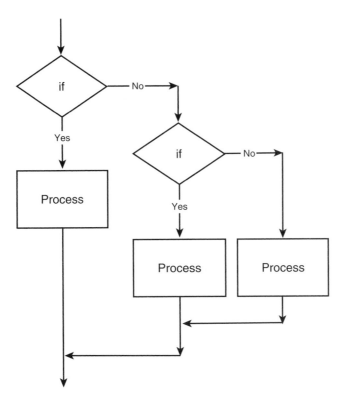

The Program Bit

The flow chart just described translates into the code fragment shown in the next figure.

The code fragment of the nested if else statement.

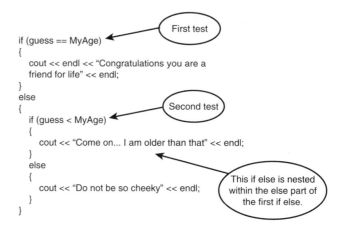

```
if (guess == MyAge)
{
    cout << endl << "Congratulations you are a
    friend for life" << endl;
}
else
{
    if (guess < MyAge)
    {
        cout << "Come on... I am older than that" << endl;
    }
    else
    {
        cout << "Do not be so cheeky" << endl;
    }
}
```

First test

Second test

This if else is nested within the else part of the first if else.

The Full Program: Time to Lie About Your Age

At last, you arrive at the full working program...well, assuming you type it in correctly. Enter and run Listing 7.4, in which you will be invited to enter your age. The program will check this age and deliver an appropriate message. Remember, *computers never lie*, so don't let anyone ever tell you, "It was a computer error." It was the person who entered the data who got it wrong, not the computer.

Listing 7.4 An Example of the Nested if else Statement

```
#include <iostream.h>

#define MyAge 21     // Don't laugh!

main()
{
    int guess;

    cout <<"Guess my age : ";
    cin >> guess;
    if (guess == MyAge)
    {
            cout << endl
                << "Congratulations you are a friend for life"
                << endl;
    }
    else
    {
      if (guess < MyAge)
      {
            cout << "Come on...I am older than that" << endl;
```

```
        }
        else
        {
                cout << "Do not be so cheeky" << endl;
        }
    }
    return(0);
}
```

Here is a description of the actions taken in this program:

➤ The first `if` statement tests the truth of the guess.

```
if (guess == MyAge)
```

➤ If the guess is correct, a message is issued.

➤ If the guess is incorrect (whether high or low), a second `if` statement, nested within the `else` part of the first, tests to see whether the guess is too low.

```
if (guess < MyAge)
```

➤ If this second test is true, an alternative message is given out.

➤ If both tests are false, the only remaining conclusion is that the guess must be too high, and an appropriate message is issued.

A Left-Hand Choice

It is also quite acceptable for nesting to live within the first part of the `if else` statement. I do not intend to develop a full program, but in the figure, the program fragment does the deed. If you are really brave, try taking this piece of code and constructing the rest of the program around it.

Techno Talk

A *program fragment* is a small piece of code. Although it isn't enough to work on its own, it can be plugged into a C++ program containing `main()`, and then it will work. It is used to focus in and demonstrate a point of program theory without having the distraction of the rest of the program.

The program fragment of an `if else` nested within the `if` part of an outer `if else` statement.

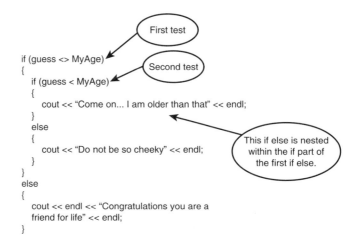

```
if (guess <> MyAge)
{
    if (guess < MyAge)
    {
        cout << "Come on... I am older than that" << endl;
    }
    else
    {
        cout << "Do not be so cheeky" << endl;
    }
}
else
{
    cout << endl << "Congratulations you are a
    friend for life" << endl;
}
```

First test

Second test

This if else is nested within the if part of the first if else.

A Left-Hand and Right-Hand Choice

It is possible to nest `if else` statements in both the `if` and `else` parts. This is shown in the figure; follow the logic path through the chart.

An if else nested in both legs of the outer if else statement

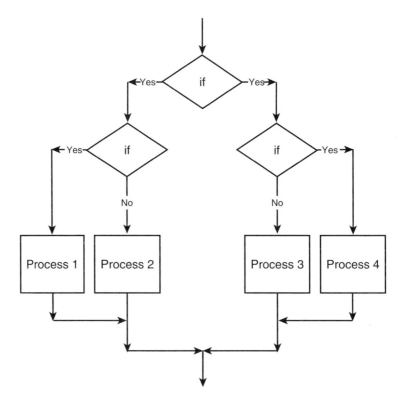

Just to be really smart, take a look at a mind-blowing problem and construct a program from it. By chance, it happens to fall into the `double_compound_if` category. Now, isn't that convenient. Here is the problem.

Write a program that will accept an age as input and then will issue one of the following messages, depending on the age category:

Age group	Message
Less than 5	Under school age
Less than 16	Of school age
Less than 65	Of working age
65 or over	Over the hill

The solution is Listing 7.5, which conveniently demonstrates a nested `if else` program. Enter and run the program and try to follow the logic. A big clue is that I tested for the middle-age range first, using `if age < 16`, and thus split the choices into two convenient halves. Each half also fell into two convenient halves and solved the problem. Don't worry, program design comes with a lot of practice and cheating! Keep on plugging away, and you'll get the hang of it.

Listing 7.5 An Example of a Heavily Nested `if else` Program

```
#include <iostream.h>

main()
{
    int age;

    cout << "Enter your age : ";
    cin >> age;

    if (age < 16)
    {
        if ( age < 5)
        {
            cout << "Under school age" << endl;
        }
        else
        {
            cout << "School age" << endl;
        }
    }
    else
```

continues

Listing 7.5 An Example of a Heavily Nested if else Program
CONTINUED

```
    {
        if (age < 65)
        {
            cout << "Working age" << endl;
        }
        else
        {
            cout << "Over the hill" << endl;
        }
    }
    return(0);
}
```

Some Words of Wisdom from One Who Has Fallen into the Trap

It is always possible to nest further if else statements within the second level of nesting. In fact, the process can be extended indefinitely. However, lots of nested if else groups do not make for easy program reading or design. (And who fell into this trap? No comment.)

The Least You Need to Know

➤ The purpose of the if else statement is to check whether a condition is true. If so, a particular action is performed. If the condition is false, an alternative action is performed.

➤ A simple statement is a single line of code that performs a single action.

➤ A compound statement is several lines of code that are grouped together with braces. As a group, they perform a single sequence of actions.

➤ The else part of the if else statement is sometimes not required. In such cases, the else is simply omitted.

➤ The term *nesting*, in the context of computer programming, means that further if else statements can be contained within if else statements, thus giving multiple choices.

➤ Nested if else statements should be used with care because too great a depth of nesting makes programs difficult to design and read.

Chapter 8

If You Are Spoilt for Choice, the switch case Sometimes Helps

In This Chapter

➤ The logic involved in the switch case statement

➤ The syntax and use of the switch case statement

➤ How to write a menu-driven program

➤ The meaning of the term *program fragment*

One Choice from Many

In the last chapter, we investigated the if else statement and how choices could be made. However, there is another way of making choices in C++. This tool is the switch case statement, and you shall learn it now.

The Up Side

The chances are that you found the solution to the latter examples posed in the last chapter rather long winded, and so you should have. Nested if else statements become very complicated, and an alternative strategy is wise. Fortunately, C++ offers just such a mechanism; it is called the switch case statement. The switch case statement enables all the wanted conditions of a variable to be listed and the required action to follow if that condition is true.

The following flow chart shows the typical routes through a switch case statement. You drop in through the top and establish the value of a variable. You then go on to check that value against a list of wanted values. If there is a match, you then do the process associated with that value. It's as simple as that. After you have done that process, you join up at the bottom and carry on with whatever comes next in the program. Note that only one of the processes is carried out; the others are ignored.

The routes through the `switch case` *statement.*

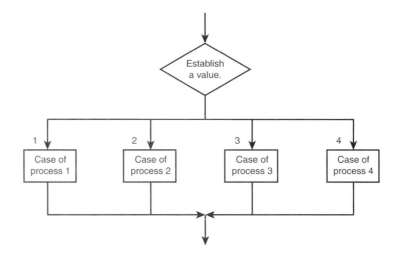

Within any of the process boxes, both simple and compound statements are allowed.

Simple and Compound, What Was That Again?

A *simple* statement is a single line of code that performs an action. A *compound* statement is several lines of code, enclosed in braces, that perform a single action.

The `switch case` is designed to capture specific requests, and as long as you know what you want, it will work wonders. There is even an optional default statement that can be used to mop up any unwanted values. I will return to this default later in this chapter.

The Downside

So far, I have told you all the good things about the `switch case`, but unfortunately there tend to be downers along with the uppers. I will quickly tell you the downside, and then we will move on as if nothing were said.

The restriction placed on the `switch case` statement is that the established value being compared with the wanted list must be of an ordinal data type.

The Ordinal Data Type Explained

An *ordinal data type* is one that follows a definite pattern and whose sequence never changes. Such sequences are integer values, that is, 1, 2, 3, 4, and so on. Another common sequence is the alphabet, that is, *a, b, c, d,* and so on.

The only ordinal types so far covered are `int` and `char`, so you will use these. Note, however, that `string` and `float` are NOT ordinal because they have an infinite number of combinations. For this very reason, they cannot be listed in the wanted conditions, so you don't use them. At this juncture, I want to make something very clear, so sit up and take notice because your very future as a C++ programmer is at stake. When I talk about using only ordinal data types in the list of wanted conditions, I am definitely not talking about the actions in the process box that were led to by the condition. In that process, you can use any data type that you want. The compiler doesn't care, I don't care, and Mr. Microsoft doesn't care, so carry on.

The C++ Syntax of `switch`

Having learned the (boring) theory, I know that you are just dying to see a real `switch case` statement. To keep you on the edge of your seat, though, I'm going to introduce it a bit at a time (sorry).

How It Really Works

Before we dive in up to our necks, let's pause for breath and digest the next fragment, which explains how the `switch case` really works in terms of C++.

In the next diagram, the variable `letter` holds a value. The code checks to see whether that value matches any of the listed cases. If there is a match, the action associated with that case is executed.

A new keyword is introduced at this point, and that word is `break`. The function of `break` is to force the action to jump outside the current set of braces where play is taking place. The effect of this action is to omit any lines of code that lie after the `break` but before that brace.

The `switch case` fragment explained.

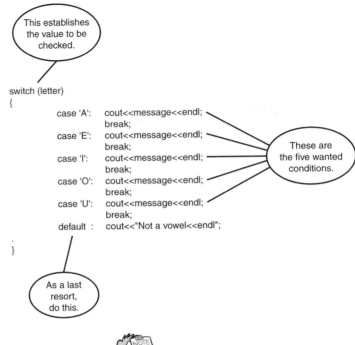

This establishes the value to be checked.

```
switch (letter)
{
          case 'A':   cout<<message<<endl;
                      break;
          case 'E':   cout<<message<<endl;
                      break;
          case 'I':   cout<<message<<endl;
                      break;
          case 'O':   cout<<message<<endl;
                      break;
          case 'U':   cout<<message<<endl;
                      break;
          default :   cout<<"Not a vowel<<endl";

}
```

These are the five wanted conditions.

As a last resort, do this.

Break for a Ghostly Occurrence

Be observant at this juncture. It's easy to forget to include all the necessary break statements. The program will still run, but strange things will happen. The best way to see these weird ghostly occurrences is to deliberately omit a break and observe the result.

This code fragment also contains a last-resort get out (escape). If none of the conditions listed are recognized, the default action takes place. That's it really, nothing to worry about.

Do You Know Your Vowels?

At last, let's cut the waffle and do some real big-time coding. The following program determines whether a letter entered by the user is a vowel. It's basically the code fragment just described, with some additional code to make it user friendly. Cast your mind back all the way to the for loop in Chapter 5, "One More Time with the for

Loop (or *Noch Einmal*, as They Say in Germany)." Do you remember the toupper command that changed a lowercase letter into uppercase? If not, you are reprimanded. Stand in the corner for ten minutes and then read that part again. The computer, once again being really stupid, assumes lowercase and uppercase to be different values, so you have two choices for the vowel program. You either list ten wanted cases or convert all lowercase inputs into uppercase and run with five wanted cases. As I said earlier, computer programmers are inherently lazy beasts, so we will go for the second option. Here's how it's done. Observe and learn.

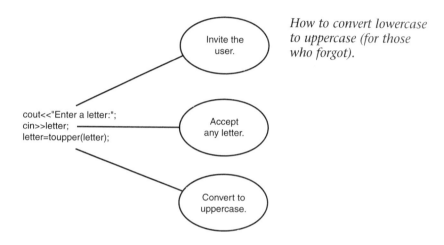

How to convert lowercase to uppercase (for those who forgot).

Try the next program and see the results. Entering any vowel, regardless of case, produces the following screen output:

```
This is a vowel
```

Listing 8.1   The Vowel Test

```cpp
#include <iostream.h>
#include <ctype.h>
#define message "This is a vowel"

main()
{
    char letter;

    cout << "Enter a letter : ";
    cin >> letter;
    letter = toupper(letter);
    switch (letter)
    {
```

continues

Listing 8.1 **The Vowel Test** CONTINUED

```
        case 'A' :     cout << message << endl;
                       break;
        case 'E' :     cout << message << endl;
                       break;
        case 'I' :     cout << message << endl;
                       break;
        case 'O' :     cout << message << endl;
                       break;
        case 'U' :     cout << message << endl;
                       break;
        default  :     cout << "Not a vowel" << endl;
    }
    return(0);
}
```

Nesting Revisited, Then Kicked into Touch

Functionality

Functionality is a big word used by computer people to describe how a computer program appears from the end user's point of view. Programs can be written using many variations of code and yet still achieve identical inputs and outputs.

To demonstrate how the nested if else statement could be used to achieve the same functionality as the previous program, I now give a sample program. If you read through the code, you should notice how long and unwieldy it is. This is a good example of when to choose the solution given in the preceding program in preference to the solution shown in the next program. Both programs work without problem and would satisfy the customer requirements (assuming you can find a customer who doesn't know which letters are vowels).

The next program is included to show you how much more work it takes to do the vowel program with if else statements. It can be done this way, but I would advise against this. You can type in and try out the program if you become really bored at some point.

Listing 8.2 The Vowel Test in a Nest (THIS IS MEANT TO BE A BAD EXAMPLE)

```
#include <iostream.h>
#include <ctype.h>
#define message "This is a vowel"

main()
```

```cpp
{
    char letter;

    cout << "Enter a letter : ";
    cin >> letter;
    letter = toupper(letter);
    if (letter == 'A')
    {
        cout << message << endl;
    }
    else
    {
        if (letter == 'E')
        {
            cout << message << endl;
        }
        else
            if (letter == 'I')
            {
                cout << message << endl;
            }
            else
            {
                if (letter == 'O')
                {
                    cout << message << endl;
                }
                else
                {
                    if (letter =='U')
                    {
                        cout << message << endl;
                    }
                    else
                    {
                        cout << "Not a vowel" << endl;
                    }
                }
            }
    }

    return(0);
}
```

Introducing the Menu-Driven Program

Many programs ask the user to select an option, and then they go on to perform one of several possible tasks as a result of this option. You could once again use an `if else` or a `switch case` statement to achieve this aim, but believe me, the `switch case` is much easier. Not only is it easier to write, but also it's easier to understand if you ever have to modify the code.

An Airport Booking

In the following program, several new points are worth learning, and I will list them one at a time. The program is the front end of an airline booking system. The back end is not implemented and would typically use electronic commerce, which, although incredibly interesting, is beyond the scope of this book.

Front End, Back End, What's the Difference?

The *front end* of a program is what the end user sees and interacts with. The *back end* is all the programming that ticks away to achieve the required functionality that is unseen by the end user.

Programmers Versus Marketing

As an aside, I was recently working on this type of project. The people who were writing the functionality dived straight in and wrote the code with the attitude of "who cares what it looks like, as long as it works," whereas the marketing people held the view of "who cares whether it works, as long as it looks good." Obviously the answer lies in between these two opposing views, but it goes to show that the culture that you work in dictates your standpoint.

The Key Points Revealed

Listing 8.3 is an example of a menu-driven system. Take a quick glance through the code now before you read the following key points of how it works:

➤ The menu system is just a few lines of text that tell the user what is available.
➤ The user is then invited to enter his selection.
➤ The `switch case` acts on that selection.
➤ The entire menu and select process is wrapped up inside a `do while` loop to keep it repeating until the user selects the quit option and exits from the program. Ironically, the command to exit the program is called `exit()` and is contained in the `stdlib.h` library.

Caps Lock On/Caps Lock Off

Make a special note of the next point: If more than one choice leads to the same action, they can be listed one after the other. In the example, quit can be achieved by selecting *q* or *Q*.

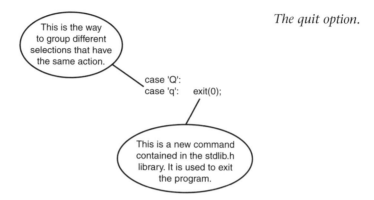

The quit option.

A Step over the Line

I don't know whether you've realized this yet, so I'm going to tell you anyway. You can split a line of code over several lines. This makes it easier to lay out your code in a professional manner, thus making it easier to read. It has no effect on the operation of the program. Here is a diagram to show what I mean.

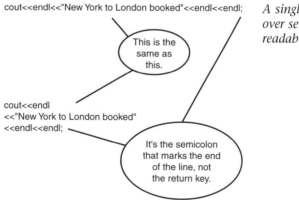

A single line of code split over several lines to aid readability.

Let's Make That Booking

Enter, save, and run the program—but don't expect a return ticket to Sydney to arrive in the mail. Remember, the back-end electronic commerce bit is missing.

Caps On, Caps Off

The only difference between *q* and *Q* is the caps lock. If you leave it to the user to distinguish between the two, you are asking for trouble. I once had a student who spent three hours debugging a program because he didn't know that the caps lock was on.

Listing 8.3   Demo of a Menu-Driven Program

```cpp
#include <iostream.h>
#include <stdlib.h>

main()
{
    char choice;

    do
      {
        // This is the menu displayed to the screen

        cout << "FLIGHT BOOKING SYSTEM" << endl << endl;
        cout << "1..New York to London Heathrow" << endl;
        cout << "2..New York to Vancouver" << endl;
        cout << "3..New York to Sydney" << endl;
        cout << "4..New York to Cape Town" << endl;
        cout << "Q..Quit" << endl;

        // This reads in the user selection.

        cout << endl << endl << "Enter your choice : ";
        cin >> choice;

        // This section acts on the user selection.

        switch (choice)
        {
            case '1' :      cout << endl
                                 << "New York to London booked"
                                 << endl << endl;
```

```
                            break;

            case '2' :      cout << endl
                                 << "New York to Vancouver booked"
                                 << endl << endl;
                            break;

            case '3' :      cout << endl
                                 << "New York to Sydney booked"
                                 << endl << endl;
                            break;

            case '4' :      cout << endl
                                 << "New York to Cape Town booked"
                                 << endl << endl;
                            break;

        case 'Q' :
        case 'q' :          exit(0);
      }
    } while(1);
    return(0);
}
```

Do You See What I See?

The text menu that appears onscreen will look like this:

```
FLIGHT BOOKING SYSTEM

1..New York to London Heathrow
2..New York to Vancouver
3..New York to Sydney
4..New York to Cape Town
Q..Quit


Enter your choice :
```

If you select option 4, for example, the following should appear on the screen:

```
New York to Cape Town booked
```

A Final Point for the Observant

Did you spot the trick? You did? Well done. On the off chance you missed it, I'll tell all. What was the data type of the user input selection? A char, I hear you cry. Well spotted, but weren't the menu items numbered 1, 2, 3 and 4? Correct again. Now then, everything on the keyboard is in fact a character, so we didn't actually read in 1, 2, 3, or 4. We actually read in '1', '2', '3', or '4', and this is dead sneaky because you cannot crash the program by selecting bogus inputs. Why? Because there aren't any bogus keys!

When Is an Integer Not an Integer?

When it's a char. Everything read in from the keyboard is an ASCII character code, which stands for *American Standard Code for Information Interchange*. The ASCII characters are a numeric sequence from 0 to 255 that represents every possible single keystroke (and a few more) on the keyboard. When you set up a variable as a char and then enter a value via the keyboard, your C++ program automatically converts that ASCII input into a char. The same thing happens with an integer and a float. All this conversion happens without you actually realizing it. Who said computers were stupid?

The Least You Need to Know

➤ The switch case statement enables all the wanted conditions of a variable to be listed and the required action to follow if that condition is true.

➤ Nested if else statements become very complicated, but the switch case is short and to the point.

➤ The restriction placed on the switch case statement is that the values in the wanted list must be of an ordinal data type.

➤ The switch case statement is an ideal tool for writing menu-driven systems.

➤ If more than one choice leads to the same action, they can be listed one after the other and that action written only once.

➤ The exit() is contained in the stdlib.h library and is used to quit the program.

➤ ASCII stands for *American Standard Code for Information Interchange*. The ASCII characters are a numeric sequence from 0 to 255 that represents every possible single keystroke (and a few more) on the keyboard.

Chapter 9

Beyond the Simple, Into the Compound Arrays

In This Chapter

➤ The theory of arrays

➤ How to store and retrieve data by using an array in C++

➤ Some more C++ shorthand

➤ How to neatly format columns of data in C++

➤ How to read in spaces within a string

Structured Variables! What Are They?

In the previous chapters, you have learned about and played with a few of the many data types available in C++. You will now build on that knowledge and learn about structured variables. "What are they?" I hear you call. Arrays, my friend, arrays.

New Types for Old

The examples encountered so far have used variables of type integer, float, and char (forget about string for the moment). These three types are collectively known as *simple data types* and are *predefined* in C++. That is, they are part of the programming language. A variable that is of a simple data type can hold only one value at any one point in time. If you are unsure about this, have a look again at Chapter 2, "From Absolutely Nothing to Screen a Display." However, much of computing is concerned with collections of related data (databases and spreadsheets, for example), and it's often more appropriate to use variables that are capable of holding more than one value at a time. These variables are called *structured variables*, and their structure is composed of simple data types. This is the concept of an array.

That Box Trick Again

An array can be pictured as a collection of boxes piled one on top of the other with the following rules applied:

Underlying Data Type

The term *underlying data type* means the simple data type that is used to build a structured data type.

➤ Each box in the pile is an element of the array.

➤ All elements in the array must be of the same simple data type.

➤ You cannot mix data types.

Let us construct an array of six numbers. The simple underlying data type of the numbers will be integer, so the array will be an array of integer.

A pile of boxes representing the array.

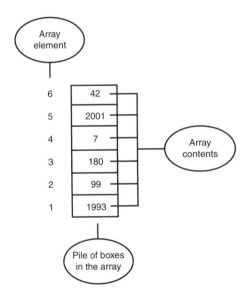

I Do Declare! A C++ Array

In C++, an array is declared like any other variable by stating the data type and giving the identifier a name. In addition to this, the number of elements contained in the array is placed in brackets after the variable. This tells C++ how many boxes are in the pile, and how big the boxes are. Easy!

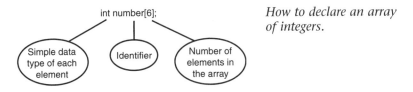

How to declare an array of integers.

Accessing the Array: The Dreaded Offset

In any program that uses arrays, you access an array element by specifying the identifier of the array along with an index, contained in brackets, that describes how far that element is displaced from the initial element of the array. You *do not* specify the element number.

The first element in the array would be described as shown in the figure. It is displaced by zero positions from the first element. It is the first element!

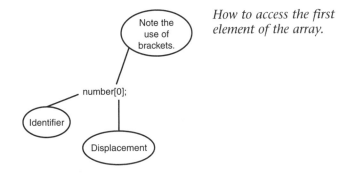

How to access the first element of the array.

The second element is displaced by one position from the first element, so you use the syntax in the next figure.

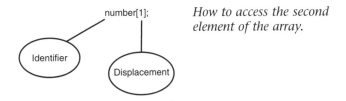

How to access the second element of the array.

And so the process continues. The number describing the displacement is known as the *offset*, and it is always one less than the array element. This relationship is shown in the next diagram.

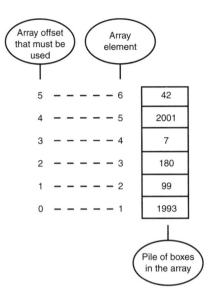

The relationship between the number of array elements and their offset.

A Peek in the Box

To print the first element of the array to the screen, you simply use the offset 0 to access that array element. If you look at the array in the first figure, you will find that offset 0, which is array element 1, contains the integer value 1993. This is the value that would appear onscreen.

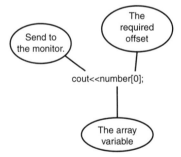

How to send the contents of a single element of the array to the screen.

A Poke at the Box

To place a value into an array element, you use the normal assignment operation. In addition, you must specify the offset, thus describing exactly where in the array you are storing the data.

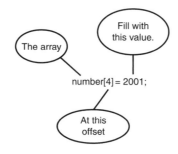

How to assign a value to a single element of the array.

A Technical Description of the Memory Model

When you declare any variable, you are grabbing a chunk of computer memory large enough to store the data. In an array, you need several consecutive chunks of memory. Where this memory starts is called the *base address*, and it is symbolized and known to the compiler by the identifier of the variable. As far as the computer is concerned, when you state the identifier, it knows where the base address of the array lives in memory. In the example, the array is of type integer, and in modern C++ compilers, an integer occupies 4 bytes of memory. For offset 0, it is the base address plus 0 bytes. For offset 1, it is the base address plus 4 bytes. For offset 2, it is the base address plus 8 bytes, and so on.

Story Time

So far so good. We've covered some pretty heavy stuff, and I haven't told you any stories. Let's remedy that now before pressing on and seeing a full program.

Several years ago, when C++ was young and networks were trusting little animals, a top student of mine wrote a program, a very good program. It was getting late, and the program was running well when, for no apparent reason, the computer locked up. Then, again for no apparent reason, the network fell over (crash). It was late, so the class went home.

Bright and early the next day when I showed up for class, the network manager was going ballistic. Someone, somehow, had got past his precious security and wiped the operating system from the server, thus decimating the network. Nothing worked any more.

The Dreaded Offset *Bytes* Back

Have you thought to yourself, "What happens if I go beyond the offset?" In other words, if the array has six elements, what will happen if I try to access a seventh element? Well, C++ is perfectly happy to allow this, but be it on your own head and conscience. If you just peek at the seventh element, there isn't a problem. You simply see the contents of that memory location, which is probably just random garbage. If you poke at memory, you don't know what you are overwriting. This can potentially be catastrophic, especially if by some chance you poke into the computer operating system. On the other hand, you might poke to an area of free memory—no problem and no harm done. Go on, I dare you! It's your computer, not mine.

Later that week when things had calmed down and the network was feeling better, I took a look at my top student's C++ program. "Oh my God" was my reaction. He had specified the element number instead of the offset and gone one step beyond the top of the array. By a freak chance, the program had somehow tapped into a network command that was interpreted as self-destruct, and self-destruct it did.

Keep this story secret because no one knows the identities of those involved. The moral is, be careful with offsets and don't tell network managers your secrets.

Program Time

Values are assigned to the six elements of the array—a technique known as *initialization*—before they are written to the screen, using a `for` loop. This program demonstrates all the issues described in this chapter, so have a good read before running it. I have initialized the array, starting at 5 and going down to 0; this is only to keep the same order as shown in previous diagrams. You don't have to do it that way. In fact, you can initialize in any random order that is appropriate. When you run the program in Listing 9.1, all six elements of the array will print to the screen as shown here:

```
42
2001
7
180
99
1993
```

Listing 9.1   Demo of a Six-Element Array

```
#include <iostream.h>

main()
{
    int number[6];          // an array of integer
    int index;              // loop control variable

    number[5] = 42;         // initialize the array
    number[4] = 2001;
    number[3] = 7;
    number[2] = 180;
    number[1] = 99;
    number[0] = 1993;

    for (index = 0; index <= 5; index++)
    {
        cout << number[index] << endl;
    }
    return(0);
}
```

I Do Declare in Shorthand

An alternative shorthand method to initialize an array is available to the C++ programmer and is demonstrated in Listing 9.2. Several advanced features are introduced in this program, and I will deal with them one at a time.

Listing 9.2   An Array of Integers That Demonstrates the Alignment of Columns

```
#include <iostream.h>

#define MAX 20

main()
{
    // declare and initialize an array
    int number[MAX] = {12,33,45,66,43,1,56,78,101,99};
    int index;

    cout.setf(ios::right);
    for (index = 0; index < MAX; index++)
```

continues

```
    {
        cout << endl
            << "THE CONTENTS OF ARRAY ELEMENT";
        cout.width(4);
        cout << (index + 1)  <<  " IS :";
        cout.width(4);
        cout << number[index];
    }
    cout << endl << endl;
    return(0);
}
```

Old Topics, New Context

The program defines MAX to be 20. This is used to create a 20-element array called number. It is also used to specify the maximum value in the for loop. The loop is used to send the contents of the array to the screen just to prove that it works.

MAX for Everything

If you change MAX, you simultaneously change the size of the array and the number of iterations of the for loop. This is a crafty trick used by the professionals, so learn it and better still, use it.

New Topics, Old Context

Immediately after the declaration of the array, its first 10 elements are initialized to the values within the braces. This is similar to the declare and initialize shorthand introduced for simple variables in Chapter 3, "The Old Box of Variables Tricks."

Because only 10 elements were initialized, the remaining 10 values are automatically set to zero.

New Topics, New Context

In case you think you have the hang of C++ and are sneering at the ease of the language, I have decided to introduce some new, nasty, confusing topics. It's all tied up with OOP, of which you will learn shortly. If you find some of the syntax strange, don't worry, it's supposed to be. Just use it and don't ask questions—all will be well.

The new OOP program statements are to tidy up the screen display and arrange figures into nice neat columns. To do this, you must set column widths and set up display justification. The command `cout.setf(ios::right)` is used at any convenient point before you want right justification to begin. After you've set it, it stays set until you tell the program differently.

The `cout.width(4)` sets up the column width as four. The cout command that follows inserts its data into the right-justified, four-digit–wide column. The `cout.width` command works only once; if you want further data in the column, you must use it again. I have used a column width of four. To increase or decrease column widths, simply change the 4 to the required value.

Justification

Justification dictates whether the output lines up with the left or right side of the column it is placed in.

Now that you grasp the new concepts, it's time to put them to work. Enter and run the program. You will get an output as shown in the next screen display.

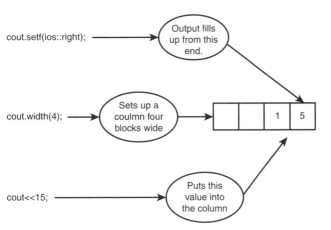

Setting up right justification and column width.

Here is the screen output for Listing 9.3, showing right justification of the data in a width 4 column:

```
THE CONTENTS OF ARRAY ELEMENT  1 IS :  77
THE CONTENTS OF ARRAY ELEMENT  2 IS :  23
THE CONTENTS OF ARRAY ELEMENT  3 IS :   6
THE CONTENTS OF ARRAY ELEMENT  4 IS : 100
THE CONTENTS OF ARRAY ELEMENT  5 IS :  43
THE CONTENTS OF ARRAY ELEMENT  6 IS :   1
THE CONTENTS OF ARRAY ELEMENT  7 IS :  56
THE CONTENTS OF ARRAY ELEMENT  8 IS :  78
THE CONTENTS OF ARRAY ELEMENT  9 IS : 101
THE CONTENTS OF ARRAY ELEMENT 10 IS :  99
```

Check This Out

Try changing the width value from 4 to the values 6,8,20,2. Run the program each time and note the results.

Arrays Are Easy, Tell Me More

Now that you have the hang of what arrays are all about, let's dive in a little deeper and have a look at some further options.

Populating an Array at Runtime

So far, you have seen the contents of the array set up when you wrote the code. This technique is okay if you know the values and do not want them to change. Of course, this will not always be the case. In the next program, an array of four elements is created, and the user is prompted to enter values at runtime using the cin command. When all four pieces of data have been collected, they are displayed onscreen. Try out the program a few times and enter different sets of data. Note that the program defines the size of the array and iterations of the loop through the constant MAX; try changing the value of MAX. Here's a tip: Don't change MAX to a ridiculously large figure unless you really love typing into the computer and have countless hours to waste.

Listing 9.3   Creating an Array of Integers Example #1

```
#include <iostream.h>

#define MAX 4

main()
{
    int number[MAX];          // declare empty array
    int index;

    // gather the data and put it in array
    for (index = 0; index < MAX; index ++)
    {
        cout << "Enter a number ";
        cin >> number[index];
    }

    // show array contents to screen
    for (index = 0; index < MAX; index++)
    {
        cout << endl
             << "THE CONTENTS OF ARRAY ELEMENT "
             << (index + 1) << " IS : ";
        cout << number[index];
    }
    cout << endl << endl;
    return(0);
}
```

When you run this program, you will be invited to enter four integer values. When all four values have been entered, they are all shown onscreen as follows:

```
Enter a number 77
Enter a number 23
Enter a number 6
Enter a number 100

THE CONTENTS OF ARRAY ELEMENT  1 IS : 77
THE CONTENTS OF ARRAY ELEMENT  2 IS : 23
THE CONTENTS OF ARRAY ELEMENT  3 IS : 6
THE CONTENTS OF ARRAY ELEMENT  4 IS : 100
```

Hiding the Empty Spaces

The program given in Listing 9.3 assumes that you required a fixed number of data entries with the use of a for loop. This might not always be the case. One method of

93

getting away from the fixed quantities of data is given in Listing 9.4. You declare an array of sufficient size to cope with the largest number of elements that you are ever likely to encounter. Then, with the aid of a `while` loop, you read in the list of data to be entered. After each data entry, the program asks the user whether any more data is to be entered. If the answer is `'y'`, a variable called `count` is incremented and the process repeated. The purpose of `count` is to keep track of how many elements in the array have been filled. The loop is terminated when the user replies `'n'`.

The next action is for all elements of the array that have been assigned data to be written to the screen. Unused array elements are omitted because `count` is used as the upper limit of the `for` loop. Although this method is rather wasteful in terms of computer memory (alternative methods are available), at this stage the technique suits your purposes extremely well. Try this program with different numbers of data entries, anything from zero to forty entries.

Anything Goes

In Listing 9.4, the user is asked to enter `'y'` or `'n'`. The action to terminate is specifically `'n'`. However, any other character, not just `'y'`, will keep the loop operating.

Listing 9.4   Creating an Array of Integers Example #2

```cpp
#include <iostream.h>

#define MAX 40

main()
{
    int number[MAX];      // declare empty array
    int index;            // loop control variable
    int count = 0;        // keep count of elements used
    char more;            // is there more data?

    // gather the data and put it in array
    while(1)
    {
        cout << "Enter a number ";
        cin >> number[count];
        cout << "Any more items to enter y/n : ";
```

```
    cin >> more;
    if (more == 'n')
    {
        break;
    }
    else
    {
        count++;
    }
}
// show contents of array element
//which contain data
for (index = 0; index <= count; index++)
{
    cout << endl
         << "THE CONTENTS OF ARRAY ELEMENT "
         << (index + 1) << " IS : ";
    cout << number[index];
}
cout << endl << "ARRAY ELEMENTS USED = " << count+1;
cout << endl << endl;
return(0);
}
```

Arrays That Float

So far, you have dealt only with arrays of type integer, but this need not be the case, of course. You can have arrays of any data type that you want. If you require an array of floats, you simply declare it to be so. The next diagram shows how to declare an array of 20 elements of float. Displaying the contents and populating the array are exactly the same as in an integer.

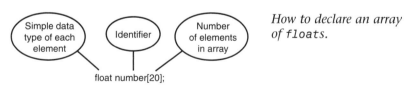

How to declare an array of floats.

Character Arrays: A String in Disguise

As I said earlier, you can have an array of any data type, so you can also have an array of characters, which would be declared just like any other array. Look at the next diagram.

A string is an array of characters.

char name[20];

Now I hear you say, "But haven't I seen this before?" And so you have. We used this when we first introduced strings, and a string is actually an array of characters, so the previous figure is an array that holds 20 characters. Just to recap, here is Listing 9.5, which is a program that uses an array of characters and a special string function called `getline` contained in the `string.h` library. On investigating the program, you should find nothing new except the line of code shown in the next diagram. This is another part of that mysterious OOP stuff that you will learn later (and love). This command reads in a string and stores it in the variable called `name`. "Hold it, hold it!" I hear you scream. "Why didn't we just use `cin`?" Well, this command reads the spaces within a string; `cin` throws away the characters after a space. You didn't know that, did you?

Look, I can do spaces.

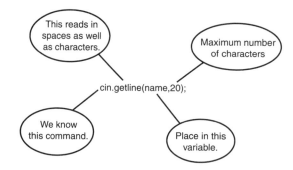

cin.getline(name,20);

Try Listing 9.5 with several different names, some with and some without spaces in them.

Listing 9.5   Example of the `getline` Function

```
#include <iostream.h>

main()
{
    char name[20];

    cout << "Enter a name ";
    cin.getline(name,20);
    cout << endl << name << endl << endl;
    return(0);
}
```

When you run this program, you will get the following screen output. Using `cin.getline` allows spaces within the test string.

```
Enter a name Bob Dylan

Bob Dylan
```

The Least You Need to Know

➤ An array is composed of several simple data types all of the same data type.

➤ In C++, an array is declared like any other variable by stating the data type and giving the identifier a name. In addition to this, the number of elements contained in the array is placed in brackets after the variable.

➤ You access an array element by specifying the identifier of the array along with an index, contained in brackets, that describes how far that element is displaced from the initial element of the array.

➤ An alternative shorthand method to initialize an array is available to the C++ programmer:

```
int number[MAX] = {12,33,45,66,43,1,56,78,101,99};
```

This is known as in-line initialization.

➤ An array can be populated at runtime by using the `cin` command just like a simple variable. However, you must specify which element in the array you are assigning data to.

➤ Justification dictates whether the output lines up with the left or right side of the column it is placed in.

➤ The command `cout.setf(ios::right)` is used at any convenient point before you want right justification to begin. After you've set it, it stays set until you tell the program differently.

➤ The `cout.width(4)` sets up the column width as four. The `cout.width` command works only once. If you want further data in the column, you must use it again.

➤ You can have an array of floats just like an array of integers.

➤ You can have an array of characters just like an array of integers.

➤ An array of characters is a string.

Chapter 10

Spread Yourself Out in Space with Multidimensional Arrays

An Array Among Arrays

In the examples met so far, the data types of the arrays have been the simple types: integer, float, char, and string. However, there is no reason why the data type of an array cannot also be a structured data type such as an array—that is, an array of arrays. Such a data type is known as a *multidimensional array*. Consider the following relatively simple example of a two-dimensional array.

Putting It into Rows and Columns

The data stored in a two-dimensional array can be pictured as a grid with rows and columns, as in the following figure. Suppose the vertical index down the side (which numbers the rows) is the five open days of a shop that sells BOTCHUPS, and the horizontal index along the top (which numbers the columns) is the week in the month. The matrix shown depicts the daily sales of BOTCHUPS over a four-week period.

The BOTCHUPS data can be pictured as a grid with rows and columns.

		Column Index		
	1	2	3	4
Row Index 1	91	22	37	40
2	58	63	99	35
3	77	81	23	62
4	92	15	33	29
5	102	73	62	64

X and Y Mark the Spot

Every item of data in the array can be pinpointed by giving the row number and the column number, in that order. For example, if you say 3,2, you are talking about the point where the coordinates given by row 3 and column 2 intersect. If you trace this out, you will find that the value 81 lives at this location.

The Treasure Declared in C++

The BOTCHUPS data can be represented by a two-dimensional array because it has two coordinates. It is simply a matter of giving the declaration of the array two numbers instead of one. First of all, you need to declare and initialize the array. The row index representing days comes first, and the column index representing weeks comes second. It is dead easy to get these coordinates mixed up, so be very careful.

Declaration of the array showing the number of rows and columns required.

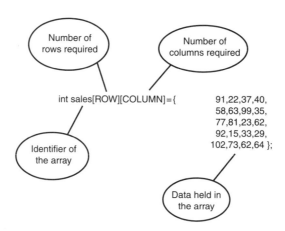

The Offset Strikes Again

To specify a data item in a C++ array is now very easy. You know that you must give the row and column number in the correct order, and you know how to use cout, so, no problem. Ah ah. Haven't we forgotten something? Oh yes, the dreaded offset! Remember that the first row offset is actually zero, not one. Similarly, the first column offset is also zero, not one. To output a data item from the array, you must give the array identifier, followed by the row offset in brackets and the column offset in brackets. Remember that the offset in C++ is always one less than the element or index number. Earlier I talked about the coordinates 3,2 pointing to the data item with a value of 81. Well, a C++ offset would be 2,1 to point to that same piece of data. Confusing, isn't it? This is shown in the next diagram.

cout with a two-dimensional array item as the data.

Neat Data!

In the source code, I have laid out the data array in rows and columns. You don't have to do it that way. You can just type in the data in a straight line with each data item following the next. But believe me, it's really difficult to read. Try it out if you want, but don't blame me when you hit snags.

A Program on the Table

Using your newly acquired knowledge of arrays, you can build the program in Listing 10.1 to write out all the data items stored in the array. Because two offsets are required to manipulate a two-dimensional array, it is convenient to use a for loop nested within another for loop. Remember nesting? And you thought that you could forget it, didn't you? It works like this:

➤ Using the outer of the nested for loops, you set the value of down to 0. This is the first row offset.

➤ Entering the inner for loop, you sweep across the entire column offsets from 0 to 3.

101

- Having done this, you find yourself back at the outer `for` loop where the value of down increments to 1.

- Once again, you enter the inner `for` loop and sweep across the entire column offsets from 0 to 3.

- This process continues until all the data items have been visited and displayed onscreen.

When you run the program, you will have a nicely formatted screen that looks similar to this:

```
 91  22  37  40

 58  63  99  35

 77  81  23  62

 92  15  33  29

102  73  62  64
```

Listing 10.1   Demo of a Two-Dimensional Array

```cpp
#include <iostream.h>
#define ROW 5          // FIVE WORKING DAYS
#define COLUMN 4       // FOUR WEEKS IN MONTH
main()
{    int sales[ROW][COLUMN] = { 91,22,37,40,
                                58,63,99,35,
                                77,81,23,62,
                                92,15,33,29,
                                102,73,62,64};
      int down;        // go down the rows
     int across;       // go across the columns

     cout.setf(ios::right);
     cout << endl;
     for (down = 0; down < ROW; down++)
     {
       for (across = 0; across < COLUMN; across++)
       {
           cout.width(4);
           cout << sales[down][across];
       }
       cout << endl << endl;
     }
     return(0);
}
```

The Daily Sales Figures Observed

Listing 10.1 displays all the data to the screen in a nice set of rows and columns, but it might be that you are interested in only certain sections of the data. If so, read on, amigo.

A Day in the Month

Suppose you want to list all BOTCHUPS sold on the first working day of each week. You would need to select offset 0 (which is row 1) and keep this fixed. Then you would need to sweep across all the columns. To achieve this task, you could use a single `for` statement in the manner of this diagram:

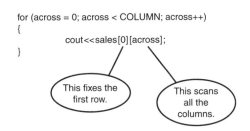

The `for` loop to scan a single row of the array.

Enter and observe Listing 10.2, which pulls all the points together. The Monday sales display as follows:

        91   22   37   40

I Don't Like Mondays

Okay, so change the 0 to either 1, 2, 3, or 4, and you can observe any day that you want. Now *there's* a challenge for you.

Listing 10.2   Using a Two-Dimensional Array to List a Particular Row

```
#include <iostream.h>

#define ROW 5
```

continues

Listing 10.2   Using a Two-Dimensional Array to List a Particular Row CONTINUED

```
#define COLUMN 4

main()
{
        int sales[ROW][COLUMN] = {    91,22,37,40,
                                      58,63,99,35,
                                      77,81,23,62,
                                      92,15,33,29,
                                     102,73,62,64};
        int across;          // This is the columns

        cout.setf(ios::right);
        cout << endl << "A Day In The Month";
        cout << endl << endl;
        for (across = 0; across < COLUMN; across++)
        {
          cout.width(4);
          cout << sales[0][across];
        }
        cout << endl << endl;
        return(0);
}
```

A Week in the Month

Having listed a particular day, it would be grossly unfair to the ~~weak~~ week supporters if you didn't include them. So here you go. If you want to list all the BOTCHUPS sold in the second week of the month, you simply fix the second coordinate to an offset of 1 and scan down that column.

Using the for *loop to scan a single column of the array.*

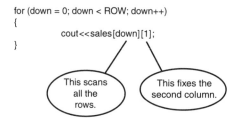

At last, the program. I hope that you haven't cheated and already typed in Listing 10.3. Good, so type it in now as a reward. Your screen view will show the following BOTCHUPS sales in the second week of the month:

```
22
63
81
15
73
```

I Don't Like Being Second

Okay, so change the 1 to either 0, 2, 3, or 4, and you can observe any week that you want. Now there's a second challenge for you.

Listing 10.3   Using a Two-Dimensional Array to List a Particular Column

```cpp
#include <iostream.h>
#define ROW 5
#define COLUMN 4

main()
{
int sales[ROW][COLUMN] = {    91,22,37,40,
                              58,63,99,35,
                              77,81,23,62,
                              92,15,33,29,
                              102,73,62,64};

        int down;          // This is the row

        cout.setf(ios::right);
        cout << endl << "A Week In The Month Observed.";
        cout << endl << endl;
        for (down = 0; down < ROW; down++)
        {
          cout.width(4);
          cout << sales[down][1] << endl;
        }
        cout << endl << endl;
        return(0);
}
```

A Three-Dimensional World

I have taught C++ in face-to-face class situations for many years now. When it comes to this part of the course, most people understand one- and two-dimensional arrays, so I'll tell you a secret that I don't tell my classes. The reason for this is that you can't attack me in the corridor after class. You can have more than two dimensions. Now that didn't sound too bad, did it? But wait, until you try to implement the next example of a three-dimensional array, the concept is easy enough, but entering the data plays havoc with the typing fingers.

Putting It into Rows, Columns, and Pages

If you are working in a three-dimensional array, you need three coordinates, so you just add the extra dimension to your C++ declaration, as shown in these figures.

The data can be pictured as a grid with rows and columns, as well as pages that give the extra dimension.

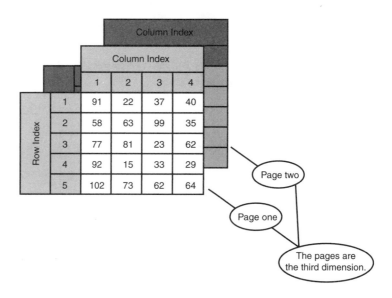

Declaration of the three-dimensional array showing the number of rows, columns, and pages required.

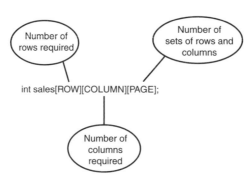

106

X, Y, and Z Mark the Spot

When you output data to the screen, you must specify three coordinates, as shown in the following diagram.

cout<<sales[down][across][back];

Three coordinates

A three-dimensional array requires three coordinates.

A (Very Long) Program with Pages

Now for the program. You're really going to love me for this one! Notice that I have changed the way in which I initialize the data items in the array. There are two reasons for this. The first one is a good educational reason because it shows you how to assign data to an individual element of the array. You can use this method to set up an array at runtime. The second reason is my cowardice in attempting to write and explain how to use the in-line style of the last program. I think I'll settle for the educational reason. Now try the program, and I apologize for the amount of typing required.

May I Have Some More Pages, Please?

Sure you can. Just increase the value of PAGE. I settled for two pages because my keyboard began to overheat, but you are quite welcome to add extra data if you want.

In Listing 10.4, you should observe the sale of BOTCHUPS over a two-month period, as shown here:

```
91  22  37  40

58  63  99  35

77  81  23  62

92  15  33  29
```

```
              102  73  62  64

               12  23  27  42

               59  83  79  75

               77  71  63  72

              110 105 103 109

              102  83  61  63
```

Listing 10.4   Demo of a Three-Dimensional Array

```cpp
#include <iostream.h>

#define ROW 5                   // FIVE WORKING DAYS
#define COLUMN 4                // FOUR WEEKS IN MONTH
#define PAGE 2                  // MONTHS 1 AND 2

main()
{
    int sales[ROW][COLUMN][PAGE];
    int down;
    int across;
    int back = 0;

    sales[0][0][0] = 91;
    sales[0][1][0] = 22;
    sales[0][2][0] = 37;
    sales[0][3][0] = 40;

    sales[1][0][0] = 58;
    sales[1][1][0] = 63;
    sales[1][2][0] = 99;
    sales[1][3][0] = 35;

    sales[2][0][0] = 77;
    sales[2][1][0] = 81;
    sales[2][2][0] = 23;
    sales[2][3][0] = 62;

    sales[3][0][0] = 92;
    sales[3][1][0] = 15;
    sales[3][2][0] = 33;
    sales[3][3][0] = 29;
```

```
sales[4][0][0] = 102;
sales[4][1][0] = 73;
sales[4][2][0] = 62;
sales[4][3][0] = 64;

sales[0][0][1] = 12;
sales[0][1][1] = 23;
sales[0][2][1] = 27;
sales[0][3][1] = 42;

sales[1][0][1] = 59;
sales[1][1][1] = 83;
sales[1][2][1] = 79;
sales[1][3][1] = 75;

sales[2][0][1] = 77;
sales[2][1][1] = 71;
sales[2][2][1] = 63;
sales[2][3][1] = 72;

sales[3][0][1] = 110;
sales[3][1][1] = 105;
sales[3][2][1] = 103;
sales[3][3][1] = 109;

sales[4][0][1] = 102;
sales[4][1][1] = 83;
sales[4][2][1] = 61;
sales[4][3][1] = 63;

cout.setf(ios::right);
cout << endl;
for (down = 0; down < ROW; down++)
{
    for (across = 0; across < COLUMN; across++)
    {
        cout.width(4);
        cout << sales[down][across][back];
    }
    cout << endl << endl;
}
back++;
cout << endl << endl;
for (down = 0; down < ROW; down++)
{
```

continues

Listing 10.4   Demo of a Three-Dimensional Array CONTINUED

```
        for (across = 0; across < COLUMN; across++)
        {
            cout.width(4);
            cout << sales[down][across][back];
        }
        cout << endl << endl;
    }
    return(0);
}
```

Get In-Line

In-line was briefly mentioned in the last chapter, but I'll recap. There are two ways to initialize an array. The first is to declare and initialize just like a simple variable:

```
int demo[4] = {33,75,12,92};
```

This is referred to as *in-line*.

The second way is the longhand method. You specify every offset and manually add data to each element:

```
demo[0] = 33;
demo[1] = 75;
demo[2] = 12;
demo[3] = 92;
```

Character Arrays Are Still Strings in Disguise

The next step is to describe the representation and use of strings within multidimensional arrays. Recall from the last chapter that a single string is simply a one-dimensional array of char, so an array that contains several strings is a two-dimensional array of char.

Take a look at Listing 10.5, which contains an array of names of famous people. The representation is virtually identical to that in previous examples in this chapter.

Just as in the previous examples, you can sweep through the rows in the array with the use of the variable called index, but take note that I have given only a single coordinate. The clever compiler assumes the second coordinate to be a zero—in other words, the first letter in the name—so you display each name in full. Clever things these computers.

When you type in and then run Listing 10.5, you will see a list of four famous people appear onscreen. Here is the Hall of Fame screen display:

```
DAVY CROCKETT
JOHN LENNON
MOHAMMED ALI
WILLIAM WALLACE
```

How Many Dimensions Are There?

How many do you want? You can go on indefinitely creating four-, five-, or six-dimensional arrays (and so on), but the overhead becomes immense. Arrays are memory-hungry monsters, and you should take care with your design. I would question the validity of anything beyond a three-dimensional array, but there again, I'm not into multidimensional particle physics.

Listing 10.5 Example of a Two-Dimensional Array of Characters

```
#include <iostream.h>

#define MAXNAMES 4          // FOUR NAMES IN ARRAY
#define MAXLENGTH 20        // NOT MORE THAN 19 CHARACTERS

main()
{
     char name[MAXNAMES][MAXLENGTH] =      {
                                            "DAVY CROCKETT",
                                            "JOHN LENNON",
                                            "MOHAMMED ALI",
                                            "WILLIAM WALLACE"};

     int index;

     for (index = 0; index < MAXNAMES; index++)
     {
       cout << endl << name[index];
     }
     cout << endl << endl;
     return(0);
}
```

The Least You Need to Know

➤ A multidimensional array is an array with an array as its underlying data type.

➤ A two-dimensional array has rows and columns and forms a matrix with X and Y coordinates in which data can be stored.

Have I Lost a Letter Somewhere?

The answer is yes. If a string is declared as being an array of 20 elements, it can hold only 19 characters. The final element is reserved for a special character called NULL. The NULL character is used by C++ to mark the end of the string and to assist in special string operations.

➤ To access a two-dimensional array in C++, you must supply two coordinates to specify an array element.

➤ To scan across the rows of a two-dimensional array, you make the first coordinate a fixed value and increment the column coordinate.

➤ To scan across the columns of a two-dimensional array, you make the second coordinate fixed and increment the row coordinate.

➤ A three-dimensional array in C++ has an X, Y, and Z set of coordinates giving it length, height, and depth.

➤ To access three-dimensional array elements in C++, you must specify three coordinates.

➤ A single string is simply a one-dimensional array of char, so an array that contains several strings is a two-dimensional array of char.

➤ The NULL character is used by C++ to mark the end of the string and to assist in special string operations.

➤ In theory, you can build an array of an infinite number of dimensions. For every additional dimension, you must provide another coordinate.

Chapter 11

Take a Trip Around the Solar System in a Parallel Array

In This Chapter

➤ The theory and use of parallel arrays

➤ How to neatly space columns of data with the TAB character

➤ How to initialize a string variable by using the strcpy command

---

How Do You Mix Data Types? Enter the Parallel Array

From Chapter 9, "Beyond the Simple, Into the Compound Arrays," and Chapter 10, "Spread Yourself Out in Space with Multidimensional Arrays," you know that all elements of an array must be of the same data type. But what happens if you want to represent a mixture of data types? This can be overcome by the use of two or more parallel arrays, which are accessed by a common index. Suppose you want to draw a table of the planets in the solar system and their distance from the sun. The planet names will be of type string, and their distance from the sun will be of type integer. You must therefore create two parallel arrays from the information shown in the planet table.

There are nine known planets, so your two arrays must have room for nine elements. This is defined at the start of Listing 11.1 with #define MAX 9. Don't forget that you use an offset of 0 to 8 inclusive, which is nine.

The data for the nine known planets.

Index	Planet	Distance
1	Mercury	58
2	Venus	108
3	Earth	150
4	Mars	228
5	Jupiter	778
6	Saturn	1427
7	Uranus	2869
8	Neptune	4498
9	Pluto	5900

Listing 11.1   A Parallel Array

```
#include <iostream.h>
#include <string.h>

#define MAX 9        // There are 9 known planets
#define LENGTH 8     // No name is longer than 7
                     // characters
#define TAB '\t'     // Define a tab character

main()
{
    char planet[MAX][LENGTH];    // planet names
    int  distance[MAX];          // distance from sun
    int  index;

    // INITIALIZE THE TWO ARRAYS
    strcpy(planet[0],"MERCURY");
    distance[0] = 58;
    strcpy(planet[1],"VENUS");
    distance[1] = 108;
    strcpy(planet[2],"EARTH");
    distance[2] = 150;
    strcpy(planet[3],"MARS");
    distance[3] = 228;
    strcpy(planet[4],"JUPITER");
    distance[4] = 778;
    strcpy(planet[5],"SATURN");
    distance[5] = 1427;
    strcpy(planet[6],"URANUS");
    distance[6] = 2869;
```

```
strcpy(planet[7],"NEPTUNE");
distance[7] = 4498;
strcpy(planet[8],"PLUTO");
distance[8] = 5900;

cout << TAB << TAB << "PLANET" << TAB << TAB
                << "DISTANCE" << endl << endl;
for (index = 0; index < MAX; index++)
{
    cout << TAB << TAB << planet[index];
    cout << TAB << TAB << distance[index] << endl;
}
cout << endl;
return(0);
}
```

No planet has more than seven letters in its name, and to allow for the NULL terminator, you define the number of letters with #define LENGTH 8.

Within the main body of the program, you must create two arrays, one for each column. The first is a two-dimensional array of characters (which you now know is also an array of string) and an array of integers.

```
char planet[MAX][LENGTH];
int  distance[MAX];
```

The final step is to initialize the arrays to hold the names and distance from the sun of the nine known planets. That data can be seen in the previous table. When setting up the contents of these two variables, you must adhere to the index order. This is essential. You don't want the name MARS matched up with the distance of SATURN. That would really upset the Martians, never mind NASA.

The Planets: A Program Fit for NASA

Without much effort, you now have a complete program. You have met all the programming concepts before; they've just been rearranged slightly.

As you traverse the loop, the index is incremented by one, so first the data for the planet Mercury is written to the screen. Next time around the loop, the data for Venus is shown, then Earth, then Mars, and so on. Nothing to write home about for us professional programmers, so just to stop you from becoming bored, I thought that I'd throw in a couple of new features.

TAB *That Screen*

The first one is the TAB, which is used to line up screen data. Control characters in C++ are prefixed by the \ symbol, whereas the letter that represents TAB is t. When

115

you combine the symbol and the letter, you get a control character that I have set up using #define TAB '\t'. You can now use the word TAB anywhere in your program to insert a TAB space. Obvious really!

The String.h Library Observed

You know that strings are actually arrays of characters, and in keeping with their elevated status, they refuse to behave like common garden variables. The most obvious difference is that you cannot initialize a string in the same manner as an integer or a float. To overcome this minor problem, those nice people who produce C++ compilers have a special library called string.h, which contains functions to do these special jobs. The first one that you encounter is strcpy.

The strcpy command is used to initialize a string variable with string data.

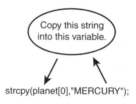

Copy this string into this variable.

strcpy(planet[0],"MERCURY");

How to Say strcpy

strcpy is an abbreviation for string copy, and C++ programmers pronounce this as *string copy*. Now that's really cool.

Try running the planets program now and observe the output to the screen. It should look remarkably like the output shown here:

PLANET	DISTANCE
MERCURY	58
VENUS	108
EARTH	150
MARS	228
JUPITER	778
SATURN	1427
URANUS	2871
NEPTUNE	4497
PLUTO	5914

Stop Press. Vulcan Discovered at Last!

A new planet called Vulcan has just been discovered. Its distance is 8,992 million kilometers from the Sun. NASA rushes to update its database.

The scientists have done the hard work. Now as professional programmers, we are paid megabucks to update the database (if only that were true). At the start of this chapter, we set up the number of planets with this statement, #define MAX 9. That meant that there are 9 planets. With the addition of Vulcan, we now have ten. So all we have to do is change the 9 to 10, and that's all folks, we have the space.

Adding the new data is easy. NASA gave it to us. This demonstrates the different way in which you initialize a string and a simple variable.

```
strcpy(planet[9],"VULCAN");
distance[9] = 8992;
```

Listing 11.2 is the full program with Vulcan added to the list. When you run the program, you will find that Vulcan has indeed joined our solar system, as can be observed in the following output:

PLANET	DISTANCE
MERCURY	58
VENUS	108
EARTH	150
MARS	228
JUPITER	778
SATURN	1427
URANUS	2871
NEPTUNE	4497
PLUTO	5914
VULCAN	8992

Programmers Love to Copy

When you are modifying an existing program, don't type the whole thing in again. Programmers always take existing code, modify it, and then save it under a different name. The old saying "Time is money" really is true here. Why waste time retyping old code when you can hack the code from someone else?

Listing 11.2   Vulcan Discovered At Last

```
#include <iostream.h>
#include <string.h>

#define MAX 10       // There are NOW 10 known planets
#define LENGTH 8      // No name is longer than 7
                      // characters
```

continues

Listing 11.2   Vulcan Discovered At Last CONTINUED

```
#define TAB '\t'        // Define a tab character

main()
{
    char planet[MAX][LENGTH];     // planet names
    int  distance[MAX];           // distance from sun
    int  index;

    // INITIALIZE THE TWO ARRAYS
    strcpy(planet[0],"MERCURY");
    distance[0] = 58;
    strcpy(planet[1],"VENUS");
    distance[1] = 108;
    strcpy(planet[2],"EARTH");
    distance[2] = 150;
    strcpy(planet[3],"MARS");
    distance[3] = 228;
    strcpy(planet[4],"JUPITER");
    distance[4] = 778;
    strcpy(planet[5],"SATURN");
    distance[5] = 1427;
    strcpy(planet[6],"URANUS");
    distance[6] = 2869;
    strcpy(planet[7],"NEPTUNE");
    distance[7] = 4498;
    strcpy(planet[8],"PLUTO");
    distance[8] = 5900;
     strcpy(planet[9],"VULCAN");
    distance[9] = 8992;

    cout << TAB << TAB << "PLANET" << TAB << TAB
                       << "DISTANCE" << endl << endl;
    for (index = 0; index < MAX; index++)
    {
        cout << TAB << TAB << planet[index];
        cout << TAB << TAB << distance[index] << endl;
    }
    cout << endl;
    return(0);
}
```

A Fatter Parallel Array

NASA has decided to spend some more dollars to update its database again. It has given the following specification:

It has been decided to add the number of moons belonging to each planet to the database. Given the additional information, create the necessary parallel arrays in the manner used in the old database. The extra information must be printed to the screen in a similar fashion to the existing information.

Index	Planet	Moons	Year	Distance
1	Mercury	0	0.024	58
2	Venus	0	0.625	108
3	Earth	1	1	150
4	Mars	2	1.91	228
5	Jupiter	16	12	778
6	Saturn	18	29.9	1427
7	Uranus	15	85.24	2869
8	Neptune	8	167.19	4498
9	Pluto	1	251.29	5900

The additional information for the planets program.

Because the new data contains four columns, all connected by a common index, it is appropriate to use four arrays in parallel.

```
char   planet[MAX][LENGTH];
int    moons[MAX];
float  year[MAX];
int    distance[MAX];
```

The big problem associated with this type of program is the amount of initialization required. Personally, I hate typing in data, so I cut and paste wherever possible. I advise you to do the same. Here is the program.

Listing 11.3   Four Parallel Arrays

```
#include <iostream.h>
#include <string.h>

#define MAX 9          // There are 9 known planets
#define LENGTH 8       // No name is longer than 7
                       // characters
```

continues

Listing 11.3   Four Parallel Arrays CONTINUED

```
#define TAB '\t'      // Define a tab character

main()
{
    char  planet[MAX][LENGTH];    // planet names
    int   moons[MAX];             // number of moons
    float year[MAX];              // length of year
    int   distance[MAX];          // distance from sun
    int   index;

    // INITIALIZE THE FOUR ARRAYS
    strcpy(planet[0],"MERCURY");
    moons[0] = 0;
    year[0] = 0.24;
    distance[0] = 58;
    strcpy(planet[1],"VENUS");
    moons[1] = 0;
    year[1] = 0.625;
    distance[1] = 108;
    strcpy(planet[2],"EARTH");
    moons[2] = 1;
    year[2] = 1;
    distance[2] = 150;
    strcpy(planet[3],"MARS");
    moons[3] = 2;
    year[3] = 1.91;
    distance[3] = 228;

    cout << TAB << TAB << "PLANET"
         << TAB << TAB << "MOONS"
         << TAB << TAB << "YEAR"
         << TAB << TAB << "DISTANCE"<< endl << endl;
    for (index = 0; index < 4; index++)
    {
        cout << TAB << TAB << planet[index];
        cout << TAB << TAB << moons[index];
        cout << TAB << TAB << year[index];
        cout << TAB << TAB << distance[index] << endl;
    }
    cout << endl;
    return(0);
}
```

Five Planets Go Missing

As a lazy programmer, I have set up the four arrays for the nine planets but added the data for only the first four. This is a valid way of testing a program. When you are sure that it works correctly, pass it on to the junior programmer to populate the rest of the arrays.

The Least You Need to Know

➤ All elements of an array must be of the same data type, but this can be overcome by the use of two or more parallel arrays, which are accessed by a common index.

➤ A C++ program uses two parallel arrays by declaring two normal arrays and tying them together with a common index.

➤ Parallel array elements are initialized in exactly the same way as normal array elements. However, care must be taken to use the common index.

➤ The elements in the parallel array are accessed in exactly the same manner as in the normal array. However, care must be taken to use the common index.

➤ Additional elements can be added to the parallel array in exactly the same manner as a normal array. However, care must be taken to use the common index.

➤ Control characters in C++ are prefixed by the \ symbol, whereas the letter that represents TAB is t. When you combine the symbol and the letter, you get a control character that can be set up using `#define TAB '\t'`. You can then use the word TAB anywhere in your program to insert a TAB space.

`float` at the `double`

In the fatter parallel array program in Listing 11.3, I have sneaked in a new data type called `double`. This data type is actually a very big `float` and is needed in this program because C++ constants with a decimal point are also `doubles`. These constants are used to hold the year length and are copied across in the program. They don't actually cause a problem, but they cause a warning to be generated when you compile the program, and this at your tender stage of development might frighten you. Now wasn't that considerate of me?

➤ Because a string is really an array of characters, you cannot use the equals sign to copy a string into a string variable. You must use the strcpy command that is contained in the string.h library.

➤ To write a C++ program that uses several parallel arrays, you simply increase the number of normal arrays that are accessed by the common index.

Chapter 12

Divide and Conquer: Functions Rule Okay

In This Chapter

➤ The reason why you use functions

➤ How you write functions in a C++ program

➤ How you use functions in a C++ program

➤ The meaning of the phrase *pass by value*

➤ The meaning of the term *internal variable*

➤ The meaning of the term *external variable*

Five Good Reasons to Use Functions

In the real world, programs tend to be extremely large and complicated. To manage such complexity, there is a widely used program development technique known as *top down design*. Top down design is the art of decomposing a complex problem into smaller more manageable tasks. These small tasks form the basis for writing a set of modules that can be linked together to make a complete program. Many advantages are gained by this, but some of the main ones are discussed here.

Short Code Is Best

Each module is reasonably short and therefore much easier to compose. I'm all in favor of making life easy.

Beat the Bugs

Each module can be tested as a standalone piece of code, making the removal of bugs (fault location) much easier.

It's a Team Game

In a team, each software engineer can work on a separate module. When all modules have been developed, they can be linked together as a complete program. This speeds developing the overall working program. If one person had been given the task of writing Windows 98, it probably would have been ready for release by the year 2098. However, lots of people worked on the product, and hey, presto, we have Windows 98 in 1998. And a wonderful product it is, too. Keep up the good work, Bill—any jobs going?

The Kiddies and The Pros

Having worked for lots of years training computer people, I am forever amused at how many of the kiddies believe that programmers sit in a corner and work in isolation. It's all about having a good time swapping ideas and working as a team, but try telling the kiddies this. No way, so let's keep the perks for the pros.

Call Again

Certain actions might be needed many times in a program, and it would be very inefficient to write those actions time and time again. A module need only be written once but can be used every time that action is required.

In the Library

When a module defines a particular action, it can be stored in a software library and used by future programs. We do not re-invent the wheel every time we make a car. How we actually do this is dealt with in Bonus Chapter 2, "Reusable Code, or How to Let Someone Else Do the Work."

A Revision of the Rules of the Game

A module in C++ is known as a *function* and consists of a prototype and a definition. We must redefine the C++ program format because C++ prototypes and definitions should follow the layout described in the rest of the book. I know some of you are going to tell me that you don't have to do it this way, but I am anyway. These are my house rules, and if you wanna be a programmer, you have to live with rules. So tough. Here are my house rules.

➤ The prototype comes before the main program begins.

➤ Definitions come after the main program has finished.

The Prototype Comes First

As I stated earlier, the prototype comes before the start of the main program and is made up of the following list of components. It is analogous to the age-old IT model of input-process-output.

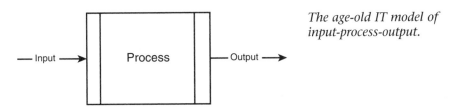

The age-old IT model of input-process-output.

➤ The function inputs are enclosed in parentheses and are known as *input parameters*, but really they are just like the variables that you already know and love. You must always specify the data type of the parameter and give it an identifier name, as done in the main program since Chapter 2. The difference is that these variables belong solely to this function and nowhere else. They are known as *local* or *internal variables*.

➤ The function is given its own unique name. You may call it anything you like, as long as it's not a keyword in C++.

➤ Specify the data type to be returned by the function. When the function finishes its work, it will give some data back to the main program. All you are doing here is specifying the data type to be handed back. A key point to note is that a function can return only one simple data item, no more and no less. The only simple types that you have looked at so far are int, char, and float. This means that strings and arrays cannot be returned from a function in this manner. Oh dear!

"What's a Prototype?" He Asked, Surprised

A *prototype* is just a single line of code that states the inputs and output of a function. It performs no action other than to warn the compiler of what to expect later in the function definition.

When you translate these rules into C++, the prototype looks like that shown in the next diagram. I am using a prototype from a program that you will encounter very shortly. It's simple and doesn't do very much, but it emphasizes the key points. A new data type is introduced here. It is called void and means that the function doesn't return anything. In our IT model, it doesn't have an output.

The C++ prototype of a function.

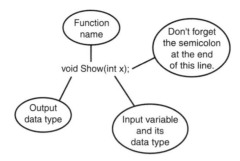

Let's Define the Function

The body of a function is just like a normal C++ program and may include its own variables, statements, and operations, all enclosed in braces. These definitions belong solely to the particular function you are defining and have no effect elsewhere. They are local, or internal, to this function.

As you can see, the format of a function is similar to the format of the main program, and you write the actual programming statements in exactly the same fashion as you have learned in the previous chapters. The definition of the Show function is given in the next diagram.

The definition of the Show function.

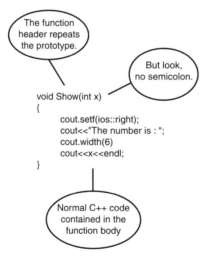

Call the Function into Life

This is the easy bit. All you do is call the function name and it jumps up like your pet dog. Because the function requires an integer input, you must supply a value in the parentheses. The function doesn't return anything, so you don't have to worry about it. The appearance of the function, as you will shortly see, depends on its name, its return data type, and its input parameters.

Semicolon or No Semicolon?

Note that the first line of the function is the same as its prototype except that there is no semicolon at the end. This point is crucial! Lots of students become confused here and cause distress both to themselves, their teacher, and the compiler. To stress the point, the prototype has a semicolon at the end; the first line of the definition does not. Forget this gem of wisdom at your peril.

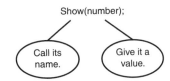

Calling the function into life.

A Functional Program

Now that I have discussed the pieces of the program, let's put it all together. Here it is in Listing 12.1, so give it a whirl. Check out the function prototype, the function call, and the function definition. Wow, now you're a modular programmer!

Listing 12.1   A Simple Function

```
#include <iostream.h>

// Here is the function prototype
void Show(int x);

main()
{
    int number;

    cout << "Enter a number : ";
    cin >> number;
    Show(number);
    return(0);
}
```

continues

Listing 12.1   A Simple Function CONTINUED

```
// Here is the function definition
void Show(int x)
{
    cout.setf(ios::right);
    cout << "The number is : ";
    cout.width(6);
    cout << x << endl;
}
```

When you run this program, you will be prompted to enter a number.

In Full Flow

The flow of the program can be described in three steps:

1. You call the function into life and give it a value within the main program block.

2. You jump from the main program block into the function and execute the code within the function.

3. On finishing the code in the function, you return to the next line in the main program after the function call.

The flow of the program.

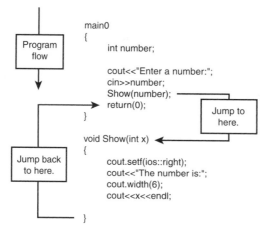

A Fully Functional Program

Now that you have the idea of what a function is, let's create a fully modular program based on functions. You already have a function called Show that receives and displays a formatted integer to the screen. You know it works because we used it in the last program, so let's reuse the code and save ourselves some work. That's modular programming. You will develop a function that accepts an integer from the keyboard and another function that finds the square of that number. It isn't rocket science, but you have to start somewhere.

Integer Out, Nothing In

This function is used to read an integer value from the keyboard. It has the following prototype:

```
int Gather(void);
```

which requires the following definition:

```
int Gather(void)
{
    int n;

    cout << "Enter a number : ";
    cin >> n;
    return(n);
}
```

which results in the following signature:

```
number = Gather();
```

Integer In, Integer Out

This function accepts an integer value as input and returns an integer value as output. It has the following prototype:

```
int Square(int x);
```

which requires the next definition. Notice how you take an integer input and store it in the variable x. To square a value, you multiply it by itself and store it back in x. You met a similar technique when you wrote the running total programs back in Chapters 5 and 6.

```
int Square(int x)
{
    x = x * x;
    return(x);
}
```

This definition results in the following signature:

```
answer = Square(number);
```

Sign Here, Please

The appearance of a function is known as its *signature* and is a direct result of its name, its return data type, and its input parameters. All these must be different for each individual function. The analogy is that every individual has a unique signature. Learn the jargon.

Catch the Result

From the prototype, it can be observed that the function Gather returns an integer. It is therefore necessary to catch that integer value after the function has executed. Hence, the use of number to catch that result. Take a look back at the call to function Show, where you can observe we didn't catch a result. This is because Show has a void return, meaning there is nothing to catch.

The Program in Full

The purpose of the demonstration program in Listing 12.2 is to show you how to construct a modular program and use parameters. "What are parameters?" I hear you ask. Ah-ah, you've forgotten already, so I'll repeat what I said earlier in this chapter. The function inputs are enclosed in parentheses and are known as input parameters, but really they are just like the variables that you already know and love. It follows that an output parameter is just an output from the function, which in the case of C++ is a single simple data type. It's time to try out the program, so roll up your sleeves and off you go.

The user will be asked to enter a value, which the program will then square and show the result.

Listing 12.2   A Fully Modular Program Uses Three Functions

```
#include <iostream.h>

// Here are the function prototypes
void Show(int x);
int Square(int x);
int Gather(void);

main()
{
    int number;
    int answer;
```

```
        number = Gather();
        answer = Square(number);
        Show(answer);
        return(0);
}

// Here are the function definitions
void Show(int x)
{
    cout.setf(ios::right);
    cout << "The number is : ";
    cout.width(6);
    cout << x << endl;
}

int Square(int x)
{
    x = x * x;
    return(x);
}

int Gather(void)
{
    int n;

    cout << "Enter a number : ";
    cin >> n;
    return(n);
}
```

The Secret Language Revealed, Pass by Value

Here is the definition of the top secret *pass by value* phrase. This sort of jargon is used by professionals who disguise their trade behind such mumbo jumbo. When I was young and in my prime, I dared to ask, "What is *pass by value*?" I was met with looks of surprise and disgust. "Don't you know what that is?" was the general response from the professionals. I'm still waiting for the answer. All IT establishments where I have worked do this, and the spoken language descends into a string of incomprehensible acronyms and phrases. The first few months of any new contract seem to be spent learning the inhouse language.

When a value is passed as an input parameter to a function, the contents of that variable are copied to the internal variable declared in the function header. Within the function, only the copied value is manipulated; the original value remains unchanged. It is the result of the manipulated value that is returned and is totally independent of the original. This is shown in the next diagram.

A diagram showing the flow of events in pass by value.

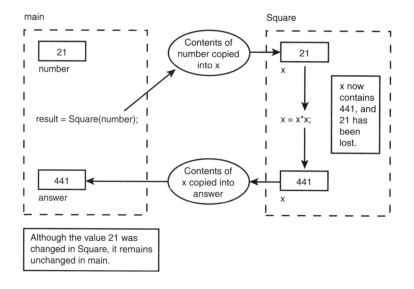

main

| 21 |
number

result = Square(number);

Contents of number copied into x

Square

| 21 |
x

x = x*x;

x now contains 441, and 21 has been lost.

| 441 |
answer

Contents of x copied into answer

| 441 |
x

Although the value 21 was changed in Square, it remains unchanged in main.

Functions and `floats`

Until now, we have restricted ourselves to functions that use integer and void as their data types. However, other simple data types can be used as parameters in exactly the same manner. Let us examine Listing 12.3. This program is virtually the same as the example in Listing 12.2 except that floats replace all integer parameters. The operation of the program is otherwise identical in every detail. As you can see, you simply specify a float as an input or output parameter, just as you would with an integer. Couldn't be easier, eh! When you run this program, remember to enter some numbers containing decimal points. After all, that's the whole point of using floats.

When you run your program, your screen will be very much like the preceding program except that you can use decimal places.

Listing 12.3   An Example of `floats` in Functions

```
#include <iostream.h>

// Here are the function prototypes
void Show(float x);
float Square(float x);
float Gather(void);


main()
{
    float number;
    float answer;
```

```
        number = Gather();
        answer = Square(number);
        Show(answer);
        return(0);
}

// Here are the function definitions
void Show(float x)
{
    cout.setf(ios::right);
    cout << "The number is : ";
    cout.width(6);
    cout << x << endl;
}

float Square(float x)
{
    x = x * x;
    return(x);
}

float Gather(void)
{
    float n;

    cout << "Enter a number : ";
    cin >> n;
    return(n);
}
```

A Useful Piece of Shorthand Revealed

Let's re-examine the function Square, which by now you fully understand and consider a close friend.

```
float Square(float x)
{
    x = x * x;
    return(x);
}
```

It has one line of code that performs the calculation and one line of code that returns the result of the calculation. C++ programmers love to take shortcuts, and the function can be rewritten as follows:

```
float Square(float x)
{
```

```
        return(x * x);
    }
```

You simply put the calculation directly into the return statement. This is the preferred method!

Functions and chars

Having seen how functions deal with the data types void, integer, and float, you will not be surprised to find that chars are dealt with in exactly the same manner. Listing 12.4 reads a character from the keyboard, finds the next character, and displays both of them to the screen. Here is a description of the actions of the program:

➤ First of all, a character is entered at the keyboard via the function GetData.

➤ The character returned from GetData is placed in the variable choice.

➤ It is then passed as a parameter into the function NextCharacter. This function contains a single line:

```
        return(++beta);
```

➤ Remember that beta is an internal variable that was temporarily assigned the value held by choice. Therefore, ++beta is the character after beta because this is the value in the parentheses that is returned by the function and assigned to the variable changed in the main program.

It's in the Scale of Things

Packing the calculation into the return statement doesn't seem to save much work. But remember, you are dealing with only tiny, trivial programs to demonstrate the concepts. The example did save a line of code, but behind the scenes the computer had one less action to take, and this saved a few microseconds of processing time. Scale this up to a million-line program, and you potentially save a few thousand lines of code and a few thousand microseconds. That is significant in terms of performance, and performance sells programs.

Pre- or Post-beta? That Is the Question

I first had the idea of the next program when I was learning C++ (or was it C?). Anyway, I thought it was a good idea. When I ran the program, the letter didn't change to the next one, and no matter what I tried, I couldn't get the program to work. After several bottles of beer, the penny dropped. I was using postfix notation with beta++ rather than prefix notation, as in ++beta. Did I feel a fool? No way, I was a still a student—and a rather intoxicated one at that. Give it a try (Listing 12.4, that is) and see the lack of incremented letters.

When you run Listing 12.4, enter a letter, and the computer will work out the next letter for you.

Listing 12.4   An Example of chars in Functions

```
#include <iostream.h>

char GetData(void);
void Show(char alpha);
char NextCharacter(char beta);

main()
{
    char choice;
    char changed;

    choice = GetData();
    changed = NextCharacter(choice);
    Show(choice);
    Show(changed);
    return(0);
}

char GetData(void)
{
    char data;

    cout << "Enter a character : ";
    cin >> data;
    return(data);
}

char NextCharacter(char beta)
{
    return(++beta);
}

void Show(char alpha)
{
    cout << "The character is " << alpha << endl;
}
```

Some Key Points

At this point, it is worth highlighting some important features of functions. It might not have struck you, but

1. A function can return only a single result. If you want two results, you need two functions or two calls to the same function.

2. The result returned by a function must be of a simple data type. You cannot return an array from a function. How to get around this problem is dealt with in the next chapter.

Internal and External Variables

In C++ there are two general types of variables: those that are internal and those that are external. The jargon is widely used, but for anyone coming from some other language, these terms mean the same as *local* and *global*, respectively.

External (or Global)

Anything that is declared prior to the keyword main is known as *external* (or global) and can be used by any statements contained anywhere in the program. You have seen #define, #include, and function prototypes that are in fact externals. They may also be used by any function that has not used the same identifier within its own declarations. This enigma is explained in the next paragraph because these are internal (or local) variables.

Internal (or Local)

An *internal* (or local) variable is a declaration that is within a function. These declarations belong to that function and cannot be accessed from elsewhere. In other words, the main body of the program cannot access a variable declared within a function, nor can it be accessed by any other function. Without this feature, many advanced programming techniques could not be implemented.

Keep In with the Professionals

It is good programming practice to use internal variables wherever possible and pass information between functions via parameters. Modules can manipulate external variables, but in programming circles this is generally frowned on. If you are writing a program for a nuclear power plant, you don't want any Frank, Buddy, or Elvis opening the reactor door by accidentally accessing a freely available external variable. It does happen!

The Least You Need to Know

➤ Five good reasons why you use functions are

1. You have chunks of code that are relatively short.
2. It's easier to locate errors in short pieces of code.
3. It enables people to work in teams to rapidly produce a finished product.
4. A function need only be written once yet can be used many times.
5. After a function is written and proven to work, it can be stored in a library for use by other programs and programmers.

➤ A function prototype comes before the main program. It consists of a line of code that describes the return data type, the name of the function, and the function inputs and their data type enclosed in parentheses and terminates with a semicolon.

➤ The format of a function definition is similar to the format of the main program, and you write the actual programming statements in exactly the same fashion as you learned in the previous chapters. The definition header is the same as its prototype except that there is no semicolon.

➤ A function is called from the main program by calling its name, giving it the correct parameters, and collecting the result.

➤ When a value is passed as an input parameter to a function, the contents of that variable are copied to the internal variable declared in the function header. Within the function, only the copied value is manipulated; the original value remains unchanged. It is the result of the manipulated value that is returned and is totally independent of the original.

➤ A function can return only a single data item of a simple data type.

➤ An internal, or local, variable is a declaration that is within a function. It belongs solely to that function and cannot be accessed from elsewhere.

➤ Anything that is declared prior to the keyword main is known as external and can be used by any statements contained anywhere in the program. It can also be used by any function that has not used the same identifier within its own declarations.

Chapter 13

Functions Can Talk to Arrays

In This Chapter

➤ Arrays as inputs to functions

➤ An introduction to pointers

➤ Pass by reference

➤ A simple bubble sort

➤ How to compare strings

Arrays as Function Inputs

In Listing 13.1, you will see how an array of integers can be passed to a function. When we dealt with arrays in Chapter 9, "Beyond the Compound, Into the Simple Array," I gave a description of how an array variable specifies a base address in memory. Fortunately, you don't have to worry too much about that because it is totally invisible to the programmer. You will be pleased to hear that you simply tell the function to expect an array as its input and then treat the variables in the normal manner prescribed for arrays.

Listing 13.1   An Example of Passing an Array to a Function

```
#include <iostream.h>

#define MAX 10

void Show(int n[MAX]);

main()
{
// numbers can store 10 integers.
    int numbers[MAX] ={12,99,77,34,6,45,199,38,123,91};

    Show(numbers);
    return(0);
}

void Show(int n[MAX])
{
    int index;

    for (index = 0; index < MAX; index++)
    {
        cout << "ARRAY ITEM  " << index
            << " IS " << n[index] << endl;
    }
}
```

The function Show is very similar to what you have seen before; it returns nothing and accepts a reference to an array of integers. Take special note here that you are declaring an array, not a simple variable, by the specific use of n[MAX]. You offer the reference held by numbers to the function, where it is copied into the internal variable n. Within the function, all values in the array are written to the screen with the use of a for loop. Here is what the screen will look like:

```
ARRAY ITEM 0 IS 12
ARRAY ITEM 1 IS 99
ARRAY ITEM 2 IS 77
ARRAY ITEM 3 IS 34
ARRAY ITEM 4 IS 6
ARRAY ITEM 5 IS 45
ARRAY ITEM 6 IS 199
ARRAY ITEM 7 IS 38
ARRAY ITEM 8 IS 123
ARRAY ITEM 0 IS 91
```

More Secret Language: The Dreaded *P* Word and Pass by Reference

Pointers are a subject that you cannot avoid in C++. I will deal with them now as swiftly and as painlessly as possible. It's still going to hurt.

The Dreaded P Word

Until now, I have deliberately avoided the subject of pointers code, named *the dreaded P word*. The reason for this is twofold. First, it scares most students (it scares me), and second, it's really no big deal after you come to grips with it. I do not intend to dwell on the subject for long, but you do need a basic understanding of the topic to progress further.

In Chapter 2, "From Absolutely Nothing to Screen a Display," I introduced the concept of a variable. You should recall that a *variable* is a box that can hold a data item such as an integer or a `float`. However, professional programmers sometimes prefer to use pointers (or a *pointer variable*, as it's correctly called) when they are dealing with memory-hungry programs such as database applications or with direct memory manipulation when writing operating systems.

This is the definition of a *pointer*: A pointer variable is a variable that contains the address of the memory location of an area of memory where the data is stored.

Now that sounds rather complex and weird, so look at the following diagram.

A pointer variable pointing to a memory location.

That's all you need to know for the moment. Dead easy, isn't it? I'll say no more for now!

Pass by Reference

Here is the definition of *pass by reference*. It sounds rather complex, so read it in conjunction with the associated diagram.

When an external pointer variable is passed as an input parameter to a function, the contents of that variable, which are an address, are copied to the internal pointer variable declared in the function header. Because an address points to a memory location within the computer, this means that both the external and internal pointer variables point to the same place. That area of memory can thus be manipulated from within the function or from the main program because they both contain variables that point to the same place. This is *shared memory*.

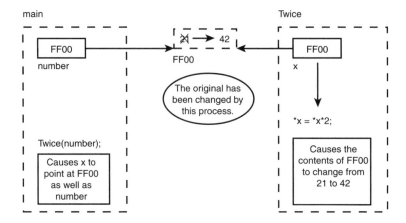

A diagram showing the flow of events in pass by reference.

Twice the Program It Was

Listing 13.2 is a program that demonstrates pass by reference. It also serves as a brief but fleeting glance at pointers.

➤ You set up a pointer variable with the following line. Notice how the star is used to distinguish between a normal and a pointer variable.

```
int* number;
```

➤ You set up and initialize a normal variable.

```
int Num1 = 77;
```

➤ Now you copy the address of the normal variable into a pointer variable. Notice the use of the ampersand & sign.

```
number = &Num1;
```

➤ You output the contents of the memory location pointed to by number with this line. Note the use of the star prefixing the identifier.

```
cout << *number << endl;
```

➤ Now you pass the address of the data to the function Twice, where the content of that memory location is doubled. Note that there is no * before the identifier; this means it is the contents of, not the memory location pointed to, that we are talking about.

```
Twice(number);
```

➤ When you output the contents of number again, it has indeed doubled. You have manipulated the original data item.

```
cout << *number << endl;
```

Here is a screen display of the dastardly deed as it happens:

77
154

Listing 13.2   Pass by Reference—An Example of Pointers and Functions

```
#include <iostream.h>

void Twice(int* x);

main()
{
    int* number;
    int Num1 = 77;

    number = &Num1;
    cout << "Address of Num1 is                          : " << &Num1
        << endl;
    cout << "Contents of number is                       : " << number
        << endl;
    cout << "Data pointed to by number before function   : " << *number
        << endl;
    Twice(number);
    cout << "Data pointed to by number after function    : " << *number
        << endl;
    return(0);
}

void Twice(int* x)
{
    *x = *x * 2;
}
```

The novice must take care when using this method, because side effects can occur. However, the experienced programmer, especially working at machine level, will find this route extremely inviting.

Warning! Achtung! Atención!

When you are working in a modern operating system such as Windows 95 or 98, it's very dangerous to go poking around in memory. The operating system contains its own memory management system and allocates resources when requested.

143

A Simple Sort of Demo

Now that you know about such complicated topics as arrays, functions, pointers, and pass by reference, let's take a look at a descent size program. This is a real step up from the demonstrations that you are used to, so get some coffee and hang in during the description because it's not as bad as it sounds after the tenth reading. The overall purpose of the program is to read in four numbers, store them in an array, sort them into ascending order, and then display them onscreen. Now that sounds easy enough, doesn't it?

Side Effects

Side effects in programming jargon are the result when the deliberate action of a piece of your code causes something else to happen somewhere else in the system. Such an event could be caused by pass by reference when two or more areas of code can access the same shared memory location. By changing the contents of that memory location with one piece of code, you run the risk of altering the outcome of the piece of code, should it draw data from the shared memory location.

A Bubbly Overview

This is what is going on in the program:

➤ An array, called `data`, of `MAX` integers is set up, and the pointer to the first item in the array is passed by reference to the function `GetData`.

➤ The internal pointer x now holds the same address as that of `data`, so they can both access the same area of memory (the place where the data held in the array elements is stored).

➤ Within `GetData` you simply read in some integers and place them in the array.

➤ Make a special note that you are using pass by reference and do not need to return anything to the main program, because you are writing directly to the area of memory occupied by the array.

➤ Having collected and stored the data, you display it to the screen with the `Show` function, which you have met before.

➤ Now you pass the address of the data to the sort function. This is quite involved and deserves some explanation because it is a widely used concept. It is known as a *bubble sort*.

Break Out the Bubbly: The Bubble Sort Explained

The following flow chart explains the steps involved in the sort, but the swap needs a little more explanation. It is really cunning and is worth learning. I make no apologies for using boxes again. I like boxes!

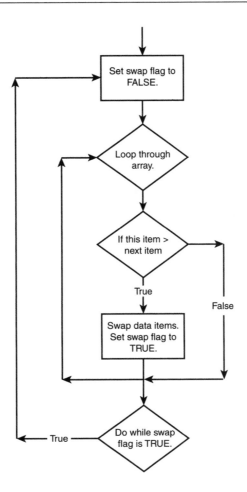

The flow chart of the bubble sort.

Let's Swap Details

The next figure shows in three steps how to swap the contents of an element a with the contents of an element b. Bear in mind that a box can hold only one value at a time and cannot remember what it contained, once overwritten.

The steps involved in swapping a and b.

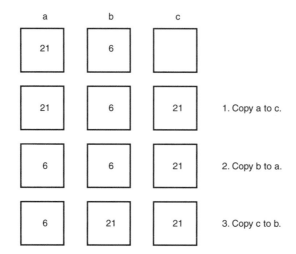

a	b	c	
21	6		
21	6	21	1. Copy a to c.
6	6	21	2. Copy b to a.
6	21	21	3. Copy c to b.

A Bubbly Sort in Practice

Now that you understand the theory, let's try the program in Listing 13.3 and enter four random integers. The program will do the sort and show you the results. Your screen will look something like this—you don't have to put the same numbers in that I have, but make sure they are integers:

```
Enter a number : 13
Enter a number : 4
Enter a number : 77
Enter a number : 42

BEFORE THE SORT
13
4
77
42

AFTER THE SORT
4
13
42
77
```

Listing 13.3   Pass an Array by Reference to Its Address

```
// Simple sort demo

#include <iostream.h>
```

```
#define MAX 4

void GetData(int x[MAX]);
void Sort(int x[MAX]);
void Show(int num[MAX]);

main()
{
    int data[MAX];

    GetData(data);
    cout << endl << "BEFORE THE SORT" << endl;
    Show(data);
    cout << endl;
    Sort(data);
    cout << "AFTER THE SORT" << endl;
    Show(data);
    cout << endl;
    return(0);
}

void GetData(int x[MAX])
{
    int loop;

    for (loop = 0; loop < MAX; loop++)
    {
        cout << "Enter a number : ";
        cin >> x[loop];
    }
}

void Show(int x[MAX])
{
    int loop;

    for (loop = 0; loop < MAX; loop++)
    {
        cout << "Array item " << loop
<< " contains " << x[loop] << endl;
    }
}

void Sort(int x[MAX])
{
```

continues

147

Listing 13.3   Pass an Array by Reference to Its Address
CONTINUED

```
    int loop;
    int swapflag = 0;
    int temp;

    do
    {
        swapflag = 0;
        for (loop = 0; loop < MAX - 1; loop++)
        {
            if (x[loop] > x[loop+1])
            {
                temp = x[loop];
                x[loop] = x[loop+1];
                x[loop+1] = temp;
                swapflag = 1;
            }
        }
    }while (swapflag != 0);
}
```

Functions and Multidimensional Arrays

In this section, you'll combine what you already know and apply the bubble sort to an array of strings. This is a very useful program because names do tend to be sorted in alphabetic order.

A Recurring Nightmare

Having described how arrays can be manipulated via pass by reference, I will give a similar demonstration using a multidimensional array. Such an array could well be a two-dimensional array of char, which is in fact a one-dimensional array of string. Listing 13.4 is a program that will sort a list of strings into ascending alphabetic order. The concept is identical to the preceding bubble sort program, so all the previous diagrams and flow charts hold true. The main effect of switching to strings is that you must use the string.h library provided by those lovely writers of the compiler. Cheers, guys, job well done, saves us some work.

Try out the program and enter four names. The screen shot of the four names looks like this:

```
Enter a name : Crockett Davy
Enter a name : Wallace William
Enter a name : Ali Mohammed
Enter a name : Keegan Kevin
```

```
Crockett Davy
Wallace William
Ali Mohammed
Keegan Kevin

Ali Mohammed
Crockett Davy
Keegan Kevin
Wallace William
```

Listing 13.4   Demo of an Array of Strings

```cpp
#include <iostream.h>
#include <string.h>

#define MAX 4
#define LENGTH 20

void GetData(char s[MAX][LENGTH]);
void Show(char s[MAX][LENGTH]);
void Sort(char s[MAX][LENGTH]);

main()
{
    char people[MAX][LENGTH];

    GetData(people);
    cout << endl;
    Show(people);
    cout << endl;
    Sort(people);
    Show(people);
    cout << endl;
    return(0);
}

void GetData(char s[MAX][LENGTH])
{
    int loop;

    for (loop = 0; loop < MAX; loop++)
    {
        cout << "Enter a name : ";
        cin.getline (s[loop],20);
```

continues

Listing 13.4   Demo of an Array of Strings CONTINUED

```
    }
}

void Show(char s[MAX][LENGTH])
{
    int loop;

    for (loop = 0; loop < MAX; loop++)
    {
        cout << s[loop] << endl;
    }
}

void Sort(char x[MAX][LENGTH])
{
    int loop;
    int swapflag = 0;
    char temp[LENGTH];

    do
    {
        swapflag = 0;
        for (loop = 0; loop < MAX - 1; loop++)
        {
            if (strcmp(x[loop],x[loop+1]) > 0)
            {
                strcpy(temp,x[loop]);
                strcpy(x[loop],x[loop+1]);
                strcpy(x[loop+1],temp);
                swapflag = 1;
            }
        }
    }while (swapflag != 0);
}
```

How Do You Compare Strings?

From this I hope you can perceive that the technique is identical, the only difference being that a two-dimensional array has two offsets to specify. Within the function bodies, the actions taken are identical except that for convenience you are using the string.h library functions. Even the swap function works in the same way, although it's worth taking a look at the line that initiates the swap.

```
    if (strcmp(x[loop],x[loop+1]) > 0)
```

The line revolves around the function strcmp, which is contained in the string.h library and checks the alphabetic relationship between the first parameter x[loop] and the second parameter x[loop+1]. It returns one of these three possible integer values:

```
if x[loop] = x[loop+1]  strcmp  returns = 0

if x[loop] > x[loop+1]  strcmp  returns > 0

if x[loop] < x[loop+1]  strcmp  returns < 0
```

The integer result is checked by the if statement to determine what action is to be taken—in our case, a swap. If the first item is greater than the second, strcmp returns a value of greater than zero, so a swap takes place. Zero, or less than zero, results in no swap being required.

How Do I Get the Reverse?

Rather than use the strcmp to check for greater than, you can change the comparison to less than:

```
if (strcmp(x[loop],x[loop+1]) < 0)
```

Now you have the reverse.

The Least You Need to Know

➤ When you pass an array variable into a function, you are actually passing the address in memory where the data contained in the array lives.

➤ A pointer variable is a variable that contains the address of the memory location of an area of memory where the data is stored.

➤ When an external pointer variable is passed as an input parameter to a function, the contents of that variable, which are an address, are copied to the internal pointer variable declared in the function header. Because an address points to a memory location within the computer, this means that both the external and internal pointer variables point to the same place. That area of memory can thus be manipulated from within the function or from the main program because they both contain variables that point to the same place.

➤ A bubble sort is a section of code—normally, a function—that is used to check whether data is in the correct order. Typically, it can sort integers into ascending value or names into alphabetic order. It isn't the most efficient method of sorting, but it is simple and easy to understand.

➤ You can use pass by reference as a tool to manipulate an external variable from within a function, because pass by reference gives the function the external address of the data. Any manipulation done inside the function thus affects the original data stored in main memory.

➤ The `strcmp` function, which is stored in the string.h library, is used to compare the value of two strings or string variables. If the two are the same, a value of `0` is returned. If the first sting is alphabetically before the second string, a negative value of less than zero is returned. If the first sting is alphabetically after the second string, a positive value of greater than zero is returned.

Chapter 14

The Parallel Array Is Dead, Long Live the Structure

In This Chapter

➤ The definition of a structure in C++

➤ Dot notation

➤ A C++ program that uses structures

➤ An array of structures

➤ C++ programs that manipulate arrays of structures

So What Is Structure Anyway?

In Chapters 9, 10, and 11, you investigated a data structure known as an *array*. You found that all elements of the array have to be of the same underlying data type and that the solution to the problem of mixed data types is a parallel array. C++ offers a means of handling mixed data types with the structure, which in many instances, but not all, can be a better solution than parallel arrays. We shall examine this topic now.

Records, Fields, and All That Database Stuff

You might have heard of the term *record*. A record is one of the most commonly used structures in data processing (computerized or not). It consists of collections of related data, not necessarily of the same type, that convey some form of information about a subject. The data contained within the record must be of a predefined order, each piece having a distinct identifier.

These next two facts will be used in this chapter's investigation into simple database technology:

➤ A field is just a variable—which you've seen in previous chapters.

➤ A single record is made up of several fields.

➤ Many records constitute a database.

This abstract record data type has a concrete counterpart in C++, known as a *structure*.

Defining the Structure

For an example, I will return to the discussion of the solar system, which you met in Chapter 11, "Take a Trip Around the Solar System in a Parallel Array." At that point, we represented the information with a number of parallel arrays to overcome the problem of mixed data types. This can also be achieved with the use of a structure. First, you need to define the structure that you require. This is done at the start of the program and is shown in the following diagram.

This is the way a structure is made up.

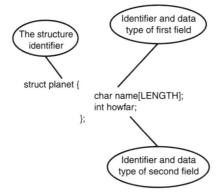

I Declare This Structure to Be...

The structure called `struct planet` that you have just defined is in fact a user-defined data type. You can assign an identifier to it, thus creating a variable of type `struct planet`, which we shall call `solar`. This variable will contain the two fields contained in the structure definition—that is, a string called `name` and an integer called `howfar`. You now have a variable that can hold the data on a single planet. You declare it like this:

```
struct planet solar;
```

154

Introducing Dot Notation

You access the individual fields of the structure by what is known as *dot notation*. Dot notation syntax is shown in this next diagram.

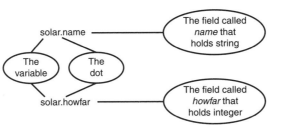

The syntax of dot notation in our solar variable.

Assigning the Data

To assign information to the fields of a structure is just a matter of using the normal rules of C++. You must specify both variable and field name in dot notation. For a string, you use the strcpy function:

```
strcpy(solar.name,"EARTH");
```

You assign a numeric value as follows:

```
solar.howfar = 150;
```

Accessing the Data

If you want to write the contents of a structure to the screen, again you use dot notation and the cout command. For the string field, it looks like this:

```
cout << solar.name;
```

For the numeric field, it looks like this:

```
cout << solar.howfar;
```

Abstract and Concrete

An *abstract* data type is a purely conceptual idea used as a design tool. It can be written down, manipulated by mathematics, and discussed, but it has no actual implementation in a computer programming language. A *concrete* data type is the physical implementation of a data type. It can physically occupy computer memory and hold data. This data can be used and manipulated by a computer program.

The Single Record Database

Now let us examine a complete program that has a single structure. As described earlier, you create a structure called planet that has fields called name of type string and howfar of type integer. You then declare a variable called solar of type struct planet. The variable solar now contains two fields, name and howfar.

The two fields are initialized for the details of the planet Earth and the details sent to the screen through cout, using dot notation. Nothing too complex here, I hope. Try out Listing 14.1. Your screen will show the details of home—the planet Earth:

```
EARTH
150
```

Listing 14.1   Demo of a Structure

```
#include <iostream.h>
#include <string.h>

#define LENGTH 20

struct planet {
                char name[LENGTH];
                int howfar;
            };

main()
{
        struct planet solar;

        strcpy(solar.name, "EARTH");
        solar.howfar = 150;
        cout << solar.name << endl;
        cout << solar.howfar << endl;
        return(0);
}
```

An Array of Structures

In Listing 14.1, you might have felt that a database with only one record isn't really much use, and you were correct. So let us create a structure that can hold several items of information. After all, the solar system has nine known major planets.

I Declare This Array of Structures to Be...

One way of doing this is to create an array of structures. The data type struct planet is created as before, but when you declare a variable of that type, you declare it as an array by the inclusion of brackets and a number stating how many elements are in the array.

```
struct planet solarsystem[9];
```

Now `solarsystem` is a variable with nine elements, each of which have two fields, `name` and `howfar`.

Record *or* Element, What's in a Name?

To the C++ programmer, you are writing an array-based program that contains elements. However, to the operator who knows little of computer programming, these elements contain records of data. You might well come across these two terms being used interchangeably.

Assigning the Data

To enter data into record number 6, field 1, you must specify the variable, the offset, and the field. You use this code:

```
strcpy(solarsystem[5].name, "VULCAN");
```

Accessing the Data

To write record number 3, field 2, to the screen, you must specify the variable, the offset, and the field. The following code does the trick:

```
cout << solarsystem[2].howfar;
```

The Forgotten Offset

Over the years I have noticed that for some strange reason students often get this syntax wrong. They forget to include the index or try to put the index after the field identifier. Please read through the preceding text again to make sure that you really do understand what is discussed. Maybe because it all sounds so straightforward, it gives a problem.

The Multiple Record Database

You create a structure called `planet` that holds the name and distance from the sun of a single planet. This structure is then used as the elements of an array to create a variable called `solarsystem` that is capable of holding the information on the nine known planets. The actual main body of the program simply initializes the array before printing its contents to the screen. Now try out Listing 14.2. It appears to be a lot of typing, but do you remember the trick about testing your program with lots of data?

Being as I'm a dedicated programmer and never take shortcuts(!) (cough cough), here is the screen display for the program, with all the data included:

```
PLANET          DISTANCE
MERCURY         58
VENUS           108
EARTH           150
MARS            228
JUPITER         778
SATURN          1427
URANUS          2871
NEPTUNE         4497
PLUTO           5914
```

Selective Memory

When you have a program that contains lots of data, as in Listing 14.2, you don't need to type it all in. MAX tells us we have nine planets, so why don't we just accidentally forget the last six. Set MAX to three and enter only the data for Mercury, Venus, and Earth. When you have shaken out the bugs and know that the program works, add the rest of the data. Then you can show it off to NASA.

Listing 14.2   Demo of an Array of Structures

```cpp
#include <iostream.h>
#include <string.h>

#define MAX 9          // nine known planets
#define LENGTH 8       // name length
#define TAB '\t'

struct planet  {
                char name[LENGTH];
                int howfar;
           };

main()
{
        struct planet solarsystem[MAX];        // the array
        int index;                             // loop control

        strcpy(solarsystem[0].name, "MERCURY");
```

```
solarsystem[0].howfar = 58;
strcpy(solarsystem[1].name, "VENUS");
solarsystem[1].howfar = 108;
strcpy(solarsystem[2].name, "EARTH");
solarsystem[2].howfar = 150;
strcpy(solarsystem[3].name, "MARS");
solarsystem[3].howfar = 228;
strcpy(solarsystem[4].name, "JUPITER");
solarsystem[4].howfar = 778;
strcpy(solarsystem[5].name, "SATURN");
solarsystem[5].howfar = 1427;
strcpy(solarsystem[6].name, "URANUS");
solarsystem[6].howfar = 2869;
strcpy(solarsystem[7].name,"NEPTUNE");
solarsystem[7].howfar = 4498;
strcpy(solarsystem[8].name,"PLUTO");
solarsystem[8].howfar = 5900;

cout << "NAME" << TAB << TAB << "DISTANCE"
     << endl << endl;
for (index = 0; index < MAX; index++)
{
        cout << solarsystem[index].name;
        cout << TAB << TAB;
        cout << solarsystem[index].howfar << endl;
}
        cout << endl;
return(0);
}
```

How to Steal a Record

Often the user wants to extract a specific item of data rather than view the entire contents of the database, so who are we to argue. In C++ it is possible to copy a single element from an array of structures. The simple model that I will demonstrate enables the user to type in a number. The program copies that record and then displays it to the screen, the theory being that if you can copy it, you can do something with it. The process goes like this:

1. You declare a variable called `oneplanet` of type `struct planet`.

2. Then a single element of the array `solarsystem` (say, element 5) can be transferred using the following code:

   ```
   oneplanet = solarsystem[4];
   ```

3. You now have a copy of the data from the database and can play with the copy instead of the original data.

Listing 14.3 is a program that enables the user to select a single planet from the array of structures by copying an element into a variable of the same underlying data type. You will be invited to enter a planet in order of merit from the Sun. For example, 3 represents Earth and 4 represents Mars.

```
Enter the planet [1 to 9]: 4

PLANET          DISTANCE

EARTH           150
```

But They Are Different Data Types, Aren't They?

oneplanet and solarsystem appear to be of different data types; oneplanet is a structure and solarsystem is an array. They seem to be incompatible. However, because each individual element of solarsystem is, in fact, of type struct planet, it has the same underlying data type as oneplanet, which is also of type struct planet. Therefore, they are compatible; they are said to have the same underlying data type.

Listing 14.3   Demo of Copying a Single Element

```
#include <iostream.h>
#include <string.h>

#define MAX 9
#define LENGTH 8
#define TAB '\t'

struct planet {
                char name[LENGTH];
                int howfar;
              };

main()
{
    struct planet solarsystem[MAX];
    int index;
    struct planet oneplanet;
```

```
strcpy(solarsystem[0].name, "MERCURY");
solarsystem[0].howfar = 58;
strcpy(solarsystem[1].name, "VENUS");
solarsystem[1].howfar = 108;
strcpy(solarsystem[2].name, "EARTH");
solarsystem[2].howfar = 150;
strcpy(solarsystem[3].name, "MARS");
solarsystem[3].howfar = 228;
strcpy(solarsystem[4].name, "JUPITER");
solarsystem[4].howfar = 778;
strcpy(solarsystem[5].name, "SATURN");
solarsystem[5].howfar = 1427;
strcpy(solarsystem[6].name, "URANUS");
solarsystem[6].howfar = 2869;
strcpy(solarsystem[7].name, "NEPTUNE");
solarsystem[7].howfar = 4498;
strcpy(solarsystem[8].name, "PLUTO");
solarsystem[8].howfar = 5900;

cout << "Enter the planet [1 to 9] : ";
cin >> index;
cout << endl;
oneplanet = solarsystem[index - 1];
cout << "NAME" << TAB << TAB << "DISTANCE"
     << endl << endl;
cout << oneplanet.name << TAB << TAB
     << oneplanet.howfar;
cout << endl << endl;
return(0);
}
```

Putting You in the Picture

In case you are finding it difficult to wrap your mind around the database, record, and field stuff, I thought I'd draw you a picture.

Now isn't this better than a story? The picture shows the relationship between our solar system (the database), each element (a record), and each field (a field!).

161

The relationship between the database, the record, and the field.

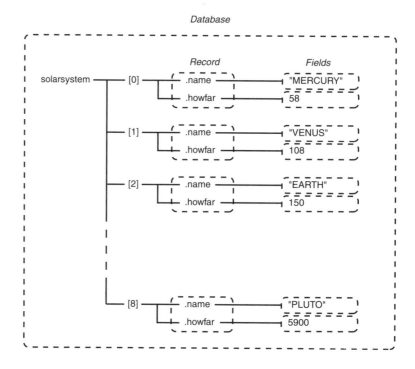

The Least You Need to Know

➤ A database is a collection of related information. It is made up of many records.

➤ A record is a single item of related data. It is made up of several fields.

➤ A field is a single data item.

➤ A structure in C++ is a collection of related information of different data types. It is the C++ version of a record.

➤ Individual fields within a C++ structure are accessed using dot notation. You must specify the variable name, followed by a full stop, and then the individual field name.

➤ Data is assigned to a field in the same way as normal data except that you must specify the variable name, followed by a full stop, and then the individual field name.

➤ An array of structures is defined in exactly the same way as normal data type. It has the following format:

```
struct planet solarsystem[9];
```

➤ A single structure can be copied from an array of structures because they have the same underlying data type. That is, they are constructed from the same building blocks.

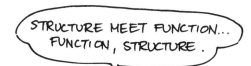

Chapter 15

The Best of Both Worlds: Structures Meet Functions

In This Chapter

➤ How structures are returned from functions

➤ How structures are passed to functions

➤ How to define an array of structures

➤ How arrays of structures are passed to functions

➤ Functions with more than one input parameter

➤ Command-line programming

The Planets Revisited

In Chapter 12, "Divide and Conquer: Functions Rule Okay," and Chapter 13, "Functions Can Talk to Arrays," we looked at how simple data types and arrays can be passed between functions. We now revise and extend this process by investigating how they can also be used as function parameters. The program in this section is based on the planets example in Chapter 14, "The Parallel Array Is Dead, Long Live the Structure." It demonstrates how a structure can be returned from a function and how a structure can be supplied to a function.

Structure In, Nothing Out

First of all, you will examine how a structure can be returned from a function. The relevant code fragment is given here, followed by a description of the actions in the code:

```
struct planet Gather(void)
{
    struct planet temp;

    cout << "ENTER THE PLANET NAME ";
    cin >> temp.name;
    cout << "ENTER THE PLANET DISTANCE ";
    cin >> temp.howfar;
    return(temp);
}
```

➤ The function header tells you that a structure defined by struct planet will be returned to the main program, that the function is called Gather, and that no input parameters are required.

➤ Within this function, an internal variable called temp of type struct planet is defined.

➤ The next two lines enable the user to input a planet name.

➤ The next two lines enable the planet's distance to be entered.

➤ Now that the relevant data to the internal structure has been assigned to temp, the contents of temp are returned to the main program.

➤ Within the main program, the result of Gather is assigned to the variable third; this was intended to be the details for Earth, presuming that you are still in this solar system:

```
third = Gather();
```

Nothing Out, Structure In

The next step is to show the details that you have just collected. You do this by using the Show function, whose relevant code fragment is repeated as follows:

```
void Show(struct planet p)
{
    cout << endl << p.name << TAB << TAB;
    cout << p.howfar << endl;
}
```

➤ From the main program, the contents of the variable third are copied into the variable p, which is internal to the function Show. Once again, this is virtually identical to the way that you treat simple variables. Can you spot the difference in the next line of code? I certainly can't—because there isn't any difference unless you know it's a structure. You can tell only by looking at the prototype:

```
Show(third);
```

➤ Two cout statements are then used to output the name field and then the howfar field to the screen.

Nothing too difficult there, I hope. In fact, it's virtually a repeat of what has gone before, except that you are using a structure instead of simple variables.

The Earth as a Structure

Here is the full program, in Listing 15.1. Try it out by entering the details for the planet Earth.

When Is a Compound Statement Not a Compound Statement?

When it's a structure! Although compound in nature and composed of several simple types, a structure is treated exactly the same as simple data types such as integer or float and can be returned from a function.

As you are prompted to enter the data, your screen will show something like this:

```
ENTER THE PLANET NAME : Earth
ENTER THE PLANET DISTANCE : 150
```

After the data is entered, it's sent to the screen.

Listing 15.1   Demo of Functions and Structures—The Planets Revisited

```
#include <iostream.h>

#define LENGTH 20
#define TAB '\t'

struct planet {
            char name[LENGTH];
            int howfar;
        };

struct planet Gather(void);      // structure as output
void Show(struct planet p);      // structure as input

main()
{
    struct planet third;
```

continues

```
    third = Gather();        // get details for earth
    Show(third);             // display the details
    return(0);
}

struct planet Gather(void)
{
    struct planet temp;

    cout << "ENTER THE PLANET NAME ";
    cin >> temp.name;
    cout << "ENTER THE PLANET DISTANCE ";
    cin >> temp.howfar;
    return(temp);
}

void Show(struct planet p)
{
    cout << endl << p.name << TAB << TAB;
    cout << p.howfar << endl;
}
```

Structures, Arrays, and Functions Join Forces

The next step is to extend the program to accommodate more than one structure of planet information. This can be achieved by modifying the preceding program to use an array of structures.

The function Gather is used four times to collect the planet data for the first four planets. Notice that Gather returns a single structure and must therefore be invoked four times to achieve this task. Remember that a function is written once but can be used many times. If you recall, this is discussed in Chapter 5, and we agreed that it's good practice to get into this habit. The returned data is stored in the variable system, which is an array of structures. An interesting section of this function is the code that converts all inputs into uppercase. The subject is briefly mentioned a couple times in earlier chapters, but for reference purposes, here it is again:

```
for (x = 0; x < strlen(temp.name); x++)
{
        temp.name[x] = toupper(temp.name[x]);
}
```

The first time around the loop, we are examining the first element of the character array, offset zero. The toupper function checks whether the character is uppercase. If not, it converts it; otherwise, it leaves it unchanged. The resultant character is written over the first element in the array. Thus you have an uppercase letter in this location. The second time around the loop, the process is identical except that you are looking at the second element, offset one. The process continues until you reach the end of the string. And how do you know how long the string is? That's where strlen comes in. It is a function, contained in the string.h library, that works out how many letters are in the string. By using it in the loop control, you can dictate how many times a loop will repeat for any string.

The Show function accepts an array of structures as input. Because it's an array, recall that this is known as *pass by reference*. Within the function body, a for loop is used to skim through the array and output the formatted data to the screen.

Being Positive

In Listing 15.2's Gather function, you will see the declaration unsigned int x. This is called a *modifier* and means that the integer value of x is limited to only positive values rather than positive or negative values. You need to do this because the strlen function returns only positive values; you don't get negative-length strings. Without the modifier, the compiler would give a warning. It would still work, but we can't go around upsetting compilers, can we?

The following shows the data entered as lowercase letters but displayed in uppercase. This is because of the code that forces conversion to uppercase.

```
ENTER THE PLANET NAME : Mercury
ENTER THE PLANET DISTANCE : 58
ENTER THE PLANET NAME : Venus
ENTER THE PLANET DISTANCE : 108
ENTER THE PLANET NAME : Earth
ENTER THE PLANET DISTANCE : 150
ENTER THE PLANET NAME : Mars
ENTER THE PLANET DISTANCE : 208

MERCURY        58
VENUS          108
EARTH          150
MARS           208
```

Here is the program, in Listing 15.2. Give it a try and enter the details of the first four planets in the solar system.

The Solar System According to the Romans

This example, which has only four planets in the solar system, is historically correct, assuming it was written in 100 B.C. The alternative explanation is that the author of the code was an extremely lazy programmer who didn't enjoy typing in data at runtime. (I wonder who that was?) In defense, good programmers use only small amounts of data to test their program. When they know it works, they extend the program and have the junior programmer enter the data in its entirety. Over to you!

Listing 15.2   Demo of Functions and Arrays of Structures

```
#include <iostream.h>
#include <string.h>
#include <ctype.h>

#define LENGTH 20
#define MAX 4
#define TAB '\t'

struct planet {
            char name[LENGTH];
            int howfar;
        };

struct planet Gather(void);
void Show(struct planet p[MAX]);

main()
{
    struct planet system[MAX];
    int index;

    for (index = 0; index < MAX; index++)
    {
        system[index] = Gather();
    }
    cout << endl;
    Show(system);
```

```
        return(0);
}

struct planet Gather(void)
{
    struct planet temp;
    unsigned int x;

    cout << endl;
    cout << "ENTER THE PLANET NAME " ;
    cin >> temp.name;
    // Convert to uppercase
    for (x = 0; x < strlen(temp.name); x++)
    {
        temp.name[x] = toupper(temp.name[x]);
    }
    cout << "ENTER THE PLANET DISTANCE ";
    cin >> temp.howfar;
    return(temp);
}

void Show(struct planet p[MAX])
{
    int loop;

    for (loop = 0; loop < MAX; loop++)
    {
        cout << p[loop].name << TAB << TAB;
        cout << p[loop].howfar << endl;
    }
    cout << endl;
}
```

In reality, you haven't learned anything new here, and you probably had quite an easy ride. However, this does reinforce some earlier concepts, and that's worthwhile. Now that I have lulled you into thinking that C++ is dead easy and you can walk tall with the professionals, read on. You are now up and running with the college kids who sound convincing. The next chapter takes it up a gear and moves into the world of the real programmer.

While We Are on the Subject of Functions...

So far so good. We've covered a lot of ground, but there are still a few things we need to mop up, so I'll cover them now.

Functions with More Than One Input

In every example that you have seen so far, only void and single parameters have been passed into functions. As stated earlier, this need not be the case, and a function may have several input parameters. The next program contains a simple demonstration of a function that requires two input parameters. It also contains three other functions (Gather, Show, and Pause) that you already understand, so I will describe only the new function, Add.

The prototype of Add is given in the figure. It returns an integer result. But look inside the brackets. There are two inputs, each of type integer, which are separated by a comma.

In the definition of the function, you can see that the two inputs are assigned to the internal variables one and two. Within the function, they are added up and the answer assigned to res. Finally, res is returned to the main program.

```
int Add(int one, int two)
{
        int res;

        res = one + two;
        return(res);
}
```

The format of a function with more than a single input parameter.

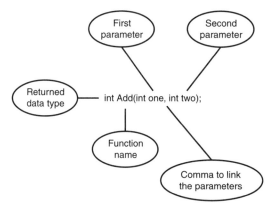

Two Inputs in a Working Program, Now You Are Getting Technical!

Listing 15.3 gives the complete program, and I will briefly explain its operation to you.

➤ Within the main body of the program, two calls are made to the function Gather. These values are assigned to the variables first and second.

170

➤ The function Add is then invoked, with first and second passed as its two parameters. The output is assigned to result.

➤ The sum of the two variables is displayed to the screen via the function Show.

These actions are shown in the following screen output, where the program performs the monumental task of adding 5 to 4 and giving 9:

```
ENTER A NUMBER 4
ENTER A NUMBER 5

THE TOTAL IS 9
```

The Add function caught in the act.

NoteWrite Once, Use Often

Remember, one of the reasons for writing programs in a modular fashion is to reduce code size. Here is an example of writing a function once, yet using it twice. If this were a real-world program, it would be much bigger, and the number of times you would call the function would typically be a lot more than twice.

Listing 15.3 Functions with More Than One Input Parameter

```cpp
#include <iostream.h>

int Gather(void);
int Add(int one, int two);
void Show(int total);

main()
{
    int first;
    int second;
    int result;

    first = Gather();
    second = Gather();
    result = Add(first,second);
    Show(result);
```

```
            return(0);
      }

      int Gather(void)
      {
            int x;

            cout << "ENTER A NUMBER ";
            cin >> x;
            return(x);
      }

      int Add(int one, int two)
      {
          int res;

          res = one + two;
          return(res);
      }

      void Show(int total)
      {
          cout << endl << "THE TOTAL IS  " << total << endl;
      }
```

A Word of Warning

The list of input parameters can be extended indefinitely, but it's bad practice to use too many, because reading the code becomes very difficult.

Mix and Match

The input parameters need not be of the same data type; you are quite at liberty to mix them. Take a look at the following prototype, which contains three inputs. The first is a character, the second an integer, and the third is a float:

```
int Example(int alpha, char beta, float gamma);
```

172

I have established that the function `Example` requires three inputs—no problems there. However, you must take care when you call this function. The parameters must be passed in the correct order; nothing else will do. Look at the next figure as an example. The prototype states that the `char` must be the first parameter, the integer must be second, and the `float` third. This rule must be strictly adhered to. If you don't, your program will not work properly, so be warned. Here is the screen output of my attempt:

```
42
a
9.275
```

Listing 15.4 An Example of a Multiple Input Function with Inputs of Different Data Types

```cpp
#include <iostream.h>

void Example(int alpha, char beta, double gamma);

main()
{
    int a = 42;
    char b = 'a';
    double g = 9.275;

    Example(a,b,g);
    return(0);
}

void Example(int alpha, char beta, double gamma)
{
    cout << alpha << endl;
    cout << beta << endl;
    cout << gamma << endl;
}
```

Some Functional Shorthand for the Lazy Programmer

Earlier in the book, I promised that I would introduce pieces of C++ shorthand when I could, and this is one of those times. The program given in Listing 15.5 does exactly the same as Listing 15.3 but has some striking differences, which I will outline now.

When Is a char Not a char?

If you are feeling really brave, try this out. In the call to the function `Example` in Listing 15.4, try swapping the order of the variables a and b and see the outcome. Your computer should live to fight another day, but then again, would you trust this man?

Listing 15.5   A C++ Shorthand Method for Passing Parameters

```cpp
#include <iostream.h>

int Gather(void);
int Add(int one, int two);
void Show(int total);

main()
{
      Show(Add(Gather(),Gather()));
      return(0);
}

int Gather(void)
{
       int x;

       cout << "ENTER A NUMBER ";
       cin >> x;
       return(x);
}

int Add(int one, int two)
{
       // another piece of shorthand
       return(one + two);
}

void Show(int total)
{
       cout << endl << "THE TOTAL IS  " << total << endl;
}
```

The major difference is, in fact, within the main program:

```cpp
main()
{
    Show(Add(Gather(),Gather()));
    return(0);
}
```

First of all, notice that there are no variables! "How do you achieve this wondrous feat?" I hear you ask. Easy! Look at this line:

```cpp
Show(Add(Gather(),Gather()));
```

This replaces the following four lines in the original program:

```
first = Gather();
second = Gather();
result = Add(first,second);
Show(result);
```

Read this paragraph in conjunction with the next diagram. It should make more sense if you do it this way. The topic can become quite confusing and should not be read when you are feeling tired. Notice that Add requires two parameters of type integer. Gather readily plugs in to these inputs because it returns an integer value. Add returns an integer value, and the input to Show is also of type integer, so these two functions mesh. Because you are passing function results to and from functions, you do not require any variables to act as go-betweens—clever, eh!!

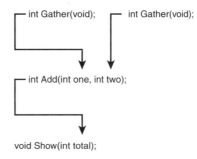

How the functions mesh and do not need variables as go-betweens.

Another difference occurs in function Add: It has only one line of code instead of the original two. The internal variables one and two that were assigned directly from the main program call produce a single result when added together, which is exactly what return requires. By adopting this technique, you save on declaring an internal variable, adding two figures together and then giving this figure to be returned:

```
return(one + two);
```

Function Crunching

The technique of using a function as an input to another function is known as *crunching* functions and is widely used by programmers. Not only does it save on program length, but it also speeds up the execution of your compiled program. This saving can be quite significant on a large program. The drawback, however, is that code tends to be difficult to read, especially when you are learning the language. I always try to avoid function crunching when teaching, but when you are writing real programs, it's a different ballgame.

The Return of `main`

Now this might come as a surprise to you, but the main program from where you call all other functions is, in reality, just a function that is invoked from the operating system. All your main programs to date have the following header:

```
main()
```

You should also recall that in all the functions specified so far, you always state the returning data type, even if it is void. In reality, the default return type of any function is integer, and you do not actually need to specify it. As far as our functions are concerned, we have always done this, and I hope you will continue to do so in the interest of good programming practice. So, to be absolutely squeaky clean and above board, I suppose you should declare your `main` function as returning an integer value, like so:

```
int main()
```

I rarely do, and most other programmers don't bother, so I'll let you off with this one. But there again I'm a lazy programmer!

Because your main program by default must return an integer value, you always terminate the `main()` function, and therefore the programs, with the following line:

```
return(0);
```

A Hacker's Paradise

C++ (and C) are languages that allow the programmer several ways of doing anything. The scope of the language is so vast that you can write virtually any code to achieve any task. In addition to this are many pieces of shorthand notation. This is why the language is so popular among the professionals. Compared to Visual Basic, learning the more advanced topics is much harder, but this overhead is worth it because of the inherent flexibility.

This is an integer value, and now you know why it's there and where it comes from.

An alternative to stating `return(0)` at the end of every program is to declare `main()` as a void return. Then you don't need to return anything. This is also a very popular way of doing things. I just happened to choose the integer return method because that's what I'm used to. Just for the record, Listing 15.6 is a program that uses a void return.

Listing 15.6   A Main Program Using a Void Return

```
#include <iostream.h>

void main()
{
    cout << "Look, no return needed!" << endl;
}
```

I shall now return to my hacker's way of life and continue to omit `int` before `main()`.

Warning

If you leave main() at its default setting and then miss out the return(0), the program will still compile and run. The compiler will issue a warning, but quite often C++ programmers learn to ignore some warnings. Really, I should be telling you never to ignore warnings, because there might be repercussions and side effects. I must confess, I do tend to ignore most warnings as long as the finished program works during the testing phase. With experience, you learn which warnings cause problems.

The main Entry

You should recall that parameters are passed to functions from within the brackets. With the main function, it is similar. In the good old days of command-line programming using DOS or UNIX, this method was commonplace. If you have ever worked in these environments, you will immediately recognize the technique. The technique is still alive today and even used, would you believe, in Windows programming. Unfortunately, Windows programming is beyond the scope of this book, but I'll briefly explain command-line programming.

The parameters passed through the main program header, unlike normal functions, are of a certain format that must be strictly adhered to. Nothing else will do. I will explain that format now.

Suppose you had a command-line utility called AVERAGE that could find the average value of two numbers entered with the following call:

AVERAGE 8 4

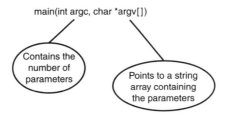

The syntax of main for a command-line program.

argc would automatically be set to 3, which means that *argv[] is an array of three elements of string. The three elements of the *argv[] array would contain the following information in the array:

    *argv[0]   "AVERAGE"

    *argv[1]   "8"
    *argv[2]   "4"

To access the name of the command-line program, you could use the first element in the array using an offset of zero:

    cout << argv[0];

177

To access the two numbers, you would access the second and third elements of the array using offsets one and two, respectively:

```
cout << argv[1];
cout << argv[2];
```

Notice that the numeric values passed through main are in fact arrays of characters and are therefore strings. Shortly, I will describe how to retrieve their numeric values. The first example, in Listing 15.7, simply adds two numbers and then displays the result onscreen. Read through the source code now.

Blank Screen, Pet Mouse, and No Windows

In the good old days when DOS and UNIX reigned supreme, the computer operator had to type in a command followed by some data. This invoked a program that analyzed the data and, if you were lucky, returned an answer that actually meant something. Those were the joys of command-line programming. The bonus was that these operating systems were lean and fit and didn't require megs of memory to work. Although much of DOS has been overtaken by Windows, a huge UNIX base is still out there, and lots of work still supports DOS-based programs.

Listing 15.7   A Command-Line Example

```
// argc is the number of parameters in argv
// argv is a pointer to the actual string parameters
// argv[0] points to the name of the program

#include <iostream.h>
#include <stdio.h>
#include <stdlib.h>

main(int argc, char *argv[])
{
     int first;
     int second;
     int third;

    // This is error checking
    if (argc < 3)
```

```
        {
            cout << "MUST BE MORE THAN ONE PARAMETER"
                << endl;
            exit(0);
        }
    // This is the calculation
        first = atoi(argv[1]);
        second = atoi(argv[2]);
        third = first + second;
    // Display program title
        cout << argv[0] << endl;
    // Display the result
        cout << "THE SUM OF " << first << " AND "
            << second << " IS " << third << endl;
        return(0);
    }
```

Running a Command-Line Program

This type of program is saved, compiled, and linked in exactly the same fashion as any other C++ program. The difference in running it is that additional information must be entered when you are calling the program. There are two ways to do this, and I will give an overview of both.

Method 1

All C++ console application programs produce an exe file when successfully linked; therefore, they all can be run under a DOS environment. Quit C++ and return to the DOS environment. Find the exe file associated with Listing 15.7. In the DOS version, I saved mine as L15_7 because DOS uses only eight-character names and doesn't allow spaces. You can run your program by typing this at the command line:

```
    L15_7  8 4
```

DOS will load up the machine code program, run it, and print 20 to the screen before returning to the DOS prompt. This is okay when the program works correctly, but if you find a bug, you must reload C++ and make corrections.

Method 2

Depending on the version of C++ that you are using, you will find within one of the pull-down menus an option that allows you to enter data. In Microsoft Visual C++, it is under Project Settings, Debug, Program Arguments. Open this box and type in the command-line data that you want to be associated with your program, as shown in the figure.

Setting up the command-line arguments in Microsoft Visual C++.

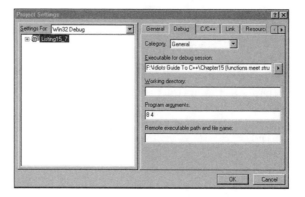

Now run the program in the normal manner. The data will be accessed as the program runs.

```
Listing15_7.exe
THE SUM OF 8 AND 4 IS 12
```

The command-line program at runtime.

Don't forget that the last method is only to test and evaluate the program. Command-line programs are meant to be run under a command-line system such as DOS.

The Program Dissected

The program conveniently falls into three sections. I will deal with them one at a time.

The Command Line

The line that enables us to pass information into the actions part of the main program is as follows:

```
main(int argc, char *argv[])
```

I have already described what this means. Make sure that you understand this concept. What I didn't emphasize was that the parameter names argc and argv are compulsory, so you cannot make up your own variable names, as in normal functions.

The Error Trap

The purpose of this program is to add two numbers and display their total. Because two numbers are needed, along with a command-line name, three parameters are required to invoke the program from the command line. The first thing to do is ensure that the correct numbers of parameters have been entered. The following test is sufficient:

```
if (argc < 3)
{
        cout << "MUST BE MORE THAN ONE PARAMETER");
        exit(0);
}
```

If anything less than a name and two values is entered, an error message is issued and the program terminated. You can enter more than three parameters, but they will be ignored.

Numbers in Disguise

As I stated earlier, the numeric values are actually string versions of numbers, and they must be converted. Within the library `stdlib.h` are several functions concerned with such conversions. You will use `atoi`, which changes ASCII characters into an integer value:

```
first = atoi(argv[1]);
second = atoi(argv[2]);
```

`first` and `second` now contain numeric values, and having done this, you can simply add the two numbers together:

```
third = first + second;
```

Just for good measure and to show how it's done, I have printed the program title to the screen. This is not compulsory:

```
cout << argv[0];
```

Finally, you display the result to the screen in the normal manner and terminate the program by returning an integer value.

```
cout << "THE SUM OF " << first << " AND "
            << second << " IS " << third << endl;
return(0);
```

The Least You Need to Know

➤ A structure, although compound in nature and made up of several simple types, can be returned from a function in exactly the same manner as simple data types such as integer or `float`.

➤ Once again, although it is compound in nature, a structure can be passed to a function in a virtually identical manner to that of a simple variable.

- ➤ Inside the function, you access the structure fields by the use of dot notation. This is exactly the same as in the main() program.
- ➤ Arrays of structures are passed to functions, using pass by reference just like any other array.
- ➤ A function can have several input parameters linked together by a comma.
- ➤ The inputs to a function do not all have to be of the same data type; they can be of any type that you want.
- ➤ If a function has several inputs of different data types, the order of the inputs must be adhered to for the function to operate correctly.
- ➤ main is itself just a special function from which all other functions are called.
- ➤ main can be used as a command-line function in non-Windows environments such as DOS or UNIX.

Chapter 16

Feel You Can't Cope Anymore? Then Take Pity on the Overloaded Operator

In This Chapter

➤ An explanation of what is meant by overloading

➤ How to overload the insertion operator

➤ How to overload the extraction operator

➤ Some fun with overloaded used cars

An Explanation Is in Order

So far, you have used the insertion and extraction operators with simple data types that are predefined in C++. Now you shall learn how to overload these operators and make them handle user-defined data types as if they were part of the language. When you overload an operator, you are giving it added functionality and customizing it to meet specific needs, such as the output of structures, or simply for a repetitive look and feel to the screen. You are taking your first real steps into the world of OOP, which is a powerful programming tool.

How to Overload <<

Your first step into operator overloading will be to output a structure to the screen. If you recall from Chapter 14, "The Parallel Array Is Dead, Long Live the Structure," you had to use dot notation to specify which field within the variable you were working with. Perhaps you felt that this was rather cumbersome to use when you had lots of data to play with. Can you imagine scaling up the planets program to several hundred star systems? Well, overloading is the answer, so read on.

What You Are Overloading

The user-defined data type in this example is a structure called data. You are fully aware of how to use structures, so here is the definition:

```
struct data    {
                char name[20];
                int  age;
                float height;
               };
```

It contains three fields whose underlying data types of char, float, and integer are part of the C++ language and can be output to the screen, using cout. You shall make use of this fact.

How Do You Overload It?

The first and only step is to add a new definition to the insertion operator <<. At first glance, this looks rather strange, so read through this code fragment and then I will explain it step by step:

```
ostream& operator << (ostream& str_out, struct data& d)
{
    str_out << d.name << tab;
    str_out << d.age << tab;
    str_out << d.height << endl;
    return(str_out);
};
```

First of all, don't panic. This is really just a function, and you know all about functions.

In the first three lines of the definition, all you are doing is pushing the field contents of the structure into str_out, using dot notation, as usual:

```
    str_out << d.name << tab;
    str_out << d.age << tab;
    str_out << d.height << endl;
```

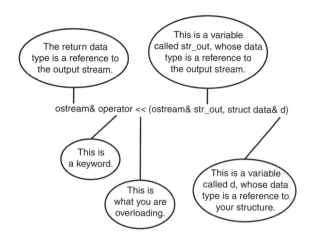

The header of the overload definition for <<.

What Is a Reference?

Do you recall that I mentioned pointers in Chapter 13, "Functions Can Talk to Arrays," and then quickly moved on? Well then, I'm going to make a confession. I don't like pointers, and wherever possible, I avoid them. If you place the ampersand sign (&) after a pointer variable, you have created a reference to it. By using a reference to a pointer, you can treat that variable like a normal variable, thus avoiding quite a bit of heartache in my opinion.

What you are actually doing here is storing the data into an area of memory called a *buffer*. Supposing the variable d held the following values:

```
d.name      "Maggie"
d.age       23
d.height    1.75
```

When the function is activated, that data would be pushed into the buffer, as shown in the figure.

185

The contents of the variable d in the buffer.

| M | a | g | g | i | e | \t | 2 | 3 | \t | l | . | 7 | 5 | \n |

The final line of the definition is

```
return(str_out);
```

which passes the contents of the buffer to the output stream and therefore to the screen. All clever stuff!

Here Is the Tune, It Goes like This

Now that I have discussed the technicalities, it's time to play. Enter the program and give it a try. Having defined the structure, you have three variables of that type, all initialized with different fictitious data. Each variable is sent to the screen, using cout. Because you have overloaded << to handle this structure, each variable is treated as if it were just another day-in-the-life. No questions, no arguments, and no problems.

When you run the program, you will get a screen display similar to this:

Cracking the Code \t\n

Did you notice the control characters in the buffer? You did! Oh well, I suppose that I had better explain then. You already know that \t is the TAB character, but what about \n? This is the new line character, and you have met it before. C++ calls it endl, but at memory level (which is low level) C++ has little say, and control characters are stored as control characters.

```
Stuart Snaith   21      2.01
Kevin Keegan    42      1.56
Mein Gott       12000   0.99
```

Extra! Extra!

Please note that this new definition is an addition to the existing predefined insertion operations of integer, char, float, and so on. It is not a replacement.

Listing 16.1   Overload <<

```
#include <iostream.h>
#define tab '\t'

struct data{
```

```
                    char name[20];
                    int  age;
                    float height;
                    };

ostream& operator << (ostream& str_out, struct data& d)
{
    str_out << d.name << tab;
    str_out << d.age << tab;
    str_out << d.height << endl;
    return(str_out);
};

main()
{
    struct data person1 = {"Stuart Snaith",21,2.01};
    struct data person2 = {"Kevin Keegan",42,1.56};
    struct data person3 = {"Mein Gott",12000,0.99};
    cout << person1;
    cout << person2;
    cout << person3;
    return(0);
}
```

It's as easy as that! When you are dealing with large quantities of data that requires formatted output, this is probably the best way to achieve the task.

Whatever << Can Do, >> Can Do Better

Your next task is to learn how to overload the extraction operator >> and store the result in a variable. It's as easy as the last time and almost identical in operation. Have a look at the code.

How Do You Overload It Again?

You simply change ostream to istream because you are dealing with the input stream and change << to >> because you are overloading the extraction operator. For easy reading, I've changed str_out to str_in, but remember, it's a variable, and you can call it anything you want.

```
istream& operator >> (istream& str_in, struct data& d)
{
        cout << "Enter Name : ";
        str_in.getline(d.name,20);
        cout << "Enter Age : ";
        str_in >> d.age;
        cout << "Enter Height : ";
```

```
        str_in >> d.height;
        str_in.get();
        return(str_in);
    };
```

The header of the overload definition for >>.

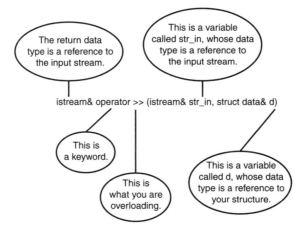

When you call >> with this particular structure as the parameter, you invoke the code in the function and are prompted to enter the required information. Within the definition, dot notation is used to transfer the data into the buffer given by the structure variable d. When all the data is collected, it's shipped to the input stream by the return statement.

Play It Again, Sam

Here is the full program that demonstrates the overloaded operators << and >>. Give it a try. Are your results like mine?

```
Enter name : Stuart Snaith
Enter age : 21
Enter height : 2.01
Enter name : Kevin Keegan
Enter age : 42
Enter height : 1.56
Enter name : Mein Gott
Enter age : 12000
Enter height : 0.99

Stuart Snaith   21        2.01
Kevin Keegan    42        1.56
Mein Gott       12000     0.99
```

Listing 16.2   Overload >>

```
#include <iostream.h>
#define tab '\t'

struct data{
            char name[20];
            int  age;
            float height;
         };

istream& operator >> (istream& str_in, struct data& d)
{
      cout << "Enter Name : ";
      str_in.getline(d.name,20);
      cout << "Enter Age : ";
      str_in >> d.age;
      cout << "Enter Height : ";
      str_in >> d.height;
      str_in.get();
      return(str_in);
};

ostream& operator << (ostream& str_out, struct data& d)
{
    str_out << d.name << tab;
    str_out << d.age << tab;
    str_out << d.height << endl;
    return(str_out);
};

main()
{
    struct data person1;
    struct data person2;
    struct data person3;

    cin >> person1;
    cin >> person2;
    cin >> person3;
    cout << endl << endl;
    cout << person1;
    cout << person2;
    cout << person3;
    return(0);
}
```

189

Programs for the Customer

A second-hand car dealer has moved into town and requires a computer program to show the goods. He has the following vast quantity of stock to sell to the public:

Make	Model	Capacity	Price in $1,000
FORD	ESCORT	1300	9.999
ROVER	216	1600	13.950
LADA	SCRAPPA	50	0.05
VW	BEETLE	1000	6.700

Our analyst programmer has come up with two possible solutions to the problem.

Case Study One

You will need to define a structure with the field names given in the shaded area of the table. Then you will need four variables of that new data type to hold the data. Because you are an OOP programmer, you will show off your skills and overload the << operator. Listing 16.3 is the solution, and here is the screen display:

```
FORD            ESCORT      1300        9.999
ROVER           216         1600        13.950
LADA            SCRAPPA     50          0.05
VW              BEETLE      1000        6.700
```

Listing 16.3   Overload << to Deal with a Structure

```cpp
#include <iostream.h>
#define tab '\t'

struct car{
        char make[10];
        char model[10];
        int  capacity;
        double price;
        };
```

```
ostream& operator << (ostream& str_out, car& d)
{
    str_out << d.make << tab;
    str_out << d.model << tab;
    str_out << d.capacity << tab;
    str_out << d.price << endl;
    return(str_out);
};

main()
{
    struct car car1 = {"FORD","ESCORT",1300,9.999};
    struct car car2 = {"ROVER","216",1600,13.950};
    struct car car3 = {"LADA","SCRAPPA",50,0.05};
    struct car car4 = {"VW","BEETLE",1000,6.700};
    cout << car1;
    cout << car2;
    cout << car3;
    cout << car4;
    return(0);
}
```

Case Study Two

You will need to define a structure with the field names given in the shaded area of the table. You will then need an array variable of four elements of that new data type to hold the data. Because you are an OOP programmer, you will show off your skills and overload the << operator. Here is the solution, in Listing 16.4. The screen display is exactly the same as for Listing 16.3.

Listing 16.4   Overload << to Deal with an Array

```
#include <iostream.h>
#define tab '\t'
struct car{
            char make[10];
            char model[10];
            int  capacity;
            double price;
          };

ostream& operator << (ostream& str_out, struct car d[4])
{
    int index;
```

continues

191

Listing 16.4 Overload << to Deal with an Array CONTINUED

```
    for (index = 0; index < 4; index++)
    {
        str_out << d[index].make << tab;
        str_out << d[index].model << tab;
        str_out << d[index].capacity << tab;
        str_out << d[index].price << endl;
    }
    return(str_out);
};

main()
{
    struct car carstock[4] = {{"FORD","ESCORT",1300,9.999},
                              {"ROVER","216",1600,13.950},
                              {"LADA","SCRAPPA",50,0.05},
                              {"VW","BEETLE",1000,6.700}};
    cout << carstock;
    return(0);
}
```

Look, No Ampersand!

Why is there no ampersand to reference the variable in the overload header? The variable is actually an array, and an array variable is a pointer. You learned this in Chapter 9, "Beyond the Simple, Into the Compound Arrays." Because the variable already is a pointer, no conversion is needed, and therefore no ampersand. Boy, do I hate pointers!

A Happy Customer

The second-hand car dealer is really happy with the computer program to show off his goods. However, he feels that he might actually sell some cars and the list could change. He would like the program modified so that he can type in the vast quantity of stock that he has available for public consumption.

Once again our analyst programmer has come up with two possible solutions to the problem.

Case Study Three

You will need to define a structure with the field names given in the shaded area of the table. You will then need four variables of that new data type to hold the data. Because you are now an experienced OOP programmer, you will show off your skills by overloading the << and the >> operators. Here is the solution. Listing 16.5 shows the data being entered, and the following shows it appearing onscreen:

```
Enter Make : Volvo
Enter Model : 213
Enter Capacity : 1600
Enter price : 1699
Enter Make : Dodge
Enter Model :
Enter Capacity : 4600
Enter price : 4500
Enter Make : Ford
Enter Model : Escort
Enter Capacity : 1300
Enter price : 1100
Enter Make : Merc
Enter Model : 5000
Enter Capacity : 2500
Enter price : 32000
```

Listing 16.5   Overload << and >> to Deal with Structures

```cpp
#define tab '\t'

struct car{
            char make[10];
            char model[10];
            int  capacity;
            double price;
          };

ostream& operator << (ostream& str_out, car& d)
{
    str_out << d.make << tab;
    str_out << d.model << tab;
```

continues

193

```
        str_out << d.capacity << tab;
        str_out << d.price << endl;
        return(str_out);
};

istream& operator >> (istream& str_in, car& d)
{
    cout << "Enter Make : ";
    str_in.getline(d.make,10);
    cout << "Enter Model : ";
    str_in.getline(d.model,10);
    cout << "Enter Capacity : ";
    str_in >> d.capacity;
    cout << "Enter price : ";
    str_in >> d.price;
    str_in.get();
    return(str_in);
};

main()
{
    struct car car1;
    struct car car2;
    struct car car3;
    struct car car4;

    cin >> car1;
    cin >> car2;
    cin >> car3;
    cin >> car4;
    cout << car1;
    cout << car2;
    cout << car3;
    cout << car4;
    return(0);
}
```

Case Study Four

You will need to define a structure with the field names given in the shaded area of
the table. You will then need an array variable of four elements of that new data type
to hold the data. Because you are an even more experienced OOP programmer, you
will show off your skills and overload the << and the >> operators while juggling with
an array. Listing 16.6 is the solution. The screen display is exactly the same as in case
study three.

Listing 16.6   Overload << and >> to Deal with Structure Arrays

```
#include <iostream. h>

#define tab '\t'

struct car{
            char make[10];
            char model[10];
            int  capacity;
            double price;
          };

ostream& operator << (ostream& str_out, struct car d[4])
{
    int index;

    for (index = 0; index < 4; index++)
    {
        str_out << d[index].make << tab;
        str_out << d[index].model << tab;
        str_out << d[index].capacity << tab;
        str_out << d[index].price << endl;
    }
    return(str_out);
};

istream& operator >> (istream& str_in, struct car d[4])
{
    int index;

    for (index = 0; index < 4; index++)
    {
        cout << "Enter Make : ";
        str_in.getline(d[index].make,10);
        cout << "Enter Model : ";
        str_in.getline(d[index].model,10);
        cout << "Enter Capacity : ";
        str_in >> d[index].capacity;
        cout << "Enter price : ";
        str_in >> d[index].price;
        str_in.get();
    }
    return(str_in);
};
```

continues

195

Listing 16.6   Overload << and >> to Deal with Structure Arrays
CONTINUED

```
main()
{
    struct car carlist[4];

    cin >> carlist;
    cout << carlist;
    return(0);
}
```

The Least You Need to Know

➤ When you overload an operator, you are giving it added functionality and customizing it to meet specific needs.

➤ You can overload any existing operator except the following:

.

.*

::

?:

➤ You can overload any existing operator again for a different structure or data type. In fact, you can overload as many times as you want.

➤ To overload the insertion operator, the first and only step is to add a new definition to the insertion operator <<.

➤ To overload the extraction operator, you simply change ostream to istream because you are dealing with the input stream and change << to >> because you are overloading the extraction operator.

➤ An array variable is a pointer. Because the variable already is a pointer, no conversion is needed when you pass it to a function, and therefore no ampersand.

Chapter 17

Not to Be Outdone, Meet Overloaded Functions

In This Chapter

➤ An explanation of what is meant by the term *overloaded function*

➤ How to overload a function

➤ The boolean data type

➤ The logical AND operator

➤ The logical OR operator

➤ The NOT operator

One Name but Many Functions

In this lesson we shall take a brief look at how groups of functions can be tailored to meet specific needs. This modification process helps make the C++ programming language extremely flexible and powerful. You have already met and used functions. You have already met and used overloaded operators. Now you look at overloaded functions.

Overloaded functions can be defined as a group of related modules that have the same name but are differentiated by the parameters that are passed to them. The prototypes of a typical group of related modules are given here:

```
int TimesTwo(int i);
double TimesTwo(double d);
char TimesTwo(char c);
```

Notice how they are all called `TimesTwo`, but note that their input and output parameters differ. This is known as the *signature* of the function, and you have met this term before. The C++ compiler is capable of evaluating the signature and calling the appropriate function, depending on the input values used within the program. The construction of the function prototypes and definitions are identical to the methods described in the earlier chapters concerning functions.

When you call the function `TimesTwo`, how does the compiler know the difference? Think of the data type as a shape. An integer is a star, a `double` is a triangle, and a `char` is a cross. When you call `TimesTwo`, it has a value as an input, which could be a star, a triangle, or a cross. The compiler tries to fit the correct shape to the shape associated with the function. When it finds a match, it invokes the code in the box above that shape. This is shown in the next diagram.

A pictorial representation of function overloading.

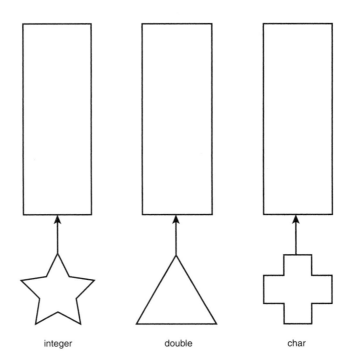

integer   double   char

The Times Two Program

The functions are all named TimesTwo, but their input parameters are different. When you call TimesTwo with an integer input, the compiler calls the correct function to do the integer calculation; the same is true for double and char. This technique can be useful. No doubt, you will come across a bit of jargon called *late binding*. This is a direct application of function overloading, and I shall explain it to you now. I don't want you to be frightened by the jargon, so read on.

Listing 17.1 is a full program that demonstrates overloaded functions. Try it out and see these results:

The Power of OOP

Overloaded functions are allowed in C++ but not in C. You are now in an area where the true power of an OOP style language begins to come through.

```
110
469.12
é
```

"How Can You Multiply Characters?" He Screamed

Yes, you can multiply letters in C++. Because characters are actually numbers! Get the men with the white coats.

Listing 17.1   Overloaded Functions

```
#include <iostream.h>

int TimesTwo(int i);     // Three overloaded functions
double TimesTwo(double d);
char TimesTwo(char c);

void main()
{
    int i = 55;
    double d = 234.56;
    char c = 'A';

    cout << TimesTwo(i) << endl;
    cout << TimesTwo(d) << endl;
    cout << TimesTwo(c) << endl;
}

int TimesTwo(int i)
{
    return(i*2);
}

double TimesTwo(double d)
{
    return(d*2);
}
```

Late Binding Versus Early Binding

At compile time, the program cannot be aware of which version of the function to use. However, it can work it out at runtime when the real data becomes available. Runtime is the latest possible time in the editing, compile, linking, and run process, hence the term *late binding*. Late binding is a dynamic process whereby the running program can determine which version of code best suits the data.

Traditional non-OOP programs that do not employ overloading use a technique known as *early binding*. All function calls are resolved at link time. This is a static process because the code is fixed and cannot alter to pick the best match for the data.

```
char TimesTwo(char c)
{
    // Yes you can multiply characters!
    return(c*2);
}
```

The Logic of Logical Operators

To work with logic, you must learn a new C++ data type. This new type is called *boolean* and has the C++ abbreviation of bool. It has only two possible values, and these are false and true, in that order. You shall learn more as you progress through this chapter, but for the moment that's all you need to know, so trust me.

C++ offers three logical operators that can be used to evaluate the overall truth of two (or more) operands. The outcome of this comparison evaluates to either false or true. The operators are now described by what is known as a *truth table*.

There's Nothing Logical About Logic

This is potentially one of the most confusing pieces of computer science you are likely to come across. At least, it seems so to the students I have taught. Don't confuse AND with addition; it has nothing to do with it. The best bet is just to learn the new operators parrot fashion and treat them as new tools to play with.

The Logical AND Operator

In C++ the logical AND operator has this syntax:

```
X && Y
```

X and Y can have the value of false or true in the combinations shown in the truth table of the logical AND operator. The result column shows the outcome of the operation, which depends on what the values are at any point in time.

The truth table of the logical AND operator.	X && Y	RESULT
	false false	false
	false true	false
	true false	false
	true true	true

> The table shows the truth of X AND Y; there are four possible combinations. The result is true only when X AND Y are true.

The Logical OR Operator

In C++ the logical OR operator has this syntax:

    X || Y

Once again, the result column shows the outcome of the operation, which depends on the values of X and Y.

The truth table of the OR operator.	X || Y	RESULT
	false false	false
	false true	true
	true false	true
	true true	true

> The table shows the truth of X OR Y; there are four possible combinations. The result is true only when X OR Y is true.

Hang On! What Is Boolean When It's at Home?

Boolean is a state of either false or true. A whole branch of mathematics, called Boolean algebra, is devoted to this subject, and, boy, is that fun! As far we're concerned as C++ programmers, we use boolean to mark a condition as being false or true, and nothing more. So don't worry your pretty little heads about anything as complicated as algebra.

The NOT Operator

In C++ the NOT operator has this syntax:

    !X

The NOT function is used to invert the truth of a boolean expression. NOT false is true; alternatively, NOT true is false. Perfectly logical, I suppose! In other words,

If X = true, then !X = false.

If Y = false, then !Y = true.

Story Time

Once upon a time there was a Irish mathematician named George Boole who was terribly concerned about the construction of railways back in the great days of steam locomotives. His big concern was about the points where the tracks change over. In his wisdom, he developed an entire branch of mathematics that could be used to predict the path on which a train would get from A to B. But poor George Boole. The people of the time thought he was mad, and the mathematics was ridiculed and largely ignored. Many years later, in the wondrous days of modern technology—the transistor, the microchip, and Coca Cola—someone suddenly said, "Hey guys, can you remember Georgie Boole?" "He invented that weird math about logic, didn't he?" "Yeh! And wouldn't it do nicely for our electronic logic systems." And so it was that Boolean algebra was reborn and lived happily ever after.

Testing George's Theory

You shall now write a program that uses Boolean logic. The logic of logic never ceases to amaze me.

Give Me an *AND*

In the next program, you use some logic to test the range of an input value. Incidentally, just because we're doing overloaded operators, to keep the theme going, I threw in two overloaded functions. Now wasn't that cunning? Before you answer no, I'll move on and describe the program to you.

There are two overloaded functions named InRange, both of which return a boolean result of either false or true. Their purpose in life is to test whether an input value falls within a given range. One overloaded function checks whether a character is a lowercase letter; the other function checks whether an integer is in the range of 0–9. The key line is the use of the && logical operator. You test to see whether x is less than or equal to 9 and whether x is greater than or equal to 0. Looking back at the truth table for AND, you can see that only when both statements are true is the overall result true.

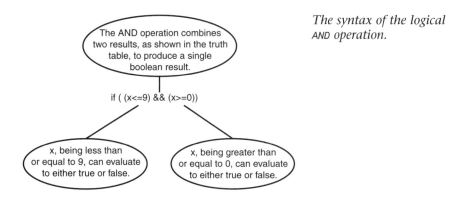

The syntax of the logical AND operation.

The if else statement determines whether the outcome of the line is true or false and returns the appropriate state to the main program via the function. The function Show simply takes that boolean condition as an input and shows the result to the screen. Try the program. With the given values, you should see the following lines appearing on the screen:

```
Test was false
Test was true
```

A screen full of logic!

Listing 17.2   An Example of Overloaded Functions and Logical AND Operators

```cpp
#include <iostream.h>

bool InRange(int x);
bool InRange(char alpha);
void Show(bool answer);

main()
{
    bool result;

    result = InRange(25);
    Show(result);
    result = InRange('v');
    Show(result);

    return(0);
}

bool InRange(int x)
{
    if ( (x <= 9) && (x >= 0))
    {
        return(true);
    }
    else
    {
        return(false);
    }
}


bool InRange(char alpha)
{
    if ( (alpha <= 'z') && (alpha >= 'a'))
    {
        return(true);
```

```
    }
    else
    {
        return(false);
    }
}

void Show(bool answer)
{
    if (answer == true)
    {
        cout << "Test was true" << endl;
    }
    else
    {
        cout << "Test was false" << endl;
    }
}
```

To prove that the program works, try changing the values and see what happens. I promise this one will not damage your precious computer, assuming you don't do anything silly, of course.

Pass the Caveat, Please

The "assuming you don't do anything silly, of course" is a get-out clause just in case things go drastically wrong. It is called a *caveat*, and all good project agreements should have lots of caveats, thereby disclaiming any responsibility for anything that might go wrong.

Give Me an OR

Moving into overtime, I will describe the use of the OR operator to determine whether an input is the letter *n* or the letter *N*. This can be useful if you are testing a user response to see whether he wants to quit from a loop. Earlier in the book, I suggested that you should convert this type of input into an uppercase letter. This is an alternative way of doing things, and I leave it to you to judge which method is the most effective.

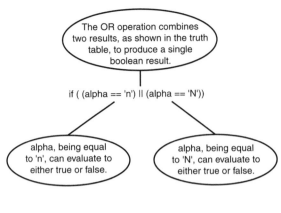

The OR operation combines two results, as shown in the truth table, to produce a single boolean result.

if ((alpha == 'n') || (alpha == 'N'))

alpha, being equal to 'n', can evaluate to either true or false.

alpha, being equal to 'N', can evaluate to either true or false.

There's Logic in That Boolean Thing

The new data type of boolean has only two values. They are false and true, in that order, which, because they follow an order, means boolean is an ordinal type. You might recall that an ordinal type can be used as the loop control variable in a for loop or a condition in a switch case statement. Because there are only two possible conditions, the for loop can loop only twice, and the switch case can choose only one of two processes. Not a lot of use, really! But there you have it. It's the sort of thing that crops up in university exams and the like. Boolean is used much more in logic and determining logical outcomes.

The OR operation works just like it reads. It asks the question, Is alpha equal to *n* or is alpha equal to *N*? Looking back at the OR truth table, you can see that either statement being true causes the overall result to be true. In the context of the next program, this causes the do while loop to terminate, whereas entering any other letter will not:

```
Enter a letter or n to quit : r
Enter a letter or n to quit : R
Enter a letter or n to quit : n
That's all folks
```

Try out the code in Listing 17.3 and experience the result.

Listing 17.3 An Example of Logical OR Operators

```
#include <iostream.h>

char GetLetter(void);
bool IsValid(char alpha);

main()
{
    bool result = false;
    char letter;

    do
    {
        letter = GetLetter();
        result = IsValid(letter);
    } while (result == false);
    cout << "That's all folks" << endl << endl;
    return(0);
}

char GetLetter(void)
{
    char in;

    cout << "Enter a letter or n to quit : ";
    cin >> in;
    return (in);
}

bool IsValid(char alpha)
{
    if ( (alpha == 'n') || (alpha == 'N'))
    {
        return(true);
    }
    else
    {
        return(false);
    }
}
```

That's NOT NOT What I Want

As a finale, I shall give some attention to NOT, just in case it is feeling left out. In the last program, you terminated the loop with the line that means "Keep going while result is false":

```
while (result == false);
```

207

However, this could have been equally well written as "Keep going while result is not true":

```
while (result != true);
```

Now, that's logic for you.

The Least You Need to Know

➤ Overloaded functions can be defined as a group of related modules that have the same name but are differentiated by the parameters that are passed to them.

➤ The data type called boolean has the C++ abbreviation of bool. It has only two possible values, and these are false and true, in that order.

➤ C++ offers three logical operators that can be used to evaluate the overall truth of two (or more) operands.

➤ The logical AND function has the syntax X && Y. The result depends on the boolean values held by X and Y.

➤ The logical OR function has the syntax X ¦¦ Y. The result depends on the boolean values held by X and Y.

➤ The NOT function is used to invert the truth of a boolean expression.

How to Annoy the Visual Basic Programmers

C++ programmers for no apparent reason tend to use the "not equal to true" solution more frequently. This is known as *negative logic*. Visual Basic programmers seem to prefer the "equal to false" solution, which is known as *positive logic*. They get really upset when they read C++ code and become confused with the negative logic. That's probably the reason why C++ programmers use negative logic, come to think of it!

Chapter 18

Don't Lose Your Data: Get a Handle on File Handling

In This Chapter

➤ The theory of file handling

➤ Storing and retrieving simple text files

➤ Storing and retrieving binary files

➤ Storing and retrieving files of structures

Okay, So What Is File Handling?

In the previous chapters, all input and output involved the keyboard and the screen. This, however, need not be the case. You can also read and write to external devices such as printers, modems, and disk drives, to name but a few. To demonstrate how data can be sent and received from external devices, I will explain a technique known as *file handling*, that is, using the disk drive on the computer to store information. This form of storage is one of the most widely used in the world of computing. You might have noticed in earlier chapters that you had to type in your data every time that you ran your program, and, boy, was that tedious. The fantastic thing about file handling is that after you have typed in your data or obtained it by some means fair or foul, that's it. It's stored forever on your disk drive.

Secondary Storage Described

Secondary storage is any device that can store electronic data that your computer can access. Such devices are hard drives or tape streamers. The data stored on a secondary device does not disappear when the computer is turned off. It sits there waiting to be used the next time the power comes back on.

My Computer and Big Brother

In the real world, huge amounts of data are stored. Modern PC computers have typically 64–128MB of RAM at their disposal within the machine. This is chicken feed compared to the sizes of stored data where you are looking at gigabytes of data. The whole point of file handling is that you can use a huge hard drive to permanently store the data and can import parts of the data when you need it.

The relationship between computer and secondary storage.

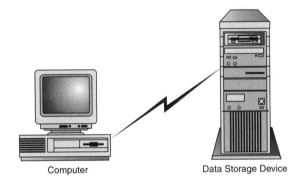

Computer   Data Storage Device

Memories Are Made of This

The technique demonstrated in this chapter is to use a single variable that requires a very small amount of memory within the computer's main RAM to hold single data items while they are processed. The main data is stored in an external file on a floppy disk. The floppy disk could equally well be the hard drive, a network drive, or a remote server in Australia. It doesn't matter, as long as it isn't main memory. This external storage is huge and cannot physically fit into the main computer memory because it's relatively small. The trick is to make a connection between main memory and external storage and then transfer small chunks from the external storage into main memory. The computer sees the external storage device as part of its own main memory and is fooled into thinking that it has huge amounts of memory. This external storage is known as *virtual memory*.

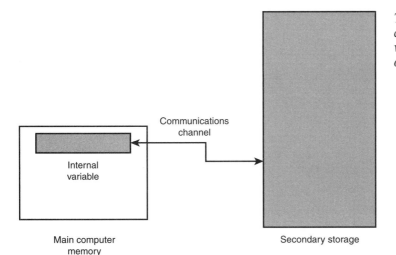

The relationship between computer memory and the virtual memory in secondary storage.

Communications channel

Internal variable

Main computer memory

Secondary storage

One Step at a Time

When you are dealing with data storage, there are two processes, these being writing the data and reading the data. We shall first deal with writing the data. There is actually a very good reason for this. If you don't write some data first, you will have nothing to read later. You might scoff at that statement, but believe me, I've lost count of the number of times I've seen it happen. In this explanation, you will encounter a few new keywords and experience a bit more of this OOP stuff. We shall properly deal with OOP starting at Chapter 19, "An Introduction to Object-Oriented Programming: A Step-by-Step Guide for the Terrified," so for the moment I must ask you to use some of the code, and all will become apparent later.

Learn to Write Your ABCs

In C++ the process of writing a file to disk is straightforward, and if you follow the list, all should be well.

1. You set up the name of the external file as it will be stored on the floppy drive:

```
char filename[20] = "a:test.txt";
```

2. Now you set up the mode in which it shall be handled; in this case, it is an output file:

```
int mode = ios::out;
```

3. Next, you set up the connection protocol to the disk drive. This is OOP, and technically fout is an instance of fstream that has access to all the member functions of the fstream class. Don't panic if you didn't understand that last sentence; just use it, and all will function. If you did understand it, then why on earth are you reading this book?

```
fstream fout( filename, mode );
```

211

The Computer Has Lost My File

This is one of the most common phrases uttered by computer students. When you save your data, you have two options. The first is just to specify the filename and let the computer decide where to put it. This is known as the *default location*. The second is to specify both the location and the filename. On a small system that you are familiar with, there shouldn't be a problem, and you should be able to find your data again. However, on a big system, your data goes shooting off down the wires and ends up who knows where. After many traumatic encounters with students who seem to believe that I was personally responsible for their lost data, I always insist now that files be stored in the second format, and the location is the student's own personal floppy disk. You are at liberty to ignore my advice, but I hold this disclaimer as my caveat.

4. Then you use standard OOP C++ code to read a character from the keyboard and send it to the external file under the name a:test.txt. The operation `cin.get(ch)` reads the data from the keyboard. Then `fout.put(ch)` is used to send it to the secondary storage device, in our case, the floppy disk.

```
while ( cin.get(ch) )
{
        fout.put( ch );
}
```

5. Finally, you must close the file. `fout.close` is a member function of the `fstream` class and is used to close the link to the secondary storage device.

```
fout.close();
```

6. When you run this program, shown in Listing 18.1, you are expected to type in a sequence of letters of your choice. To end the process and save the data to disk, press Ctrl and z together. This is an escape sequence used by the operating system, and I have used it to save additional code that might have distracted you from the task in hand, understanding simple file handling.

The following output shows data being entered from the keyboard. The Ctrl+z have not yet been pressed.

```
Ready for input: Use Control-Z to end.
Create a file on your flop
```

Listing 18.1   Create a File on Your Floppy Disk

```cpp
#include <fstream.h>

main()
{
    char ch;
    char filename[20] = "a:test.txt";
    int mode = ios::out;
```

```
fstream fout( filename, mode );      // Output file
cout << "Ready for input: Use Control-Z to end."
      << endl;
while ( cin.get(ch) )
{
    fout.put( ch );
}
fout.close();
return(0);
}
```

The Computer Didn't Save My File

This is another common cry from students (and the odd teacher). There are usually two reasons for this. The first one is that the specified location is not what you thought it was, in which case the file is hiding somewhere but does actually exist. The second one is a bit more serious. If you miss out the line fout.close(), the computer doesn't close the file, and the data is lost forever.

eof Is Not a New Swear Word

Pay attention, I'm going vto let you in on a secret. When your last program closed the file, it cunningly placed a marker called eof (which is an abbreviation for End Of File) at the end of your file. Now, this marker is really useful, and we shall pick up the story in the next section. But do you recall that I said that if you omit the close statement in your program, you lose your data? Well, this is the reason. No EOF means you don't have a file, and the close statement is responsible for placing EOF at the end of the file.

Still on this theme, I have a phobia about EOF in C++, and I'll tell you why. Many years ago I was teaching a class on how to do file handling in C (C not C++). One of the students (there's

Seeing the Light

If you are familiar with basic IT principles, have a look at your floppy disk contents. All being well, you will find that a file called a:test.txt has appeared there. If you are even more IT-literate, open this file with something such as Notepad, and what you typed in during the last program run should be contained in the file.

always one) had forgotten his floppy disk, to which I glibly said, "Oh dear, oh well, tut tut, never mind, just save your data to the hard drive," and so he did. Unfortunately, he omitted the close statement on his program. He bravely ran the program and then reported that he couldn't find his file. I took a look at the hard drive and discovered that not only was his file missing, but so were the entire contents of the hard drive. On further examination, I discovered that the hard drive not only contained no files—and also had no free space, which meant that his file did exist—but also it could not be viewed, and it occupied the entire hard drive because of the missing EOF.

At that point, I sent the class home and sneaked out the back door. Incidentally, the version of C that we were using was some obscure species, which I have thankfully never encountered again on my travels. Products such as Microsoft and Borland appear to be quite tame. Good luck!

Learn to Read Your ABCs

Having created the file, you now need a means of reading it back at a later date. That later date has now arrived, so follow the steps, and you should see some results.

1. In the first program, you set up the name of the external file that was stored on the floppy drive. You use exactly the same line of code to read it back:

   ```
   char filename[20] = "a:test.txt";
   ```

2. You set up the mode in which it shall be handled; in this case, it is an input file:

   ```
   int mode = ios::in;
   ```

3. Next, you set up the connection protocol to the disk. Once again, this is OOP, and technically fin is an instance of fstream that has access to all the member functions of the fstream class.

   ```
   fstream fin( filename, mode );
   ```

4. It's always a good idea to check that the file can be accessed; if not, you issue an error message. This is a standard piece of code and well worth learning parrot fashion:

   ```
   if (!fin)
        cerr << "Unable to open file";
   ```

5. Then you use the standard C++ code fin.get(ch) to read characters from the file and send it to the screen:

   ```
   while ( fin.get(ch) )
   {
           cout << ch;
   }
   ```

6. As long as `fin.get(ch)` reads a char, it maintains the loop. When it hits `eof`, the loop terminates.

7. Finally, you close the file:

```
fin.close();
```

Make sure your floppy disk is in place and run the program (shown in Listing 18.2). All being well, you will see in glorious black and white text the original message that you typed in during the first program run. View the following output and see whether my original file did actually work:

```
Create a file on your floppy disk
```

Listing 18.2   Read Back the File

```
#include <fstream.h>

main()
{
    char ch;
    char filename[20] = "a:test.txt";
    int mode = ios::in;

    fstream fin( filename, mode );        // Input file
    if (!fin)
        cout << "Unable to open file";
    while ( fin.get(ch) )
    {
        cout << ch;
    }
    fin.close();
    return(0);
}
```

Binary Files at the Double

So far, you have seen C++ deal with text files, which is the default setting. Text files store data in ASCII format and really need further manipulation if they are to be of any use in powerful numeric programs. However, you can override the feature and process binary files. Binary files can be of any data type and are much more useful than plain text files. The next few programs elaborate on the feature.

Learn to Write Your 1, 2, 3s

You set up the filename just as before:

```
char filename[20] = "a:xtest.dat";
```

Then you set up the mode of access. It is an output, but note how the binary mode is invoked:

```
int mode = (ios::out | ios::binary);
```

Having defined the file mode, you now invoke the file protocol just as before:

```
fstream fout( filename, mode );
```

Then, using the for loop, you simply send the data contained in the array to the external file. Here is an important point: Note that you use an endl after each item sent to the file. This is known as a *delimiter* and serves to separate each individual integer value from the next. Without it, you could not easily recover the original information:

```
for (loop = 0; loop < MAX; loop++)
{
        fout << x[loop] << endl;
}
```

Wow, It Works! But I Can't See the Error Message

That's correct. If your program worked correctly, you won't see the error message. So how do you know whether that piece of code works? Easy. Where your program says "a:test.txt", change it to a fictitious filename such as "a:wrong.txt". When you run your program, it won't find the file, and you will see the error message.

Finally, you close the file:

```
    fout.close();
```

I hope you noticed that the technique is almost identical to using text files. The only difference is that you set it up as a binary file at the beginning. Try out the program in Listing 18.3 to create the external file on disk. I've noticed over the years that my students tend to panic at this point because very little appears on the screen. The only visible sign you have is a short message that says Data written to file in whitish colored letters. However, I now believe that students have a mental block with this phrase and read it as Your program didn't work, and you should now run around screaming, call for your teacher, and generally panic. Don't worry. The message Data written to file should reassure you that everything is working fine.

Listing 18.3   Create a File Stream of Integers, Using Binary Mode File Access

```
#include <fstream.h>
#define MAX 6

main()
{
    int loop;
    int x[MAX] = {42,707,99,101};
```

216

```
    char filename[20] = "a:xtest.dat";
    int mode = (ios::out ¦ ios::binary);

    fstream fout( filename, mode );      // Output file
    for (loop = 0; loop < MAX; loop++)
    {
        fout << x[loop] << endl;
    }
    fout.close();
    cout << "Data written to file" << endl;
    return(0);
}
```

Learn to Read Your 1, 2, 3s

Now it's time to write a program to view the contents of the binary file. Once again, it's almost identical to Listing 18.2 (the text file version). The only difference worth noting in Listing 18.4 is the line that specifies the mode of access. No medals for guessing it is an input file in binary mode:

```
    int mode = (ios::in ¦ ios::binary);
```

Try out the program now and see your numbers reappear on the silver screen. No reassuring message is needed, because real data appears from nowhere:

```
    42
    707
    99
    101
    0
    0
```

The Challenge of a Lifetime

The binary files that you have seen use integer values. I challenge you to modify the files to deal with floats. If you succeed in this venture, go for the gold and attempt char.

Listing 18.4   Read a File Stream of Integers, Using Binary Mode File Access

```
#include <fstream.h>

main()
{
    int loop = 0;
    int x;
    char filename[20] = "a:xtest.dat";
    int mode = (ios::in ¦ ios::binary);
```

```
        fstream fin( filename, mode );      // input file
        if (!fin)
            cerr << "Unable to open file";
        while (fin >> x)
        {
            cout << x << endl;
            loop++;
        }
        fin.close();
        return(0);
    }
```

Compound Files—You Know It Makes Sense

Now we turn our attention to the storage and retrieval of the C++ structures that you met in Chapter 14, "The Parallel Array Is Dead, Long Live the Structure." Structures are used to represent real-world records and are collections of related information of different data types. You will be pleased to hear that the file access method is identical to the previous binary files, but for convenience, you utilize the insertion and extraction overloads discussed in Chapter 16, "Feel You Can't Cope Anymore? Then Take Pity on the Overloaded Operator." Here is the sequence of events:

1. You define a structure in the usual manner, as shown in Chapter 14.

2. You overload the insertion operator to deal with this structure, as shown in Chapter 16.

3. You set up an array containing the desired information, as shown in Chapter 15, "The Best of Both Worlds: Structures Meet Functions."

4. You define the mode and open the binary file just as before.

5. You use a for loop to send the information to the external file.

6. You close the file.

Sounds familiar, doesn't it!

Run the program in Listing 18.5 and observe the light on your disk drive blink into life. This is always a good indication that something is trying to work. For this reason, I'm not including the output here. After all, it just says Data written to file, which you know translates as "Your program didn't work, and you should now run around screaming, call for your teacher, and generally panic."

Listing 18.5   Create a File Stream of Records

```
#include <fstream.h>
struct planet     {
```

```
                          char name[10];
                          int  dist;
                    };

ostream& operator << (ostream& str_out, planet& d)
{
    str_out << d.name  << endl;
    str_out << d.dist << endl;
    return(str_out);
};


main()
{
struct planet solar[3] = {    {"MERCURY",58},
                              {"VENUS",108},
                              {"EARTH",150}};
    int x;
    char filename[20] = "a:system.dat";
    int mode = (ios::out | ios::binary);

    fstream fout( filename, mode );      // Output file
    for (x = 0; x < 3; x++)
    {
          fout << solar[x];
    }
    fout.close();
    cout << "Data written to file" << endl;
    return(0);
}
```

The Planets Revisited Again

Now it's time to write a program to view the contents of the compound binary file. Again, Listing 18.6 is almost identical to Listing 18.2 (the text version) except that you need to overload the insertion and extraction operators to handle structures and you must use binary access mode:

1. After overloading the insertion and extraction operators, you set up the protocol to handle the external file.

2. You open the file and then read in the data, using the overloaded extraction operator.

3. You close the file. Couldn't be easier!

Just to reassure you, I'll include the screen output here. Look at the nice planets.

```
MERCURY    58
VENUS     108
EARTH     150
```

219

Who Forgot the Delimiter, Then?

Oh no I didn't. Look at the overload insertion operator. That's where I hid it, and that's what I said earlier in the book. Formatting of data can be set up in an overloaded operator and then used every time it is needed, without any further coding effort. Don't you just love it when a plan comes together!

Listing 18.6   Read a File Stream of Records

```
#include <fstream.h>
#define tab '\t'

struct planet    {
                    char name[10];
                    int  dist;
                 };

ostream& operator << (ostream& str_out, planet& d)
{
    str_out << d.name << tab;
    str_out << d.dist << tab << endl;
    return(str_out);
};

istream& operator >> (istream& str_in, planet& d)
{
    str_in >> d.name;
    str_in >> d.dist;
    return(str_in);
};

main()
{
    struct planet solar;
    char filename[20] = "a:system.dat";
    int mode = (ios::in ¦ ios::binary);

    fstream fin( filename, mode );  // Input file
    if (!fin)
        cerr << "Unable to open file";
```

```
        while (fin >> solar)
        {
            cout << solar;
        }
        fin.close();
        return(0);
    }
```

Do You Like a Challenge?

Now that you have seen file handling, you might ask the question "Why didn't you show me that at the beginning of the book and saved me all that typing of the solar system?" There are two answers. The first is that several threads of technology are involved here and you probably couldn't have dealt with them all in one go. The second is that I'm really cruel to students. To make up for that, I'll set you a challenge.

Write a program that is capable of storing to secondary the following information about the solar system. *Do not* call your data file system.dat. I repeat, *DO NOT* call your data file system.dat. You will need that file in the next chapter.

PLANET	DISTANCE	MOONS	YEAR
MERCURY	58	0	0.240
VENUS	108	0	0.625
EARTH	150	1	1.000
MARS	228	2	1.910
JUPITER	778	12	12
SATURN	1427	14	29.9
URANUS	2869	5	85.24
NEPTUNE	4498	2	167.19
PLUTO	5900	1	251.29

Write another program that is capable of reading back and displaying the information about the solar system.

The Least You Need to Know

> ➤ File handling is a means of electronically storing data for later use on an external device such as a disk drive. The data doesn't disappear when the power is turned off and, theoretically, remains there forever.

➤ In the real world, huge volumes of data need to be stored, but computers have limited memory capabilities. File handling enables the computer to read in small chunks of that data, process it, and then discard it.

➤ File handling enables the computer to access secondary storage capacity and treat it as part of its own memory. This extra memory is known as virtual memory.

➤ Text files store data in a plain ASCII format.

➤ Binary files store data in a format whereby numeric and structured data can easily be accessed and manipulated.

➤ The `eof` marker is inserted by the `close` command to mark the end of the file when it is written to secondary storage.

Chapter 19

An Introduction to Object-Oriented Programming: A Step-by-Step Guide for the Terrified

OOP: What It Can Do for You

In the past, when programmers wrote code that manipulated data, the data and the code that manipulated it were treated as two distinctly separate items. Object-oriented programming, on the other hand, treats both data and code as a single entity, known as a *class*. In this chapter, we will develop a trivial example of a class and its use, with the sole intention of outlining the steps involved. When you have grasped this concept, you should be able to develop your own large, complex object-oriented programs. Incidentally, object-oriented programs are often referred to as *OOP* or *OO*.

The concept of OOP hinges on some new buzz words, these being:

CLASS

INSTANCE

OBJECT

ENCAPSULATION

DATA MEMBER

MEMBER FUNCTION

CONSTRUCTOR

I will deal with these as we need them, but for the moment take a look at the following diagram, which shows the concept of OOP by presenting an analogy to television.

The relationship between a TV circuit diagram, building a TV from that circuit diagram, and building several TVs from the one circuit diagram.

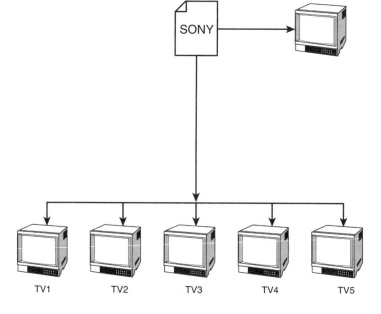

A class can be likened to a circuit diagram of a Sony television. The circuit diagram is just a piece of paper that describes how the television should be constructed; it isn't the actual television. When the circuit diagram is issued as a blueprint to construct the television, the resulting piece of equipment is a physical object that you can touch and use. You have created an instance of a single television.

You can create as many televisions as you want from a single circuit diagram—just ask Mr. Sony how many he makes from a single design. Every time you create an instance of a television from the blueprint, you end up with another physical TV set. Although every TV set is the same, each has a unique ID, which distinguishes one from another. And so it is with computer program objects. Each instance of the same class must have a unique identifier name.

Encapsulation Exposed

All OOP programs start from a class. A *class* is a data structure that contains all that is needed to store and manipulate data. In the past, we have stored our data in variables. In OOP, any variable defined inside a class is called a *data member*; it has a different terminology to distinguish it from a normal variable. The functions that manipulate the data are called *member functions*, again, to distinguish them from normal functions. It should be possible to manipulate the data members only via the member functions. External functions and commands cannot access the data members. Because of this fact, the data members and member functions are tightly bound into one entity (a class); hence, one has no effect without the other. This behavior is called *encapsulation*.

As a simple example, let us develop an OOP-based program that can calculate the area of a square. I know you will say that this is overkill, but I want to keep it as simple as possible so that you can see the mechanics behind encapsulation. What you are developing is really a template to guide you through the steps involved in writing an OOP-style program.

Note

You are now entering the realm of professional programming. All the kiddies claim to be OOP programmers because they can use cout. The OOP language called C++ was used to write cout, and using cout is just like being a copy typist.

The Painless Guide to a Working Object-Oriented Program

The next six steps are a template for building your own OOP-style programs. Follow these steps and try to get a grasp of the processes involved. When you write your own programs, substitute your own data members and member functions to achieve the desired results. I encourage you to compile at each stage; that way you can pick up errors early on. This is very important when you're learning OOP, because a single error can lead to multiple compiler-reported errors. Be warned before you start: Steps one to five run but give no screen output. You will not see any visible results until step six, so don't be impatient.

The Class Looks Like a Structure

Yes, it does, but a class is not a structure, so don't get them confused. They are very different animals.

OOP, Step One: The Construction of a Class

The first step is to create a class, which I have called shape. Take a look at the skeleton program in Listing 19.1, which does that and nothing else. This program will compile and run, but it does absolutely nothing. It is only a template.

Listing 19.1   How to Create the Class

```
#include <iostream.h>

class shape {
    // AN EMPTY CLASS
            };

main()
{
    return(0);
}
```

A class can be pictured as a circle or a "world" encompassing all the elements contained within that class. In this instance, none, because we haven't yet given any elements or functionality to shape. Look back to the declaration of the class if you don't believe me. The boundaries of what can be accessed are defined by the solid wall of the circle. In our circle, there can be no access, because no gaps are present in the circle's circumference.

The concept of an empty class.

OOP, Step Two: Adding the Data Members

The next step is to give our class some data members, that is, data that belongs solely to the class. Listing 19.2 shows how this is done.

A Class *Still* Looks like a Structure!

Right again. A class has what looks like variables of mixed data types. The only difference at this point is the jargon. You call these variables *data members*.

Listing 19.2   Adding the Data Members to the Class

```
#include <iostream.h>

class shape      {
                 // DECLARE DATA MEMBERS
```

continues

227

Listing 19.2   Adding the Data Members to the Class
CONTINUED

```
                // WHICH ARE PRIVATE BY DEFAULT
                // BUT I HAVE INCLUDED THE WORD
                // TO SHOW THE CORRECT SYNTAX
            private:
                int length;
                int height;
                int area;
                };

main()
{
    return(0);
}
```

Public and Private Explained

public—OOP uses the word *public* to describe any member of a class that can be freely accessed from outside the class.

private—OOP uses the word *private* to describe any member of a class that cannot be accessed from outside the class. These private members can be accessed only via member functions. In C++ it is a convention to make all data members private and is considered bad programming practice to do otherwise. The whole concept of OOP is to hide the data away inside a class and manipulate it via member functions. That's what we mean by encapsulation. Unfortunately, it is possible to set up a C++ class that can manipulate the data members without using member functions. This is a throwback to earlier versions of the language and included for compatibility. If you want to be an OOP programmer, do it the correct way. Unless explicitly stated, all members of a class are, by default, private.

Listing 19.2 shows how two data members called length and height are added to the class. By default, they are said to be private; that is, they cannot be accessed from outside the class boundary. Pictorially, the situation in our world now looks like this, and as you can see, length, height, and area sit within the boundary and therefore, as yet, cannot be accessed.

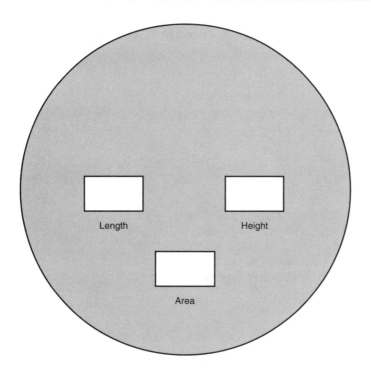

The concept of a class with three data members.

Length

Height

Area

OOP, Step Three: Prototyping the Member Functions

The next step is to create member functions that can manipulate the data members.

Structures Don't Have Functions Inside Them

Correct. You are now beginning to see the difference. By the way, don't call them *functions*. They prefer to be called *member functions*.

Listing 19.3 Adding the Member Functions to the Class

```cpp
#include <iostream.h>

class shape      {
                 // DECLARE DATA MEMBERS
                 private:
                     int length;
                     int height;
                     int area;

                 public:

                 // DECLARE MEMBER FUNCTIONS
                 // NOTE THE EXPLICIT USE OF PUBLIC
                 // THIS ALLOWS ACCESS FROM OUTSIDE
                     void CalcArea(void);
                     void ShowArea(void);
                 };

main()
{
    return(0);
}
```

The concept of a class with three data members and two member functions.

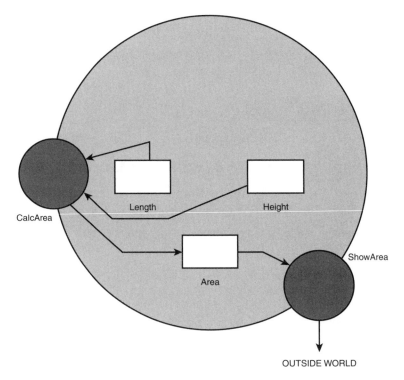

The next diagram shows the effect on our world of adding member functions to the class. Think of CalcArea as a button that, when pressed, accesses the contents of length and height and processes them before storing the result in area. The member function ShowArea is another button. It takes the contents of area, transports the data across the boundary, and displays the value to the outside world. Take a special note that at no time do the data members length and height cross the boundary. They still have not been accessed from outside the class.

Constructor...Say That Again!

A *constructor* is a special member function. You can always recognize a constructor because it has the same name as the class to which it belongs.

OOP, Step Four: The Constructor and Its Purpose in Life

The only remaining problem is, How do you put data into length and height in the first place? The model told us that we couldn't cross the boundary wall of the circle. This is usually achieved by a special kind of member function called a *constructor*. Listing 19.4 adds a constructor to our class.

Listing 19.4   Adding the Constructor to the Class

```
#include <iostream.h>

class shape {
            // DECLARE DATA MEMBERS
            private:
                int length;
                int height;
                int area;

            public:

            // DECLARE MEMBER FUNCTIONS
                void CalcArea(void);
                void ShowArea(void);
            // CREATE A CONSTRUCTOR
                shape(int l = 0, int h = 0);
        };

main()
{
    return(0);
}
```

The syntax of a constructor appears in the following figure.

It is good programming practice to give sensible default values in the declaration of the constructor, but this is not compulsory. Equally, you could well have omitted any default settings and declared the constructor as shown here:

```
shape(int l , int h );
```

*The syntax of a construc-
tor with sensible default
values.*

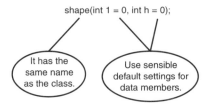

The next diagram depicts the effect on our world of adding a constructor to the class. You can see that the constructor gathers public data h and l from the outside world, transports their values across the boundary, and places those values into the private data members height and length, respectively.

*The concept of a class
with three data members,
two member functions,
and a constructor.*

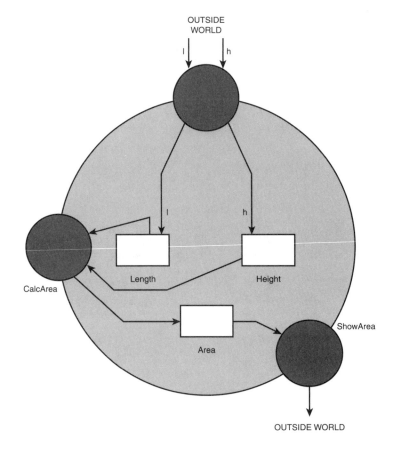

OOP, Step Five: Defining the Code of the Member Functions and Constructor

The next step is to define the member functions. You do this in a similar manner to normal C++ source code. Naturally, there are one or two minor differences. The first one is easy: All member functions are declared directly after the class definitions, using normal C++ code. The second one might sound a little odd, so take a look at the next program, in Listing 19.5.

This Looks Very Long-Winded

Yup, it is. And there's no answer to that.

Why Do We Have a Choice in Giving Default Values?

This is very much like declaring variables in traditional programming. Recall that you could declare a variable like this:

```
int number;
```

or declare and initialize like this:

```
int number = 0;
```

It might not be necessary, but it's good programming practice to set sensible default values, just in case.

Listing 19.5   Giving Definition to the Member Functions

```
#include <iostream.h>

class shape     {
                // DECLARE DATA MEMBERS
                private:
                    int length;
                    int height;
                    int area;
```

continues

Listing 19.5   Giving Definition to the Member Functions
CONTINUED

```
                        public:
                        // DECLARE MEMBER FUNCTIONS
                            void CalcArea(void);
                            void ShowArea(void);
                        // CREATE A CONSTRUCTOR .
                            shape(int l = 0, int h = 0);
                        };

// NOW DEFINE THE MEMBER FUNCTIONS

void shape::CalcArea(void)
{
    area = length * height;
}

void shape::ShowArea(void)
{
    cout << "THE AREA IS : " << area;
}

shape::shape(int l, int h)
{
    length = l;
    height = h;
}

main()
{
    return(0);
}
```

The big difference between normal C++ and OOP function definitions is that the latter specifies the class to which the definition belongs, by the use of a scope resolution operator, which is a double colon (::). This tells the compiler that the function is a member of that class, hence the name *member function*. Note that in the body of the member functions, the data members are named explicitly as if they were global variables. This isn't a problem with OOP; in fact, this is the whole point of it. You wrap up your variables in a class and access them through member functions. Then, via the scope resolution operator, you allow the compiler to sort out where the data lives.

OOP, Step Six: From Class to Object and a Running Program

Having done all this work, you will at last make the program do something. Take a look at Listing 19.6. For the first time in these program steps, there is some code in the main() program. If you cast your mind all the way back to Chapter 1, it is stated that all actions are orchestrated from main(). Now the program will actually do something.

Listing 19.6 Using the Class in the Main Program

```
#include <iostream.h>

class shape      {
                 // DECLARE DATA MEMBERS
                 private:
                     int length;
                     int height;
                     int area;

                 public:
                     void CalcArea(void);
                     void ShowArea(void);
                 // CREATE A CONSTRUCTOR .
                     shape(int l = 0, int h = 0);
                 };

// NOW DEFINE THE MEMBER FUNCTIONS
void shape::CalcArea(void)
{
    area = length * height;
}

void shape::ShowArea(void)
{
    cout << "THE AREA IS : " << area << endl;
}

shape::shape(int l, int h)
{
    length = l;
    height = h;
}

main()
{
```

continues

Listing 19.6 Using the Class in the Main Program Continued

```
        int x;
        int y;


        cout << "ENTER THE HEIGHT : ";
        cin >> x;
        cout << "ENTER THE LENGTH : ";
        cin >> y;
        // CREATE AN INSTANCE OF SHAPE
        shape square(y,x);
        // CALL THE MEMBER FUNCTIONS
        square.CalcArea();
        square.ShowArea();
        return(0);
    }
```

In the main program, you have declared two variables, x and y. These are used to collect public data from the outside world. Having read in these values, you then create what is known as an instance of the shape class, called square, and assign the values contained in x and y to the corresponding data members within the class. These new values override the default settings.

Now, returning to the diagram of the TV, the class is the circuit diagram of the TV, the constructor is the act of building the TV, and the instance is the physical object that you can watch. The values passed into the constructor are the customer requirements, such as wood cabinet or 56 cm screen. As the TV model shows, you can have as many instances of the TV as you want.

In terms of computing, you are doing the following: The class is the required memory and its configuration; the constructor claims that memory and places the appropriate code in that memory. The code is derived from the member functions. Every time that you do this action, you create a unique instance of the object living in computer memory. Each object has its own unique properties, due to the constructor input values, and its own code, derived from the member function definitions, to manipulate the data members.

Take note of the required syntax shown in the figure.

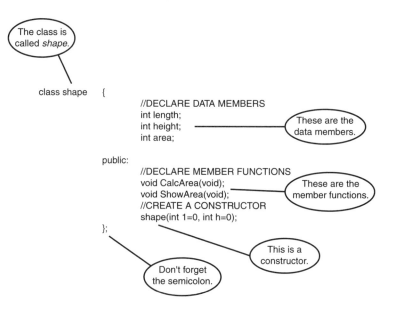

The syntax of the creation of an instance of shape.

Having created an instance of shape (called square), you now apply the member functions that manipulate the data contained within the instance. Take a look at the syntax shown in the next figure:

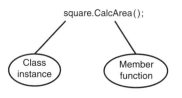

The syntax is the identifier of the instance, a dot, and then the member function and its parameter list (void, in this example).

Now, at last, after reading all the steps involved in creating object-oriented programs, you're going to run it.

Quite lengthy, wasn't it? Here is what my screen looked like when I ran the program described in Listing 19.6.

```
ENTER THE HEIGHT : 6
ENTER THE LENGTH : 7
THE AREA IS : 42
```

Now, that is really disappointing. I bet you thought that OOP was going to do some magical wondrous things. All that code to give the answer 42. It sounds like the punch line in one of my favorite sci-fi books.

OOP, like any other programming language, requires code. Where OOP does score is with a feature called *inheritance*, which I shall deal with in Chapter 21, "Inheritance! OO, Things for Free." But the underlying concept is here, and you must understand the concept.

Okay, so now you have experienced the steps involved, but that's a long way from being a fully fluent OOP programmer. It takes lots of practice to understand what's going on, so don't feel disheartened and return to traditional linear programming methods. I promise you, it's worth the effort. If nothing else, you can use the jargon and blind non-OOP people with science. On a good day, you can join the elite and strut your stuff for real. Let's try a case study and get some more practice.

The Queue (Q)

In this case study, you shall look at a Q (meaning *queue*) and define an object-oriented program solution from the specification. Actually, this is a common task in computing, so it's worth understanding the concept and the solution. Enter the given code at each step and compile it. This will minimize the number of errors you are likely to get. Don't leave it until the last program; do it step by step.

The Q Specification

A Q has the following features:

> A new Q will be empty.
> The Q will hold up to nine characters.
> Any new character can be added to only the back of the Q.
> Data can leave from only the front of the Q.
> You can view the entire Q. A message will be shown if the Q is empty.
> An error message will be shown if an attempt is made to add more than nine characters.

Based on this information, you can begin to write the OOP code to solve the problem. At each step, refer back to the earlier part of this chapter and compare it with the shape example.

238

The Six Steps to OOP

The steps described in this chapter are a guide for how to painlessly build an object-oriented program. These steps form a safety net for the reader. I will recap the steps:

1. Describe the class.

2. Add the member functions to the class.

3. Add the member function prototypes to the class.

4. Add the constructor to the class.

5. Define the code associated with each member function and the constructor.

6. Add the constructor code to the main() function that creates an instance of the class. Add the code that uses the member functions and thus manipulate the data members within the class.

Step One

First of all, you define the empty class. Remember to compile this program to make sure there are no errors. Don't run it yet, because main contains no actions, and nothing will happen.

Listing 19.7   The Q Program, Step One

```
#include <iostream.h>

class Q      {
             // an empty class.
             };
main()
{
    return(0);
}
```

continues

Step Two

Now you add the data members. From the specification, you can deduce that a nine-element array of characters would match the description of the Q. However, you also need to mark the end of the Q. I have made a design decision to use a data member called back, which will tell you how many elements of the array are currently in use. If back is set to zero, this will indicate an empty Q. The effect of this is that the array must be ten elements, not nine, because you don't use the first element but still must store nine characters.

How Do You Know When to Add Additional Variables?

Experience, my friend, experience. Don't worry about it. It takes lots of practice and heartache to become a programmer. Why do you think most good programmers have gray hair or even no hair? I've noticed that new students tend to use more variables than are actually required, but as they advance in their studies, this number starts to drop.

Listing 19.8   The Q Program, Step Two

```
#include <iostream.h>

class Q      {
             private:
                 int back;
                 char data[10];
             };

main()
{
        return(0);
}
```

Step Three

The next step is to add the member function prototypes to the class definition. The specification tells you that you need a member function to allow data to join the Q; I have called this JoinQ. Because we are adding data, I have given this member function a character input. Again, this is a design decision based on experience (and trial and error when I wrote the original program). You need a member function to allow data to leave the Q, which I have called LeaveQ. Leaving the Q requires only the command; it doesn't require any additional information. Hence, it is void. A member function to show the contents of the Q is required, so I have called it ShowQ. Once again, it requires no additional information to do this and is void.

Listing 19.9   The Q Program, Step Three

```
#include <iostream.h>

class Q {
        private:
            int back;
            char data[10];

        public:
            void JoinQ(char ch);
            void LeaveQ(void);
            void ShowQ(void);
        };

main()
{
    return(0);
}
```

How Do You Know What Member Functions Are Required?

Experience, my friend, experience. And don't worry about it—it will come with practice. The information was available with the specification, and it's a case of learning to read these specifications.

Step Four

Now for the constructor. The specification stated a new Q will be empty, so we shall oblige. I have called the constructor Q. Why? Because a constructor always has the same name as the class, so there was no choice here. The constructor requires no additional information, because the Q always starts off empty and hence is void.

Listing 19.10   The Q Program, Step Four

```
#include <iostream.h>

class Q {
        private:
            int back;
            char data[10];

        public:
            void JoinQ(char ch);
            void LeaveQ(void);
            void ShowQ(void);
            Q(void);
        };

main()
{
    return(0);
}
```

241

Step Five

And now to add the code. This is where you use the skills that you have acquired from the start of the book. All you are doing is applying normal code inside a OOP framework. You should now feel very assured. I will take you through each member function definition in turn.

The purpose of the constructor is to create an empty Q. A design decision was made to set back to zero to indicate an empty Q, and that's all the code required. This is the constructor used to set up an empty Q. Assume that if back is zero, Q is empty.

```
Q::Q()
{
    back = 0;
}
```

To add information to the Q, you apply the following code. The data is passed in via the character variable ch, and a test is applied to see whether space exists at the end of the Q. Remember that you cannot have more than 10 characters in the Q. If there is room, you increment back and add the contents of ch to the array. If the array is full, you display an error message saying that the Q is full. This member function allows a letter to be added to the end of the Q:

```
void Q::JoinQ(char ch)
{
    if (back < 9)
    {
        back++;
        data[back] = ch;
    }
    else
        cout << "Q is full" << endl;
}
```

When an item is to leave the Q, and the specification said it can leave from only the front, you can apply the following code. First of all, you must check whether there is any data in the Q; you cannot leave an empty Q. If the Q is empty, you issue a warning and take no further action. However, if there is data in the Q, read on. The trick is to shuffle the entire data one place forward in the Q, thus overwriting what was there originally. The item to leave the Q is shunted off the edge. This is done with a simple for loop. After that action, you decrement back to indicate there is one less item in the Q. The following member function allows the data item at the front of the Q to leave. All remaining items in the Q are moved up one place.

```
void Q::LeaveQ(void)
{
    int index;
```

```
        if (back > 0)
        {
            for (index = 1; index < back; index++)
            {
                data[index] = data[index + 1];
            }
            back--;
        }
        else
        {
            cout << "Q is already empty" << endl << endl;
        }
    }
```

The final member function is to show the data in the Q to the screen. If back is zero, this indicates an empty Q, so an appropriate message is given. Alternatively, a for loop is used to traverse the array elements and show their contents to the screen. Take note here that the loop starts at offset one, which is the second element. The first element at offset zero was used as a marker to indicate an empty Q. This member function is used to show the contents of the Q:

```
    void Q::ShowQ(void)
    {
        int x;

        if (back == 0)
        {
            cout << "Q is empty" << endl << endl;
        }
        else
        {
            for (x = 1; x <= back; x++)
            {
                cout << data[x] << TAB;
            }
            cout << endl << endl;
        }
    }
```

Here is the program, but remember, it still will give no results if you run it.

Listing 19.11   The Q Program, Step Five

```cpp
#include <iostream.h>

#define TAB '\t'

class Q {
        private:
            int back;
            char data[10];

        public:
            void JoinQ(char ch);
            void LeaveQ(void);
            void ShowQ(void);
            Q(void);
    };

// This is the constructor used
// to set up an empty Q.
// Assume that if back is zero, Q is empty
Q::Q()
{
    back = 0;
}

// This member function is used
// to show the contents of the Q
void Q::ShowQ(void)
{
    int x;

    if (back == 0)
    {
        cout << "Q is empty" << endl << endl;
    }
    else
    {
        for (x = 1; x <= back; x++)
        {
            cout << data[x] << TAB;
        }
        cout << endl << endl;
    }
}

// This member function allows
```

```
// a letter to be added to the
// end of the Q
void Q::JoinQ(char ch)
{
    if (back < 9)
    {
        back++;
        data[back] = ch;
    }
    else
        cout << "Q is full" << endl;
}


// This member function allows
// the data item at the front of
// the Q to leave. All remaining
// items in the Q are moved up one place
void Q::LeaveQ(void)
{
    int index;

    if (back > 0)
    {
        for (index = 1; index < back; index++)
        {
            data[index] = data[index + 1];
        }
        back--;
    }
    else
    {
        cout << "Q is already empty" << endl << endl;
    }
}

main()
{
    return(0);
}
```

Step Six

Now it's just a question of adding some code to make things happen. We've done the hard work. To verify that the program actually works, I've built up a list of three letters, using the JoinQ member function, and shown the results at each call, using ShowQ. I have then moved the data out of the Q, using LeaveQ. Before these actions could happen, I created an instance of Q called One, using the constructor.

Quirky Constructors

I find the use of a void constructor quirky. Note the correct syntax:

```
Q one;
```

There are no brackets after one, and my instinct is to put them there, through habit. So be careful.

```
main()
{
    Q One;
    One.ShowQ();
    One.JoinQ('Z');
    One.ShowQ();
    One.JoinQ('A');
    One.ShowQ();
    One.JoinQ('K');
    One.ShowQ();
    One.LeaveQ();
    One.ShowQ();
    One.LeaveQ();
    One.ShowQ();
    One.LeaveQ();
    One.ShowQ();
    return(0);
}
```

Check It Out, the Complete Q

Now that we've dissected the case study, let's give it a try. Here's the listing in full, Listing 19.12. Have fun in the Q. Your screen should look something like this:

```
Q is empty
Z
Z    A
Z    A    K
A    K
K
Q is empty
```

Listing 19.12   The Q Program

```
#include <iostream.h>

#define TAB '\t'

class Q {
        private:
            int back;
            char data[10];

        public:
            void JoinQ(char ch);
            void LeaveQ(void);
            void ShowQ(void);
            Q(void);
    };

// This is the constructor used
// to set up an empty Q.
// Assume that if back is zero, Q is empty
Q::Q()
{
    back = 0;
}

// This member function is used
// to show the contents of the Q
void Q::ShowQ(void)
{
    int x;

    if (back == 0)
    {
        cout << "Q is empty" << endl << endl;
    }
    else
    {
        for (x = 1; x <= back; x++)
        {
            cout << data[x] << TAB;
        }
        cout << endl << endl;
    }
}
```

continues

Listing 19.12   The Q Program CONTINUED

```
// This member function allows
// a letter to be added to the
// end of the Q
void Q::JoinQ(char ch)
{
    if (back < 9)
    {
        back++;
        data[back] = ch;
    }
    else
        cout << "Q is full" << endl;
}


// This member function allows
// the data item at the front of
// the Q to leave. All remaining
// items in the Q are moved up one place
void Q::LeaveQ(void)
{
    int index;

    if (back > 0)
    {
        for (index = 1; index < back; index++)
        {
            data[index] = data[index + 1];
        }
        back--;
    }
    else
    {
        cout << "Q is already empty" << endl << endl;
    }
}

main()
{
    Q One;
    One.ShowQ();
    One.JoinQ('Z');
    One.ShowQ();
    One.JoinQ('A');
    One.ShowQ();
    One.JoinQ('K');
    One.ShowQ();
```

```
        One.LeaveQ();
        One.ShowQ();
        One.LeaveQ();
        One.ShowQ();
        One.LeaveQ();
        One.ShowQ();
        return(0);
}
```

A Spicy Q

Listing 19.12 is okay for showing that our OOP Q actually worked, but it's rather static. Let's be daring and add a few refinements to make the program interactive. To do this, you need not touch the OOP bit, because you know it works. All you need to do is add a menu and a switch case as in Chapter 8, "If You Are Spoilt for Choice, the switch case Sometimes Helps." You can then view the Q, add to the Q, and leave the Q at runtime. Listing 19.13 is the complete listing, so give it a try.

Listing 19.13   Demo of OOP: The Q Program Spiced Up a Little

```
#include <iostream.h>
#include <stdlib.h>

#define TAB '\t'

class Q {
        private:
            int back;
            char data[10];

        public:
            void JoinQ(char ch);
            void LeaveQ(void);
            void ShowQ(void);
            Q(void);
        };

// This is the constructor used
// to set up an empty Q.
// Assume that if back is zero, Q is empty
Q::Q()
{
    back = 0;
```

continues

Listing 19.13   Demo of OOP: The Q Program Spiced Up a Little CONTINUED

```cpp
}

// This member function is used
// to show the contents of the Q
void Q::ShowQ(void)
{
    int x;

    if (back == 0)
    {
        cout << "Q is empty" << endl << endl;
    }
    else
    {
        for (x = 1; x <= back; x++)
        {
            cout << data[x] << TAB;
        }
        cout << endl << endl;
    }
}

// This member function allows
// a letter to be added to the
// end of the Q
void Q::JoinQ(char ch)
{
    if (back < 9)
    {
        back++;
        data[back] = ch;
    }
    else
        cout << "Q is full" << endl;
}

// This member function allows
// the data item at the front of
// the Q to leave. All remaining
// items in the Q are moved up one place
void Q::LeaveQ(void)
{
    int index;
```

```
        if (back > 0)
        {
            for (index = 1; index < back; index++)
            {
                data[index] = data[index + 1];
            }
            back--;
        }
        else
        {
            cout << "Q is already empty" << endl << endl;
        }
}

char menu(void);

main()
{
    char ch;
    char flipper;
    Q One;

    while (1)
    {
        ch = menu();
        switch(ch)
        {
            case '1' :  cout << "Enter the character : ";
                        cin >> flipper;
                        One.JoinQ(flipper);
                        break;
            case '2' :  One.LeaveQ();
                        break;
            case '3' :  One.ShowQ();
                        break;
            case '4' :  exit(0);
        }
    }
    return(0);
}

char menu(void)
{
    char choice;
```

continues

251

Listing 19.13 Demo of OOP: The Q Program Spiced Up a Little CONTINUED

```
cout << "1...Join the Q" << endl;
cout << "2...Leave the Q" << endl;
cout << "3...Show the Q" << endl;
cout << "4...Quit the program" << endl << endl;
cout << "Enter your choice : ";
cin >> choice;
return (choice);
}
```

You Don't Need a Constructor

Technically speaking, you don't need to specify a constructor. If you omit it, the compiler builds an invisible default one for you. You then create an instance of the class, just as in the Q program. This technique is fine for simple programs, apart from you having no control over the start up of your object. Personally, I like to specify a constructor, but that's just my preference.

The Least You Need to Know

➤ Object-oriented programming is usually called *OOP* or *OO*.

➤ A class is a data structure that contains all that is needed to store and manipulate data.

➤ A variable defined inside a class is called a *data member*.

➤ The functions that manipulate the data are called *member functions*.

➤ Data members and member functions are tightly bound into one entity (a class); therefore, one has no effect without the other. This behavior is called *encapsulation*.

➤ Any member of a class that is public can be freely accessed from outside the class.

➤ Any member of a class that is private cannot be accessed from outside the class. These private members can be accessed only via public member functions.

➤ In C++ it is a convention to make all data members private and is considered bad programming practice to do otherwise.

➤ Unless explicitly stated, all members of a class are, by default, private.

➤ A constructor is a special kind of member function that is used to create an instance of the class. This action causes memory to be allocated for the use of the class instance. This physical memory is known as an *object*.

Chapter 20

OOP, The Day of The Destructor

> **In This Chapter**
>
> ➤ How to define your own destructor
>
> ➤ Four case studies that use destructors and revise OOP
>
> ➤ The use of multiple constructors

Jargon Buster

In Chapter 19, "An Introduction to Object-Oriented Programming: A Step-by-Step Guide for the Terrified," you learned about object-oriented programming, and you experimented with the following C++ notions and busted the jargon:

➤ Class

➤ Data members

➤ Member functions

➤ Constructors

➤ Encapsulation

➤ Instance

➤ Object

You will now practice these techniques some more, and I will introduce another terrifying new OOP concept, called the *destructor*. Actually, it's nothing to be frightened of at all. It's just me being dramatic. The most off-putting thing about OOP is learning the jargon. When you come to grips with the buzzwords, it's quite easy. In fact, other OOP languages, such as Java, use exactly the same buzzwords, but that's another story.

The Destructor Sounds Nasty

The purpose of the destructor is to terminate an object in an orderly fashion. The programs that you wrote in Chapter 19 don't appear to have a destructor, but this is an illusion! Whenever you create an object through the constructor, a default destructor is automatically created. Clever things, these computers. You can, however, override the default destructor and add your own additional "clean-up" protocol. We shall now investigate a program that contains a user-defined destructor.

The Destructor Dissected

The sample program is about string handling and forms the basis of the four case studies later in this chapter. Here are the key points worthy of note.

The destructor is declared in a similar fashion to the constructor except it is prefixed by the ~ symbol. This prototype is placed along with the other public member functions inside the class.

```
~StringThings(void);
```

You write the definition in a similar fashion to the constructor—by stating the classname, the scope resolution operator, and then the destructor name. The destructor always has the same name as the class. I have just placed a message inside my destructor to show you how it works. You can, however, put any relevant code in there. Such things as closing any open files might be appropriate.

```
StringThings::~StringThings(void)
{
cout << endl << "THAT'S ALL FOLKS" << endl << endl;
}
```

Can we survive without a destructor? The answer is yes, for a short while. Remember that the constructor grabs memory to create an object, so every time an object is created, the amount of available memory decreases. The main task of the destructor is to release that memory for re-use. Failure to do this task is known as a *memory leak*, and too many memory leaks cause loss of memory. Eventually, the computer runs out of memory, and you have to reboot the machine. As long as your program works correctly, the default destructor will do the memory release job for you, so don't worry. However, if your program behaves abnormally and keeps crashing, you will experience memory leaks.

This sample program has a member function that finds the first letter in a static string. It's simply a matter of copying the first character of the string (which is an array of characters) into a data member that is a char variable. Error checking is required because you can have an empty string, but you cannot have an empty character. I have made a design decision to use '?' as a substitute for a nonexistent first letter. This is all done in the following member function:

```
void StringThings::First(void)
{
    if (strlen(str) < 1)
            FirstLetter = '?';
    else
            FirstLetter = str[0];
}
```

The Show member function is nothing spectacular. It just shows the contents of the data member FirstLetter to the screen.

```
void StringThings::Show(void)
{
    cout << FirstLetter << endl;
}
```

The constructor creates a StringThing object and copies the input string into the private data member str. Note the use of strcpy drawn from the string.h library.

```
StringThings::StringThings(char s[20])
{
    strcpy(str,s);
}
```

The Program Constructed

Now for the program, give it a spin. The screen output is spectacular:

```
P

THAT'S ALL FOLKS
```

The letter *P* is sent to the screen by the Show function, but the second line requires a little more explanation. Every time an object terminates, the destructor is invoked to clean up things and release memory back to the system. Additionally, the destructor contains the following line:

```
cout << endl << "THAT'S ALL FOLKS" << endl << endl;
```

Therefore, the message to the screen.

Listing 20.1 shows the complete program.

257

Listing 20.1   Introducing *The Destructor*

```cpp
#include <iostream.h>
#include <string.h>

class StringThings {
                        private:
                                char str[20];
                                char FirstLetter;

                        public :
                                void First(void);
                                void Show(void);
                                StringThings(char s[20]);
                                ~StringThings(void);
                };

void StringThings::First(void)
{
        if (strlen(str) < 1)
                FirstLetter = '?';
        else
                FirstLetter = str[0];
}

void StringThings::Show(void)
{
        cout << FirstLetter << endl;
}

StringThings::StringThings(char s[20])
{
        strcpy(str,s);
}

StringThings::~StringThings(void)
{
        cout << endl << "THAT'S ALL FOLKS" << endl << endl;
}

main()
{
        StringThings Test("PAUL");
        Test.First();
        Test.Show();
        return(0);
}
```

Practice Your Skills to Destruction

Now comes a sequence of case studies to emphasise OOP design. They start off nice and easy but become progressively more difficult.

Case Study One

The Problem

Listing 20.1 has a static string embedded at compile time. Modify the program to enable the user to input a string at runtime. Modify the destructor to show the full input to the screen as the object is destroyed.

The Solution

This is a relatively simple task. The first modification doesn't even involve writing any OOP. In the main program, you simply invite the user to enter a string; then read it in with `cin.getline`.

```
cout << "Enter the string : ";
cin.getline(data,19);
```

Modifying the destructor is just as easy. You simply add an extra cout.

```
StringThings::~StringThings(void)
{
        cout << endl << "THE FULL STRING WAS " << str;
        cout << endl << "THAT'S ALL FOLKS" << endl << endl;
}
```

As the destructor says, "That's All, Folks." Try the program in Listing 20.2 now, before things become more difficult.

Listing 20.2   Customizing the Destructor

```
#include <iostream.h>
#include <string.h>

class StringThings {
                            private:
                                    char str[20];
                                    char FirstLetter;

                            public :
                                    void First(void);
                                    void Show(void);
                                    StringThings(char s[20]);
                                    ~StringThings(void);
```

continues

259

Listing 20.2   Customizing the Destructor CONTINUED

```
                        };

void StringThings::First(void)
{
        if (strlen(str) < 1)
                FirstLetter = '?';
        else
                FirstLetter = str[0];
}

void StringThings::Show(void)
{
        cout << FirstLetter << endl;
}

StringThings::StringThings(char s[20])
{
        strcpy(str,s);
}

StringThings::~StringThings(void)
{
        cout << endl << "THE FULL STRING WAS " << str;
        cout << endl << "THAT'S ALL FOLKS" << endl << endl;
}

main()
{
        char data[20];

        cout << "Enter the string : ";
        cin.getline(data,19);
        StringThings Test(data);
        Test.First();
        Test.Show();
        return(0);
}
```

Case Study Two

The Problem

Modify Listing 20.1 by writing a new member function to find the last letter of the string. If the string is one character long, this is the last letter and is the same as the first. Rename the existing Show member function to ShowFirst, which will show the first letter to the screen just as before. Write a new member function, called ShowLast, that shows the last letter of the string to the screen.

strlen **Revisited**

The function strlen is contained in the string.h library. Its purpose is to return the length of a string. The return value is an unsigned integer, which makes sense because you cannot have a string of negative length. Recall that a string is an array of characters and you are dealing with the offset when you look at individual letters in the string. The offset is always one less than the number of elements. Therefore, you must use the expression strlen(str)-1 to find the offset of the last letter in the string.

The Solution

You add a private data member of type character that I have called LastLetter. This data member will hold the last letter of the input string.

The member function Last is very similar to First. In fact, only one line is different, and that's the line that finds the last letter. The statement strlen(str)-1 is used to find the offset of the last letter in the string. This value is plugged into the character array str. Hence, the last letter can be copied into LastLetter.

```
void StringThings::Last(void)
{
        if (strlen(str) < 1)
                LastLetter = '?';
        else
                LastLetter = str[strlen(str)-1];
}
```

The ShowLast member function is virtually identical to ShowFirst except that you display the data member LastLetter. Easy, isn't it? And you thought OOP was going to be difficult, didn't you?

Listing 20.3 **StringThings in an Object-Oriented Program**

```
#include <iostream.h>
#include <string.h>

class StringThings {
                private:
                        char str[20];
                        char FirstLetter;
                        char LastLetter;

                public :
                        void First(void);
                        void Last(void);
                        void ShowFirst(void);
                        void ShowLast(void);
                        StringThings(char s[20]);
                        ~StringThings(void);
                };

void StringThings::First(void)
{
```

continues

Listing 20.3 `StringThings` **in an Object-Oriented Program CONTINUED**

```
        if (strlen(str) < 1)
                FirstLetter = '?';
        else
                FirstLetter = str[0];
}

void StringThings::Last(void)
{
        if (strlen(str) < 1)
                LastLetter = '?';
        else
                LastLetter = str[strlen(str)-1];
}

void StringThings::ShowFirst(void)
{
        cout << FirstLetter << endl;
}

void StringThings::ShowLast(void)
{
        cout << LastLetter << endl;
}

StringThings::StringThings(char s[20])
{
        strcpy(str,s);
}

StringThings::~StringThings(void)
{
        cout << endl << "THE FULL STRING WAS " << str;
        cout << endl << "THAT'S ALL FOLKS" << endl << endl;
}

main()
{
        char data[20];

        cout << "Enter the string : ";
        cin.getline(data,19);
        StringThings Test(data);
        Test.Last();
        Test.ShowLast();
        return(0);
}
```

Case Study Three

Okay, I've let you off easy so far. Read the next statement and quake with fear: *Note that this is potentially a very difficult exercise.*

The Problem

Write a program to reverse the order of the letters in a string. If the string is one character long, this is the last letter and is the same as the first! Show the reverse string and then the original to the screen.

The Solution

We need a member function, which I shall call Reverse. That's quite descriptive because that's what the function is supposed to do. This is the difficult bit. First of all, you determine how long the string actually is. The number of characters is also the number of elements, but because you are dealing with an array, you deduct one because of the offset. If the string is empty, you just copy str into RevStr.

Now here is the crafty mathematics bit, so break out your abacus. You find the length and deduct one; therefore, last is set to two. Here is the key piece of code:

```
RevStr[index] = str[last - index];
```

As we step through the loop, index goes through 0 1 2 while the calculation last – index goes 2 1 0. Finally, you *must* add a NULL terminator to the end of your reversed string. You need to copy an empty string because the two data members are strings, and all strings have a NULL terminator at their end. You are actually copying the NULL terminator.

```cpp
void StringThings::Reverse(void)
{
        unsigned int index;
        unsigned int last;

        last = strlen(str);
        last--;
        if (strlen(str) < 1)
                strcpy(RevStr,str);
        else
        {
                for (index = 0; index < strlen(str); index++)
                {
                        RevStr[index] = str[last - index];
                }
                RevStr[++last] = NULL;
        }
}
```

263

Showing the screen output is no problem; you've seen this in every example so far. You don't want me to repeat it again, do you? Good. The specification asks that the original string be shown to the screen, so I've been dead sneaky here. Do you remember the destructor in the last case study? Did it have an output to the screen? Need I say more? Here's the full solution in Listing 20.4. It wasn't very difficult, was it?

Listing 20.4   More Practice with OOP

```
#include <iostream.h>
#include <string.h>

class StringThings {
                                private:
                                        char str[20];
                                        char RevStr[20];

                                public :
                                        void Reverse(void);
                                        void ShowRevStr(void);
                                        StringThings(char s[20]);
                                        ~StringThings(void);
                                };

void StringThings::Reverse(void)
{
        unsigned int index;
        unsigned int last;

        last = strlen(str);
        last--;
        if (strlen(str) < 1)
                strcpy(RevStr,str);
        else
        {
                for (index = 0; index < strlen(str); index++)
                {
                        RevStr[index] = str[last - index];
                }
                RevStr[++last] = NULL;
        }
}

void StringThings::ShowRevStr(void)
{
```

264

```
                cout << RevStr << endl;
    }

    StringThings::StringThings(char s[20])
    {
            strcpy(str,s);
    }

    StringThings::~StringThings(void)
    {
            cout << endl << "THE FULL STRING WAS " << str;
            cout << endl << "THAT'S ALL FOLKS" << endl << endl;
    }

    main()
    {
            char data[20];

            cout << "Enter the string : ";
            cin.getline(data,19);
            StringThings Test(data);
            Test.Reverse();
            Test.ShowRevStr();
            return(0);
    }
```

Case Study Four

The Problem

Write an OOP program to count the number of vowels in a string.

The Solution

As you should have realized by now, the OOP bit is very mechanical and always follows the same set pattern, as described in Chapter 19. Inside the member functions, you just apply the normal C++ code that we all know and love. This case study is a variation on a theme that you encountered way back with the if else and case statements. Here is the member function that contains the relevant code. A for loop skims through each letter of the data member str, and the switch case checks whether it's a vowel. When a vowel is encountered, the data member counter is incremented. The only other point worth noting is in the constructor, where counter is initially set to zero.

```
void StringThings::VowelCount(void)
{
        unsigned int index;

        for (index = 0; index < strlen(str); index++)
        {
                switch (str[index])
                {
                case  'A' :
                case  'a' :        count++;
                                   break;

                case  'E' :
                case  'e' :        count++;
                                   break;

                case  'I' :
                case  'i' :        count++;
                                   break;

                case  'O' :
                case  'o' :        count++;
                                   break;

                case  'U' :
                case  'u' :        count++;
                                   break;
                }
        }
}
```

Do you remember way back in Chapter 8, "If You Are Spoilt for Choice, the switch case Sometimes Helps," where I always converted everything into uppercase letters? This is the other way of doing it. The choice is yours.

Try out the program, in Listing 20.5, and count the vowels in your name.

Listing 20.5   Counting the Vowels Is the Object

```
#include <iostream.h>
#include <string.h>

class StringThings {
                                  private:
                                          char str[20];
                                          int count;

                                  public :
                                          void VowelCount(void);
                                          void ShowCount(void);
                                          StringThings(char s[20]);
```

```
                                           ~StringThings(void);
                              };

void StringThings::VowelCount(void)
{
        unsigned int index;

        for (index = 0; index < strlen(str); index++)
        {
                switch (str[index])
                {
                case  'A' :
                case  'a' :      count++;
                                 break;
                case  'E' :
                case  'e' :      count++;
                                 break;
                case  'I' :
                case  'i' :      count++;
                                 break;
                case  'O' :
                case  'o' :      count++;
                                 break;
                case  'U' :
                case  'u' :      count++;
                                 break;
                }
        }
}

void StringThings::ShowCount(void)
{
        cout << "The number of vowels is : "
<< count << endl;
}

StringThings::StringThings(char s[20])
{
        strcpy(str,s);
        count = 0;
}

StringThings::~StringThings(void)
{
        cout << endl << "THE FULL STRING WAS " << str;
        cout << endl << "THAT'S ALL FOLKS" << endl << endl;
```

continues

267

Listing 20.5   Counting the Vowels Is the Object CONTINUED

```
}

main()
{
        char data[20];

        cout << "Enter the string : ";
        cin.getline(data,19);
        StringThings Test(data);
        Test.VowelCount();
        Test.ShowCount();
        return(0);
}
```

Shape Up Three Times Over

In Chapter 17, "Not to Be Outdone, Meet Overloaded Functions," I discussed the subject of overloaded functions, and you probably thought, "Okay, clever but not too useful." Yes, I know what you were thinking, and I've heard all this doubt before. Now it's time to learn the whole truth and nothing but the truth. Overloaded functions really come into their own as class constructors. You can have several constructors that construct an object in different ways, depending on the input parameters. In other words, a single class can behave in different ways, depending on which constructor was used to build the object. Now that's clever!

Let's Do a Geometric Study

To demonstrate multiple constructors, we shall examine a shape, and as we all know from kindergarten, there are lots of shapes. We are interested in a circle, a rectangle, and a box. To find the area of a circle, you need only one measurement: its radius. To find the area of a rectangle, you need two measurements: its length and height. To find the volume of a box, you need three measurements: its length, height, and depth. They are all shapes but require different mathematical formulae to calculate the given properties. In old, boring, traditional programming, you could have written three separate functions and treated the three shapes as three completely isolated items. In new, exciting, dynamic OOP, you treat them as members of the same family. After all, they are all shapes.

The Construction Worker Gets a Job

Listing 20.6 has three constructors, each with different signatures. The first, with a single input, belongs to the circle; the second, with two inputs, to the rectangle; and the third, with three inputs, to the box. They are clearly related as shapes.

```
shape(int r);
shape(int l, int h);
shape(int l, int h, int d);
```

You can have many constructors as you want, as long as they all have different signa-tures. It all depends on the complexity of your class. When you define the construc-tors, you can specify the correct mathematical formula for each scenario. To aid in that task, I have defined six private data members. I will list them now and give a brief description of their purpose in life:

➤ length   Holds the data for the length dimension and is used in the rectangle and the box solution.

➤ height   Holds the data for the height dimension and is used in the rectangle and the box solution.

➤ depth   Holds the data for the depth dimension and is used only in the box solution.

➤ radius   Holds the data for the radius dimension and is used only in the circle solution.

➤ answer   Holds the result of the calculations for circle, rectangle, or box.

➤ which   Is a crafty data member used as a flag to distinguish the correct actions of the constructed object. It can have a value of 0 for a circle, 1 for a rectangle, or 2 for a box.

The circle constructor assigns the external value r to the data member radius and sets the flag to 0, thus indicating that the constructed object will be a circle.

```
shape::shape(int r)
{
        radius = r;
        which =0;
}
```

The rectangle constructor assigns the external values l and h to the data members length and height and sets the flag to 1, thus indicating that the constructed object will be a rectangle.

```
shape::shape(int l, int h)
{
        length = l;
        height = h;
        which = 1;
}
```

The box constructor assigns the external values l, h, and d to the data members length, height, and depth and sets the flag to 2, thus indicating that the constructed object will be a box.

```
shape::shape(int l, int h, int d)
{
        length = l;
        height = h;
        depth = d;
        which = 2;
}
```

There is only one member function to do the calculation. It's called `Calc`, and here's where the crafty bit comes into play. Remember that `which` is a flag that holds a value of 0, 1, or 2. You use this in a `switch` case to apply the correct formula to the object. Now that's clever, even if I say so myself. By the way, who wrote this program?

```
void shape::Calc(void)
{
        switch(which)
        {
        case 0 : answer = radius * radius * 3.14;
                 break;
        case 1 : answer = length * height;
                 break;
        case 2 : answer = length * height * depth;
                 break;
        }
}
```

The `Show` member function works in a similar fashion to `Calc`. Once again, a `switch` case interrogates the flag to establish the nature of the object and applies the appropriate message.

```
void shape::Show(void)
{
        switch(which)
        {
        case 0 : cout << "The circles area is : " << answer;
                 cout << endl << endl;
                 break;
        case 1 : cout << "The rectangles area is : " << answer;
                 cout << endl << endl;
                 break;
        case 2 : cout << "The boxes volume is : " << answer;
                 cout << endl << endl;
                 break;
        }
}
```

Oops, I Nearly Forgot the Destructor

Just to be consistent, I've decided to use a destructor that gives a user-friendly message when you close an object. You are allowed only one destructor per class. The compiler creates a default destructor if you fail to provide a custom definition. As you will learn when you study inheritance, you can redefine the destructor later on, but it effectively replaces the existing one, so you still have just one destructor.

Playtime with Shapes

Now that you know how the program works, let's run it and see the results. I'll give you a hint by showing my screen output, but for now, I'll leave you to guess why it looks like this:

```
The circles area is : 4
The rectangles area is : 24
The boxes volume is : 12.56

THAT'S ALL FOLKS
THAT'S ALL FOLKS
THAT'S ALL FOLKS
```

Now no cheating here, I'm putting you on trust. Answer the following question before you look at the answer, which follows immediately after Listing 20.6.

The Question:

Why does the line THAT'S ALL FOLKS appear three times?

Listing 20.6   Multiple Constructors

```cpp
#include <iostream.h>

class shape{
            public:
                    int length;
                    int height;
                    int depth;
                    int radius;
                    double answer;
                    int which;

            public:
                    void Calc(void);
                    void Show(void);
                    shape(int r);
                    shape(int l, int h);
                    shape(int l, int h, int d);
```

continues

271

Listing 20.6   Multiple Constructors CONTINUED

```cpp
                              ~shape(void);
                     };

shape::shape(int r)
{
       radius = r;
       which =0;
}

shape::shape(int l, int h)
{
       length = l;
       height = h;
       which = 1;
}

shape::shape(int l, int h, int d)
{
       length = l;
       height = h;
       depth = d;
       which = 2;
}

shape::~shape(void)
{
       cout << "THAT'S ALL FOLKS" << endl;
}

void shape::Calc(void)
{
       switch(which)
       {
       case 0 : answer = radius * radius * 3.14;
              break;
       case 1 : answer = length * height;
              break;
       case 2 : answer = length * height * depth;
              break;
       }
}

void shape::Show(void)
{
       switch(which)
```

continues

272

```
              {
              case 0 : cout << "The circles area is : " << answer;
                       cout << endl << endl;
                       break;
              case 1 : cout << "The rectangles area is : " << answer;
                       cout << endl << endl;
                       break;
              case 2 : cout << "The boxes volume is : " << answer;
                       cout << endl << endl;
                       break;
              }
      }

main()
{
      shape square(2,2);
      shape cube(2,3,4);
      shape circle(4);
      square.Calc();
      cube.Calc();
      circle.Calc();
      square.Show();
      cube.Show();
      circle.Show();
      return(0);
}
```

The Answer:

Okay, I know it's been bugging you, so here is the answer to the monumental question, Why does the line THAT'S ALL FOLKS appear three times? You're really going to hate me for this. The destructor is invoked every time an object completes its work. We have three objects in our program, and at program termination, the destructor is called for each of them, thus avoiding memory leaks. Therefore, the line THAT'S ALL FOLKS appears three times. And you thought that I nearly forgot to include a custom destructor, didn't you?

The Least You Need to Know

➤ The purpose of the destructor is to terminate an object in an orderly fashion. The memory grabbed by the object as it is constructed is released, thus avoiding memory leaks.

➤ Whenever you create an object through the constructor, a default destructor is automatically created.

➤ You can override the default destructor and add your own additional "clean-up" protocol.

➤ The destructor is declared as a public member function in a similar fashion to the constructor, except it's prefixed by the ~ symbol.

➤ All strings are arrays of characters and have a NULL terminator at their end.

➤ You can have several constructors that construct an object in different ways, depending on their signature.

➤ You can have as many constructors as you want, as long as each has a unique signature.

➤ You can have only one active destructor per class.

➤ The destructor is invoked every time an object completes its work. If you have three objects in our program, the destructor will be called for each of them.

Chapter 21

Inheritance! OO, Things for Free

In This Chapter

➤ Inheritance and what it really is

➤ How to use inheritance in a C++ program

➤ How to create and use your own .h header file

➤ Case studies on the use of inheritance

Back to the Television Set

In Chapter 19, "An Introduction to Object-Oriented Programming: A Step-by-Step Guide for the Terrified," I give the analogy of a class being a circuit diagram of a television. When that circuit diagram is used to construct a real television, which is an object that you can physically watch, this is the creation of an instance of a television. You can use the same circuit diagram many times over to construct lots of televisions. Let us now take the television analogy a step further.

All televisions have certain basic characteristics. They have a picture, a brightness control, sound, a volume control, a means of selecting channels, and so on. However, more upscale TV sets might have remote control and Teletext or Nicam stereo sound, yet they still require the functionality of a basic TV set. In other words, they are extensions of the basic concept, and this is the basis of inheritance.

A television with remote control is an extension of a basic TV.

You add an extra definition page to the Sony TV definition, which gives the extra functionality required for remote control. Note that the original definition still lies behind the extension.

When you create an instance of RC, you build a remote-controlled TV as the object. You can, of course, build many remote-controlled TVs from the same design.

You can still use the original design to Create a non-remote TV.

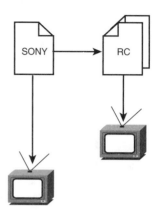

A television with Teletext is an extension of a remote-controlled TV.

You can extend the design (inherit) even further to make a teletext circuit diagram.

This extension would create a teletext TV as an object.

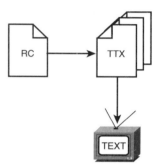

Passing On the Family Fortune

Are Superman and Clark Kent One and the Same Person?

That's a difficult question, but I can reveal that base classes and derived classes have another alias. A base class is also called a *parent class* and a derived class is also called a *child class*. The terminology is completely interchangeable, but for consistency I shall endeavor to stick with *base* and *derived*.

One of the many strengths of C++ is the capability of an existing class (known as a *base class*) to be reused and be modified by a new class (known as a *derived class*). This property is known as *inheritance*. The base class will have common properties that can be inherited by derived classes and thus be modified for specific needs without you having to rewrite entire sections of code.

A Hierarchical System Explained

The hierarchical system of inheritance can be shown in a diagram. By convention, an arrow points from the derived class up to the base class. Here is an example.

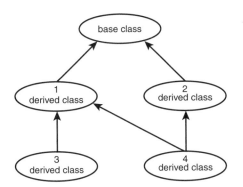

A hierarchical diagram showing inheritance.

The following key points summarize what this diagram means:

➤ The diagram shows that 1 is derived from the base class. It inherits all the properties of the base class and adds a few more to itself. The base class doesn't have the new extra properties of derived class 1.

➤ Derived class 2 also inherits all the properties of the base class and adds some new, probably different, properties. Again, the base class doesn't have the new extra properties of derived class 2.

➤ Derived class 3 inherits all the properties of derived class 1, which means it has all the properties of the base class as well. It can add new extra properties that do not exist in derived class 1.

➤ Derived class 4 is special. It derives its properties from both derived class 1 and derived class 2, which means it has all the properties of the base class and all the new properties of both derived class 1 and derived class 2. This is known as *multiple inheritance*, and you will learn about that topic in Chapter 23, "Multiple Inheritance! Even More Things for Free."

A Real Hierarchical System Explained

You have actually come across inheritance without even realizing it. Look at the next diagram.

Looking back to Chapters 8 and 9, did you notice that the programs didn't use `iostream` and yet could still use `cin` and `cout`? Did you ask yourself why? From the hierarchical chart, you can see that `fstream` is derived from `iostream` and therefore has `cin` and `cout` in its command list. That's inheritance at work.

In every program you have written in this book, you have used the `iostream` class—by using the statement `#include <iostream.h>` at the start of every program. Here's how it ties together:

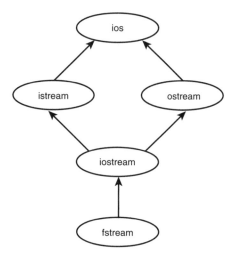

A portion of the C++ ios class that you have used in every program in this book.

➤ As you can see, iostream is derived from both istream and ostream. It's an example of multiple inheritance. You saw these when you overloaded the extraction (>>) and insertion (<<) operators. Hence, these classes are the classes that you were adding extra properties to.

➤ Both istream and ostream are derived from ios, which contains the basic input/output commands that communicate with the computer hardware.

➤ The final point is that fstream is derived from iostream, and the extra properties are those that enable file handling, as well as normal insertion and extraction operations.

Gaining Your Inheritance: A Step-by-Step Guide

To illustrate, I will use the simple example from Chapter 19 and derive a class from shape called ThreeD. We will use the simple area model and modify it through inheritance to produce a three-dimensional model.

Step One: Protect Your Data Members

The first step is to change the private data members to protected data members. If you intend your code to be used for inheritance, you should always do it this way in the first place. This means that data is still private to the class but can also be accessed by derived classes. It still remains private within these derived classes.

```
class shape      {
          // NOTE THE USE OF PROTECTED
               protected:
double length;
               double height;
```

```
        double area;
    public:
        void CalcArea(void);
        void ShowArea(void);
        shape(double l = 0,
              double h = 0);
        };
```

Preparing to Spend the Inheritance

Listing 21.1 performs in an identical manner to
Listing 19.6 in Chapter 19, despite the use of
protected, instead of private, data members. I've
sneaked in another change by changing all the
data members to the data type double. I've
done this because I know what's coming next
in the chapter, but I refuse to tell you at this
point in time. All will be revealed later.

Protected, Private, What's the Difference?

Anything that is protected behaves
as private within its own class. That
means it cannot be accessed from
the outside world. However, protected items can be inherited by a
derived class, and in the derived
class they behave as if they were
private. Incidentally, a derived class
cannot inherit private items.

Listing 21.1   Object-Oriented Programming, Creating an Inherited Class

```
#include <iostream.h>

class shape     {
            // NOTE THE USE OF PROTECTED
            protected:
double length;
            double height;
            double area;
          public:
            void CalcArea(void);
            void ShowArea(void);
            shape(double l = 0, double h = 0);
            };

void shape::CalcArea(void)
{
    area = length * height;
}

void shape::ShowArea(void)
{
    cout << "THE AREA IS : " << area << endl;
}
```

continues

279

Listing 21.1   Object-Oriented Programming, Creating an Inherited Class CONTINUED

```
shape::shape(double l, double h)
{
    length = l;
    height = h;
}

main()
{
    double x;
    double y;

    cout << "ENTER THE HEIGHT : ";
    cin >> x;
    cout << "ENTER THE LENGTH : ";
    cin >> y;
    // CREATE AN INSTANCE OF SHAPE
    shape square(y,x);
    // CALL THE MEMBER FUNCTIONS
    square.CalcArea();
    square.ShowArea();
    return(0);
}
```

Step Two: Inherit Your Class

Now you are in a position to inherit the shape class and derive a new class called ThreeD.

The first step is to define the derived class as shown in the figure.

The syntax to set up an inherited class.

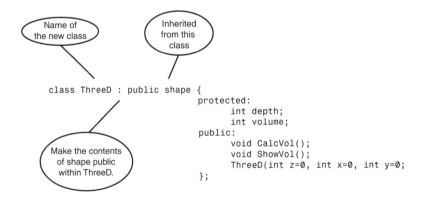

In the manner described in Chapter 19, you now list the additional data members and member functions belonging to class ThreeD. ThreeD, however, also possesses all the data members and data functions contained within shape. It has inherited them. A very important point rears its ugly head here. Please note that it's the structure of the data members and member functions that is inherited; no actual data is inherited.

As a test to see whether you've been paying attention, do the following:

a. Write down all the data members that are accessible by ThreeD.

b. Write down all the member functions that are accessible by ThreeD.

Here are the answers in reverse order. If Mozart could do this, you can as well.

Data Structure and Data, What's the Difference?

I didn't know once either, but that was a long time ago! The difference is immense, and as you grow older, you learn to recognize these subtleties. The data structure is the variables that hold the data—in other words, the physical memory locations in the computer RAM. The data is the numbers and letters that you can put into the variables; it's what you store in the physical memory locations.

a.

```
htgnel
thgieh
aera
htped
emulov
```

b.

```
aerAclaC
aerAwohS
epahs
loVclaC
loVwohS
DeerhT
```

Step Three: A Constructor to Call a Constructor

The prototype of the constructor ThreeD is the same format as any other constructor. You can see this by looking at its class. But take a look at its definition. The constructor for ThreeD accepts three parameters. The first one is assigned to its own protected data member, depth. It doesn't recognize the other two, so they are passed straight on to the constructor for the base class shape. Here they are recognized and assigned to the protected data members contained within shape, length, and height.

The definition of the
ThreeD constructor.

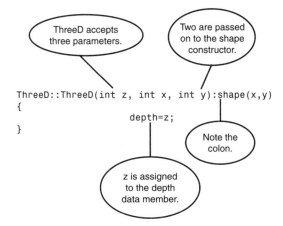

```
ThreeD::ThreeD(int z, int x, int y):shape(x,y)
{
                depth=z;
}
```

Step Four: Member Functions, No Problema

The actual definitions of the member functions CalcVol and ShowVol are nothing special, and you should be able to understand this code by now. But, because I'm a nice guy, I will describe them to you.

CalcVol simply calculates the volume of the box and places the answer into volume, which is a data member of ThreeD. Note the first line of the member function definition. CalcVol is specifically stated to be encapsulated within ThreeD, not shape.

```
void ThreeD::CalcVol()
{
    volume = depth * length * height;
}
```

Similarly, ShowVol is also specifically stated to be encapsulated within ThreeD, not shape. Its purpose is just to show the volume to the screen.

```
void ThreeD::ShowVol()
{
    cout << "THE VOLUME IS : " << volume << endl;
}
```

Within the main body of the program, you create an instance of ThreeD called box and manipulate the data via the member functions.

```
ThreeD box(z,x,y);
box.CalcVol();
box.ShowVol();
```

Notice how no mention of shape is ever made within the main body of the program. In reality, shape would be part of a separate library, and all you would need to know would be the constructor's signature and a list of the available member functions and data members. And that's what OOP and inheritance is all about. Easy!

The Mother of All Diagrams

I know you like pictures, so here is a graphical representation of the inheritance model, along with an explanation of what it means.

➤ The larger outer circle represents ThreeD and is wrapped around a slightly smaller inner circle that represents shape. The small circles stuck to the sides of the large circles represent the member functions and are "buttons" that can be "pushed." Pushing the button is analogous to calling the member function.

➤ The variables x, y, and z are collected from the outside world by the constructor ThreeD. It knows what to do with z and stores z in its own data member depth. It doesn't know anything about x and y, so it passes them on to the shape constructor. The shape constructor knows what to do with x and y and stores them in length and height, respectively.

➤ When you press the CalcVol button, it has immediate access to its own data member data, as well as inherited access to length and height within shape.

➤ When you press ShowVol, the answer is immediately available because volume is a data member of ThreeD.

➤ Even though they are within shape, the member functions CalcArea and ShowArea are available from a ThreeD object because of inheritance.

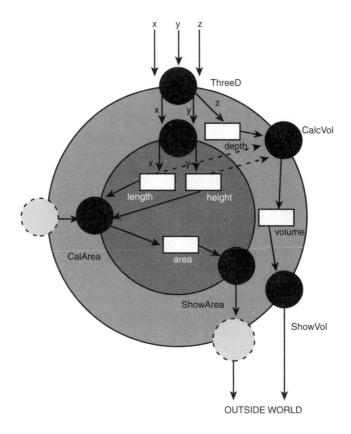

A graphical representation of inheritance.

x y z

ThreeD

x y z

depth

CalcVol

x y

length   height

volume

CalArea   area

ShowArea

ShowVol

OUTSIDE WORLD

Practically an Inheritance

Isn't It Quicker to Write a New Program?

For short programs like we are writing, the answer is a definite yes. But remember, at the moment we are looking at only the concept of inheritance. When you move on to greater things, you will thank me for showing you how to do inheritance.

Here is the full program that inherits the properties of shape and transforms them into ThreeD. I've talked theory for long enough, and I make no apology for it. This is a difficult subject, and if you are still with me, well done. But before you rush off for a coffee, I insist that you try out Listing 21.2. If you take a break at this point, you will forget all that lovely theory.

Listing 21.2   Inheritance of Data Members

```
#include <iostream.h>

class shape {
        protected:
```

```
            double length;
            double height;
            double area;
        public:
            void CalcArea();
            void ShowArea();
            shape(double l = 0, double h = 0);
        };

// THIS IS A DERIVED CLASS
class ThreeD : public shape{
        protected :
            double depth;
            double volume;
        public:
            void CalcVol();
            void ShowVol();
            ThreeD(double z=0,double x=0,double y=0);
        };

// DEFINE ThreeD CONSTRUCTOR
// NOTE HOW IT EXPLICITLY CALLS shape CONSTRUCTOR
ThreeD::ThreeD(double z, double x, double y):shape(x,y)
{
    depth = z;
}

shape::shape(double l, double h)
{
    length = l;
    height = h;
}

void shape::CalcArea()
{
    area = length * height;
}

void shape::ShowArea()
{
    cout << "THE AREA IS : " << area;
}

void ThreeD::CalcVol()
{
```

continues

Listing 21.2   Inheritance of Data Members CONTINUED

```
        volume = depth * length * height;
    }

    void ThreeD::ShowVol()
    {
        cout << "THE VOLUME IS : " << volume << endl;
    }

    main()
    {
        double x, y, z;

        cout << "ENTER THE LENGTH : ";
        cin >> x;
        cout << "ENTER THE HEIGHT : ";
        .cin >> y;
        cout << "ENTER THE DEPTH  : ";
        cin >> z;
        ThreeD box(z,x,y);
        box.CalcVol();
        box.ShowVol();
        return(0);
    }
```

I'm beginning to feel sorry for you with all this typing, so I'm going to let you in on part of a secret. Professionals don't actually type in the base class they want to inherit. That defeats the object, and you might as well just change the code to create a new class to achieve what is required. There are several ways around this, and I will show you one of them next.

It's All in the Header

An amazingly simple way of storing the shape class and all its definitions is to create a header file. This header file can then be included in any program that wants to use or inherit from shape. But what is a header file? I hear you all ask. My answer is simple. First of all, *don't panic*, you have used them in every program we have ever written, and now you will write your very own header file. I'll give you a clue by saying that all header files end with a .h extension and are included in a C++ program by the directive #include. Do you agree that you have seen this before? Good!

Knocking the Header into Shape

The process of creating the header is easy. I will give you the steps that seem to apply to every version of C++ (and C, for that matter), so here we go.

1. Open a new edit window.
2. Type in the code shown in Listing 21.3 (or cut and paste it from Listing 21.2 if you consider yourself a real IT person).
3. Save your work as shape.h on your disk.

That's it, all done, couldn't be easier.

Listing 21.3   The shape.h Header File, Containing the Definition of shape

```
class shape {
            protected:
                double length;
                double height;
                double area;
            public:
                void CalcArea();
                void ShowArea();
                shape(double l = 0, double h = 0);
            };

shape::shape(double l, double h)
{
    length = l;
    height = h;
}

void shape::CalcArea()
{
    area = length * height;
}

void shape::ShowArea()
{
    cout << "THE AREA IS : " << area << endl;
}
```

Everyone falls for this one. I'm going to warn you just once, so I'll put it in capital letters. *DO NOT COMPILE THE HEADER FILE*. Header files are text files with a .h extension and do not compile. C++ source codes are also text files, but they have a .cpp extension and they do compile. Every time I inherit a new class of would-be programmers, I warn them about this, but do they listen? Not on your life! So come on, don't let me down. Remember that you do not compile a header file.

The Invisible Shape That Can Be Seen!

Here is the trick. Take a look at Listing 21.4. It is Listing 21.2 with the shape bits surgically removed. It does, however, have a new line that looks almost, but not quite, familiar.

```
#include "shape.h"
```

When you compile Listing 21.4, the #include "shape.h" line tells the compiler to substitute in the code contained in shape.h. It is at this point that Listing 21.3 and Listing 21.4 are compiled together into one complete program.

Why does shape have "" and not <> marks around it? When you installed your C++ compiler onto your computer, everything, including lots of header files, was placed in predefined directories. By placing <> around the header file in your program, you are telling the compiler to look in that predefined place. If you use "" around the header file, you are saying, "Look in the current directory." I strongly advise you to keep all the files that you have written in the same directory.

A Warning of Impending Doom

You must make sure that you copy shape.h into the directory or disk space where you are working on this program. Failure to do so will give an error when you compile the program.

Here are the steps involved in creating the C++ program that uses the shape header file:

1. Open a new edit window.
2. Type in the code shown in Listing 21.4 (or cut and paste it from Listing 21.2).
3. Save your work as Listing 21.4 on your disk.

That's it, all done again. Now compile your program in the manner that you now should be able to do in your sleep.

When you run the program, it will perform in exactly the same way as Listing 21.2. The major difference here is that the base class shape and its definitions are hidden in the header file and can be included in any number of subsequent programs.

Listing 21.4   Inheritance, Using a Header File

```
#include <iostream.h>
#include "shape.h"

// THIS IS A DERIVED CLASS
class ThreeD : public shape{
        protected :
            double depth;
            double volume;
        public:
```

```
                void CalcVol();
                void ShowVol();
                ThreeD(double z=0,double x=0,double y=0);
        };

// DEFINE ThreeD CONSTRUCTOR
// NOTE HOW IT EXPLICITLY CALLS shape CONSTRUCTOR
ThreeD::ThreeD(double z, double x, double y):shape(x,y)
{
    depth = z;
}

void ThreeD::CalcVol()
{
    volume = depth * length * height;
}

void ThreeD::ShowVol()
{
    cout << "THE VOLUME IS : " << volume << endl;
}

main()
{
    double x, y, z;

    cout << "ENTER THE LENGTH : ";
    cin >> x;
    cout << "ENTER THE HEIGHT : ";
    cin >> y;
    cout << "ENTER THE DEPTH  : ";
    cin >> z;
    ThreeD box(z,x,y);
    box.CalcVol();
    box.ShowVol();
    return(0);
}
```

Document Your Work

Now that you know how to create a header file, I'll list the documentation that you should supply with it. If you don't supply documentation, no one else will be able to use your work. If you are like most people, you will forget how to use your work. Bear in mind that this example is a simple one, and a real single header file can contain many classes and their definitions.

- ➤ The name of the header file containing the class or classes that it contains.
- ➤ The name of the class or classes.
- ➤ All public member functions and their signatures.
- ➤ All constructors and their signatures.

A Case Study Shapes Up

The Problem

Using the previously designed code for shape, write a program that will inherit these properties and modify them to find the area of the right-angled triangle formed by height and length.

The Solution

The program to find the area of a right-angled triangle is almost the same as finding the area of a rectangle. The only difference is the formula because the area of a triangle is only half that of a corresponding rectangle.

```
area = (length * height) / 2;
```

This conveniently means that you only need to redefine the member function to calculate the area.

```
void Triangle::CalcArea()
{
    area = (length * height) / 2;
}
```

For the observant among you who spotted that CalcArea already lives in shape, well done. Before you ask, yes, you can use the name again in a derived class. The new version of CalcArea is said to override the old version of CalcArea. When you use the triangle constructor to create a triangle object, the compiler uses the new version of CalcArea. If you use the shape constructor, the compiler gives you the old version of CalcArea. Smart beasts, these here computers.

Because you are inheriting from shape, you need a triangle constructor. This constructor takes the length and height parameters and passes them immediately on to the shape constructor. This is because the protected data members are in the shape class, not the triangle class.

```
Triangle::Triangle(double x, double y):shape(x,y)
{
    // Does nothing except call shape.
}
```

There's nothing else to say about inheritance except try the program out, in Listing 21.5, and don't spend all the freebees straight away.

Oops! Don't forget to copy shape.h into the directory or disk space where you are working on this program. Failure to do so will result in a compiler error.

Listing 21.5   Inheritance, Using a Header File

```
#include <iostream.h>
#include "shape.h"

// THIS IS A DERIVED CLASS
class Triangle : public shape{
        public:
                void CalcArea();
                Triangle(double x=0,double y=0);
        };

// DEFINE Triangle CONSTRUCTOR
// NOTE HOW IT EXPLICITLY CALLS shape CONSTRUCTOR
Triangle::Triangle(double x, double y):shape(x,y)
{
    // Does nothing except call shape.
}

void Triangle::CalcArea()
{
    area = (length * height) / 2;
}

main()
{
    double x, y;

    cout << "ENTER THE LENGTH : ";
    cin >> x;
    cout << "ENTER THE HEIGHT : ";
    cin >> y;
    Triangle tri(x,y);
    tri.CalcArea();
    tri.ShowArea();
    return(0);
}
```

A Case Study Squares Up

The Problem

Using the previously designed code for shape, write a program that will inherit its properties and modify them to find the length of the hypotenuse of the right-angled triangle formed by height and length.

The Solution

Before you scream and say that it cannot be done because of the advanced nature of the mathematics, I'll give you that wonderful formula to find the hypotenuse of a right-angled triangle. Thank you, Pythagorus.

The formula to find the hypotenuse of a right-angled triangle.

$$H = \sqrt{A^2 + B^2}$$

The formula translates into this piece of C++ code:

```
hypotenuse = sqrt(pow(length,2) + pow(height,2));
```

Expand Your Power

Why not expand your mathematical power by investigating the math.h library? Use your C++ compiler documentation and see what other useful functions live in there. Then try writing a program to use them. Experimentation is the best way to learn a computer language.

Those wonderful compiler people have given us a set of tools, contained in the math.h library, that actually do mathematics. You need only pow and sqrt, although many more are in there.

pow(length,2) raises a value to a power. In our case, the value is length and the power is 2. In other words, we are squaring length. If you want to cube length, you change the 2 to a 3. sqrt(data) returns the square root of data.

This formula is all that is needed in the member function that does the advanced mathematical calculation.

```
void Triangle::CalcHyp()
{
    hypotenuse = sqrt(pow(length,2) +
                 pow(height,2));
}
```

The first step, of course, is to make the base class shape available and inherit its properties. The only ones that you will actually use are its protected data members, length and height, along with the shape constructor. Nonetheless, all the member functions are there if they are ever needed.

```
#include "shape.h"
```

```
// THIS IS A DERIVED CLASS
class Triangle : public shape{
        protected :
            double hypotenuse;
        public:
            void CalcHyp();
            void ShowHyp();
            Triangle(double x=0,double y=0);
        };
```

Remember to copy shape.h into your directory. Then try the program, which is Listing 21.6. It's as simple as that.

Listing 21.6   Inheritance, Using a Header File

```
#include <iostream.h>
#include <math.h>
#include "shape.h"

// THIS IS A DERIVED CLASS
class Triangle : public shape{
        protected :
            double hypotenuse;
        public:
            void CalcHyp();
            void ShowHyp();
            Triangle(double x=0,double y=0);
        };

// DEFINE Triangle CONSTRUCTOR
// NOTE HOW IT EXPLICITLY CALLS shape CONSTRUCTOR
Triangle::Triangle(double x, double y):shape(x,y)
{
    // Does nothing except call shape.
}

void Triangle::CalcHyp()
{
    hypotenuse = sqrt(pow(length,2) + pow(height,2));
}

void Triangle::ShowHyp()
{
    cout << "THE HYPOTENUSE IS : " << hypotenuse
        << endl;
```

continues

293

Listing 21.6   Inheritance, Using a Header File CONTINUED

```
}

main()
{
    double x, y;

    cout << "ENTER THE LENGTH : ";
    cin >> x;
    cout << "ENTER THE HEIGHT : ";
    cin >> y;
    Triangle tri(x,y);
    tri.CalcHyp();
    tri.ShowHyp();
    return(0);
}
```

The Least You Need to Know

➤ C++ has the capability to reuse an existing class, known as a *base class*, and modify that code to create a new class, known as a *derived class*. This capability is known as *inheritance*.

➤ Inheritance takes the common properties of the base class and adds additional features without you having to rewrite entire sections of code.

➤ A base class and a parent class are the same thing; only the jargon differs.

➤ A derived class and a child class are the same thing; only the jargon is different.

➤ You can show relationships between classes by using a hierarchical diagram.

➤ Data members to be inherited are declared as protected. They can then be inherited by any derived class and behave as private data members within that derived class.

➤ Member functions of the same name and signature can live in a base and derived class. The one in the derived class is said to override the base class.

➤ Classes and their associated definitions can be stored in a .h header file and thus be included in subsequent programs for reuse.

➤ If you correctly document your header files, people will know how to use them when designing their programs.

➤ The math.h library contains many useful mathematical functions, including pow and sqrt.

Chapter 22

Hail Polymorphism, The Goddess of the Design Engineer

In This Chapter

➤ Abstract classes, what they are and what they are used for

➤ Virtual functions

➤ Pure virtual functions

➤ Polymorphism described

➤ Specialist programs from abstract classes

Abstract Classes

In the world of computer programming, much effort is made in designing consistent, reliable code. It has also been discovered that many computer programs have basic similarities and differ only in small areas of their implementation. Program analysts had a vision of a tool that would solve these problems by packing the common functionality into a module and enabling the programmer to modify the relevant functions to create an outwardly unique program. Thus, object-oriented programming was born, and the core of the common functionality is the abstract class.

The *abstract class* is a design tool that enables core functionality to be defined, leaving the unique, program-specific functionality to be defined later. In the last couple chapters, we have concentrated on inheritance, and inheritance is key to using abstract classes.

Abstract classes have the following characteristics:

➤ They have at least one pure virtual member function in their class definition. Pure virtual functions are explained in the next section, which is ironically titled "Virtual Functions."

➤ Abstract classes can only be used as a base class to create derived classes.

➤ Any class that contains a pure virtual function cannot be used to create an object.

Virtual Functions

You met virtual member functions in the last chapter. They are of paramount importance to abstract classes, so I will summarize the key points.

One Function for All

A virtual member function is defined in a base class by prefixing the function prototype with the word virtual. You saw this in the last chapter. This means that derived classes share only one instance of that function to avoid ambiguity. That one definition can be used throughout the hierarchical tree, as shown in the next diagram.

The hierarchical diagram showing the virtual void f1() member function defined in the base class b1 and being shared with the derived classes d1 and d2.

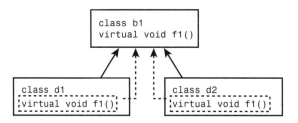

I Want My Own Function

A derived class can override the virtual member function definition by redefining its functionality. The new definition will be used in all instances of the function within objects of the derived class. In the next diagram, class d1 shares f1 with the base class, but d2 has its own unique version of f1.

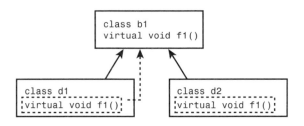

The hierarchical diagram showing the virtual void f1() *member function defined in the base class* b1 *and redefined in the derived class* d2.

When a function is declared as virtual in the base class, it remains virtual in all derived classes. You are free to include or omit the word virtual in the redefinition of the member function. In the derived class, both the following are legal and mean the same thing:

```
virtual void f1();
void f1();
```

The Purest of Functions

Earlier on, I promised to tell you what a pure virtual function is. I now will deliver that promise. A *pure virtual function* is set to zero, and you do not supply a definition for it. "What?!" I hear you cry. I agree, sounds like complete garbage, doesn't it? Look at an actual definition and see whether it makes sense.

```
virtual void f1() = 0;
```

And that's it! The virtual function f1 is set to zero, so it is now a pure virtual function without a definition. It doesn't do anything except prohibit the class from creating an instance of the object and jogging the programmer's memory into giving it a definition when they inherit the class.

Polymorphism Revealed (and Perhaps Understood)!

To claim to be an object-oriented programming language, the language must support polymorphism. Some languages support classes but not polymorphism. Do not trust these languages. They are imposters. You have seen in the last section that virtual functions enable functions of the same signature to take on different functionality when they are redefined in derived classes. It is this capability, to have different functionality at various points in the hierarchical tree, that is described as *polymorphism*.

In C++, functions must be flagged as virtual to be polymorphic functions.

A Custom-Built Class for All Occasions

As a working example, I will demonstrate a widely used university model that describes a sequence. A *sequence* in this context is a means of storing and manipulating data. The favorites are

➤ The STACK

➤ The QUEUE

➤ The LIST

➤ The DEQUE

Say It in Greek

Polymorphism is derived from the Greek word *poly*, meaning *many*, and *morph* means *shape*. So polymorphism means *of many shapes*. This is certainly true of virtual functions because many functions will have the same signature but different characteristics, depending on where they are defined in the hierarchical tree.

We shall examine these sequences (you have already met this creature) and find their common functionality. We shall incorporate the common features into an abstract class and inherit these features to create a custom STACK and a custom QUEUE.

The Sequence in a Q, the Sequence in a STACK

To get a foothold, let's take a look at the specification of a queue. I will revert to my earlier spelling of Q from this point on. Aren't programmers lazy?

A Q has the following features:

➤ A new Q will be empty.

➤ The Q will hold up to nine characters.

➤ Any new character can be added only to the back of the Q.

May I Have a Polymorphic Stack, Please?

Yup, no problem. When you inherit the sequence, you will redefine some of its functions. You will then own your very own polymorphic stack.

➤ Data can leave only from the front of the Q.

➤ You can view the entire Q. A message will be shown if the Q is empty.

➤ An error message will be shown if an attempt is made to add more than nine characters to the Q.

Now let's take a look at the specification for a STACK. A STACK has the following features:

➤ A new STACK will be empty.

➤ The STACK will hold up to nine characters.

➤ Any new character can be added only to the top of the STACK.

➤ Data can leave only from the top of the STACK.

➤ You can view only the top of the STACK. A message will be shown if the STACK is empty.

➤ An error message will be shown if an attempt is made to add more than nine characters to the STACK.

On examination of the two sequences, you can see that they have many similarities and some differences. It makes sense for a programmer to code the common features only once and then through inheritance customize them for specialization. And that's what abstract classes are for. Now isn't that a coincidence!

How to Be Common

When you examine the two sequences, the following items are obviously in common, if not identical.

1. A new STACK will be empty.

1. A new Q will be empty.

2. The STACK will hold up to nine characters.

2. The Q will hold up to nine characters.

6. An error message will be shown an attempt is made to add more than nine characters to the STACK.

6. An error message will be shown if an attempt is made to add more than nine characters to the STACK.

How to Be Unique

Having extracted the common features from the specification, you are left with the three features that make the STACK different from the Q.

3. Any new character can be added only to the top of the STACK.

3. Any new character can be added only to the back of the Q.

4. Data can leave only from the top of the STACK.

4. Data can leave only from the front of the Q.

5. You can view the entire Q. A message will be shown if the Q is empty.

5. You can view only the top of the STACK. A message will be shown if the STACK is empty.

Analyst Programmers Are Paid for Doing This

Having done this analysis, it should be obvious to you that items 1, 2, and 6 are the same thing and are prime candidates for inclusion in an abstract class. And so it shall be. I'm going to show you a trick at this point. If we are really crafty, we can cheat even more and bring another piece of functionality into the abstract class. Here is my cheat.

If you examine item 3, it says that a character joins at the top of the STACK, whereas a character joins at the back of the Q. In practice, you are placing the character at the next empty element of the array. They are actually the same action and can be coded as such in the abstract class.

So now you have four sections of the specification that you will code into the abstract class. For convenience, you will code it into a header file and inherit the class into the STACK program later on. Even later, later on you will inherit it into the Q program.

Do you remember how to create a header file? Open a new edit window, type in the text, and save it as Sequence.h—nothing for a programmer of your experience to lose sleep over, is it?

```
// Sequence.h
// AN ABSTRACT CLASS
// IN A HEADER FILE.

#include <iostream.h>

class SEQUENCE {
```

```
            protected:
                int back;
                char data[10];
            public:

                virtual void POKE(char ch);
                virtual void POP(void) = 0;
                virtual void PEEK(void) = 0;
                SEQUENCE();
            };

SEQUENCE::SEQUENCE()
{
    back = 0;
}


void SEQUENCE::POKE(char ch)
{
    if (back < 9)
    {
        back++;
        data[back] = ch;
        cout << endl;
    }
    else
        cout << endl << "SORRY - FULL"
            << endl << endl;
}
```

How Do You Know the Code Works?

Trust me, it does. But if you really want to test it, here's what you do. Write a short
`main()` program that contains `#include "sequence.h"`. Don't forget that
Sequence.h and your program must be in the same directory. In the body of your
program, create a sequence object. When you compile the program, you should
get an error message saying `Cannot create instance of abstract class` or
something similar. Why? Because you cannot create an instance of an abstract class,
as I told you in the first paragraph of this chapter. Now do you believe me?
Actually, it does work because I stole it from Listing 19.8 in Chapter 19.

The sequence code is very similar to the Q program that you met in Chapter 19. It is an array-based implementation with a data member to mark the top of the array. I have named three member functions POKE, POP, and PEEK. Finally, there is a constructor whose job it is to initialize an empty sequence. When you inherit the SEQUENCE class, you must provide implementations for POP and PEEK.

Inheritance Rears Its Ugly Head Again

Now that you have the header file that contains the abstract base class, it's time to write your STACK program. The task is to inherit the SEQUENCE and implement the pure virtual functions that it contains. You need to override the functions POP and PEEK, and that will enable you to compile and create a STACK object. I know I keep going on about this, but make sure that the sequence header file and your program are in the same directory. I've had lots of experience with students who forget to do this and then blame everyone and everything except themselves.

Here is the inheritance model of the STACK.

The Inheritance of MyStack

First, you create a new class called MyStack, which inherits from SEQUENCE. Notice that I have declared POP and PEEK without setting them to zero in this derived class. They are no longer pure, and the class can be used to create a MyStack object.

```
class MyStack : public SEQUENCE {
                public:
                    MyStack();
                    void POP(void);
                    void PEEK(void);
                };
```

Popping the Stack

Having declared POP to be not pure, you must now define it. This is the point at which you are customizing SEQUENCE for a specialist implementation. You will make it into a STACK. To remove a character from the stack, you just move the top of the stack down one. This is implemented by decrementing the member function back.

```
void MyStack::POP(void)
{
    if (back > 0)

    {
        back--;
    }
    else
    {
        cout << endl << "STACK IS EMPTY"; cout << endl << endl;
    }
}
```

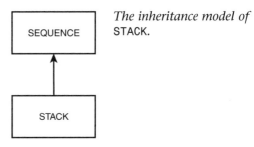

The inheritance model of STACK.

Taking a Peek

The specification tells us that we can view only the character on the top of the STACK. The inherited data member back points to that item, so it's just a question of accessing the array at that element. Because an empty stack is flagged by back being equal to zero, you must first check for that condition and then issue a message if the empty case proves true.

```
void MyStack::PEEK(void)
{
    if (back == 0)
    {
        cout << endl << "STACK IS EMPTY";
        cout << endl << endl;
    }
    else
    {
        cout << endl << data[back];
        cout << endl << endl;
    }
}
```

303

Constructing *MyStack* from an Inheritance

The `MyStack` constructor is easy. All it does is call the `SEQUENCE` constructor, which in turn sets the data member back to zero, and as I've just said, zero signifies an empty `SEQUENCE`. Our stack is constructed and empty, and just to show itself to the world, it issues an announcement: `STACK CREATED`.

```
MyStack::MyStack() : SEQUENCE()
{
    cout << "STACK CREATED" << endl << endl;
}
```

STACK the Program On the Run

All is in place. All is ready. Have you forgotten anything?

You've probably noticed that the menu function is the same as the one in Listing 19.8 in Chapter 19. Once again, guilty. I did hack it. My defense: That's what good programmers do.

Psst! What About the Header File?

Don't forget to copy Sequence.h into the same directory as your program.

All Together Now

Just in case you are having trouble with separate files, as in the preceding chapter, I've combined the codes into a single file in Appendix B, on the CD-ROM. It's under Listing B.4. Use it only if you cannot get Listing 22.1 to combine with the Sequence.h file or if you want to inspect the entire code for educational purposes.

Listing 22.1 The Implementation of a STACK, Based on the SEQUENCE Abstract Class

```
#include <iostream.h>
#include <stdlib.h>
#include "Sequence.h"

class MyStack : public SEQUENCE {
                              public:
                                    MyStack();
                                    void POP(void);
                                    void PEEK(void);
                              };

void MyStack::POP(void)
{
    if (back > 0)
    {
        back--;
    }
    else
    {
        cout << endl << "STACK IS EMPTY";
        cout << endl << endl;
    }
}

void MyStack::PEEK(void)
{
    if (back == 0)
    {
        cout << endl << "STACK IS EMPTY";
        cout << endl << endl;
    }
    else
    {
        cout << endl << data[back];
        cout << endl << endl;
    }
}

MyStack::MyStack() : SEQUENCE()
{
    cout << "STACK CREATED" << endl << endl;
}
```

continues

305

Listing 1.3 This is an example of LH

Listing 22.1 The Implementation of a STACK, Based on the SEQUENCE Abstract Class CONTINUED

```
char menu(void);

main()
{
    char ch;
    char moby;

    MyStack S;
    while (1)
    {
        ch = menu();
        switch(ch)
        {
            case '1' : cout << "Enter the character : ";
                       cin >> moby;
                       S.POKE(moby);
                       break;
            case '2' : S.POP();
                       break;
            case '3' : S.PEEK();
                       break;
            case '4' : exit(0);
        }
    }   return(0);
}

char menu(void)
{
    char choice;

    cout << "1...Join the STACK" << endl;
    cout << "2...Leave the STACK" << endl;
    cout << "3...Show the STACK" << endl;
    cout << "4...Quit the program" << endl << endl;
    cout << "Enter your choice : ";
    cin >> choice;
    return (choice);
}
```

STACK the STACK

Play with Listing 22.1 and try it in extreme conditions. By this I mean try to PEEK when it's empty and full. Try to POKE when it is full; try to POP when it is empty. If you want to be an analyst programmer, you will have to anticipate these extreme conditions for your programs. You document them in a test plan and then test the program. A good test plan will prove or disprove the validity of a program. I don't want to sound cynical here, but you should never allow programmers to test their own programs. Why? Because they cheat.

From a STACK to a Q (Sounds like a Country Western Song)

You are now going to implement the Q from the SEQUENCE abstract class. Again, all you need to do is inherit the class and provide specific functionality to the POP and PEEK member functions.

Here is the inheritance model of the Q.

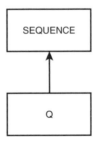

The inheritance model of Q.

Inheritance: Get in the Q

You create a new class, called Q, that inherits from SEQUENCE. Just as before, I have declared POP and PEEK without setting them to zero in this derived class. They are no longer pure, and the class can be used to create a Q object.

```
class MyQ : public SEQUENCE   {
                    public:
                        MyQ();
                        void POP(void);
                        void PEEK(void);
                    };
```

POP the Q

One of the two big differences between a STACK and a Q is the way data leaves the SEQUENCE. In a STACK implementation, you simply knock off the top element and leave the rest of the array unchanged. In a Q, you remove the data in the bottom element and shuffle any data above it down one place. How to achieve this is discussed in Chapter 19, so I hope you remember the theory. If not, stand chastised and read it again. Just kidding. Here's the code fragment:

```
void MyQ::POP(void)
{
    int index;
    if (back > 0)
    {
        for (index = 1; index < back; index++)
        {
            data[index] = data[index + 1];
            cout << endl;
        }
        back--;
    }
    else
    {
        cout << endl << "Q IS EMPTY";
        cout << endl << endl;
    }
}
```

PEEK the Q

This is the second major difference between a STACK and a Q. In a STACK, you only ever see the top element; in a Q, you see the entire contents. Again, the theory of this code fragment is discussed in Chapter 20. What you are doing here is learning the theory of abstract classes and how to override pure virtual functions.

```
void MyQ::PEEK(void)
{
    int x;
    if (back == 0)
    {
        cout << endl << "Q IS EMPTY";
        cout << endl << endl;
    }
    else
    {
        for (x = 1; x <= back; x++)
        {
            cout << endl << data[x] << TAB;
        }
        cout << endl << endl;
    }
}
```

Constructing Q from an Inheritance

Just as in the STACK, all you do is use the Q constructor to call the SEQUENCE constructor. Once again, this initializes an empty Q and provides an announcement to the world.

```
MyQ::MyQ() : SEQUENCE()
{
    cout << "Q CREATED" << endl << endl;
}
```

The Q on the Run

All is in place, all is ready, but have you forgotten something again?

Psst! What About the Header File?

Don't forget to copy Sequence.h into the same directory as your program. This really is déjà vu.

If you are still having trouble with separate files, I've combined the Q codes into a single file in Appendix B. It's under Listing B.5. Use it only to inspect the entire code for educational purposes.

Listing 22.2   The Implementation of a Q, Based on the SEQUENCE Abstract Class

```
#include <iostream.h>
#include <stdlib.h>
#include "Sequence.h"

#define TAB '\t'

class MyQ : public SEQUENCE    {
                            public:
                                MyQ();
                                void POP(void);
                                void PEEK(void);
                            };

void MyQ::POP(void)
{
    int index;

    if (back > 0)
    {
        for (index = 1; index < back; index++)
        {
            data[index] = data[index + 1];
            cout << endl;
        }
        back--;
    }
    else
    {
        cout << endl << "Q IS EMPTY";
        cout << endl << endl;
    }
}

void MyQ::PEEK(void)
{
    int x;

    if (back == 0)
```

```
        {
            cout << endl << "Q IS EMPTY";
            cout << endl << endl;
        }
        else
        {
            for (x = 1; x <= back; x++)
            {
                cout << endl << data[x] << TAB;
            }
            cout << endl << endl;
        }
    }

MyQ::MyQ() : SEQUENCE()
{
    cout << "Q CREATED" << endl << endl;
}

char menu(void);

main()
{
    char ch;
    char shark;

    MyQ Q;
    while (1)
    {
        ch = menu();
        switch(ch)
        {
            case '1' : cout <<  "Enter the character : ";
                       cin >> shark;
                       Q.POKE(shark);
                       break;
            case '2' : Q.POP();
                       break;

            case '3' : Q.PEEK();
                       break;
            case '4' : exit(0);
        }
    }
```

continues

311

Listing 22.2   The Implementation of a Q, Based on the SEQUENCE Abstract Class CONTINUED

```
    return(0);
    }

char menu(void)
{
    char choice;

    cout << "1...Join the Q" << endl;
    cout << "2...Leave the Q" << endl;
    cout << "3...Show the Q" << endl;
    cout << "4...Quit the program" << endl << endl;
    cout << "Enter your choice : ";
    cin >> choice;
    return (choice);
}
```

Break the Q

Draw up a test plan to examine the Q in normal and extreme conditions. Verify that it works correctly. This is a challenge to see how good my programming really is.

The Counter Challenge

I challenged you to verify my Q code. Now I'm going to challenge you to write two more programs based on the abstract SEQUENCE class. All the information required is in this book, and I've written the bulk of the code in the abstract SEQUENCE class already. You have no excuses, so don't let me down.

The List Challenge

The specification for a LIST is the following:

➤ A new LIST will be empty.

➤ The LIST will hold up to nine characters.

➤ Any new character can be added only to the back of the LIST.

➤ Data can leave the LIST from any place in the array by the user selecting an array element (element, not offset). Shuffling the higher-placed elements down one place will fill the empty element. The elements below will remain unchanged.

➤ You can view the entire LIST. A message will be shown if the LIST is empty.

➤ An error message will be shown if an attempt is made to add more than nine characters to the LIST.

Can you write this program? Don't forget that Sequence.h must be in the same directory as your program.

The Deque Challenge

➤ A new DEQUE will be empty.

➤ The DEQUE will hold up to nine characters.

➤ Any new character can be added to the front or the back of the DEQUE. (*Hint*: Start off by filling at the center of the array.)

➤ Data can leave the DEQUE from either the top or the bottom.

➤ You can view only the top and bottom elements of the DEQUE. If only one item is in the DEQUE, the top and bottom will be the same. A message will be shown if the DEQUE is empty.

➤ An error message will be shown if an attempt is made to add more than nine characters to the DEQUE.

The Least You Need to Know

➤ The abstract class is a design tool that enables core functionality to be defined, leaving the unique, program-specific functionality to be defined later.

➤ An abstract class has at least one pure virtual member function in its class definition.

➤ Abstract classes can be used only as a base class to create derived classes.

➤ Any class that contains a pure virtual function cannot be used to create an object.

➤ A derived class must override the pure virtual member functions of an abstract class to give them functionality. Only then can an object of the derived class be created.

➤ A virtual member function is defined in a base class by prefixing the function prototype with the word `virtual`.

➤ Derived classes share only one instance of the virtual function and thus avoid ambiguity. That one definition is used throughout the hierarchical tree.

➤ A pure virtual function is set to zero, and you do not supply a definition for it, as shown here:

```
virtual void f1() = 0;
```

- ➤ When a function is declared as virtual in the base class, it remains virtual in all derived classes. You are free to include or omit the word `virtual` in the redefinition of the member function.
- ➤ Polymorphism is the capability of a member function to have different functionality at various points in the hierarchical tree. The one that is used is the one most appropriate to the object to which it belongs.

Chapter 23

Multiple Inheritance! Even More Things for Free

Where the Paths Unite

You saw properties being passed on through inheritance in Chapter 21, "Inheritance! OO, Things for Free." Now you take another step along the road to OOP perfection and investigate multiple inheritance. *Multiple inheritance* is the art of bringing two or more classes into a single class and thus combining their properties. I give a brief example of this in the last chapter when I describe the hierarchical diagram of the iostream.h library. In this chapter, you will build your own multiple inheritance program, as well as get some more practice at plain old inheritance.

A Radio/Cassette Player Analogy

In Chapter 19, "An Introduction to Object-Oriented Programming: A Step-by-Step Guide for the Terrified," I made the analogy of a class being like a circuit diagram of a television and an object being the equivalent of building that television.

I made the comparison that adding extra functionality to the circuit is the equivalent of inheritance.

It is only fitting that we take things one step further when dealing with multiple inheritance. The next diagram shows a separate circuit diagram for the radio and a separate circuit diagram for the cassette player. When you join them, you end up with a single circuit diagram that has the functionality of both devices. That is multiple inheritance. It follows that if you construct an object from the new circuit diagram, you will create an instance of a radio/cassette player. Because the original circuit diagrams are still available, you can still create a radio and you can still create a cassette player.

The joining of two circuit diagrams to make a radio/cassette player.

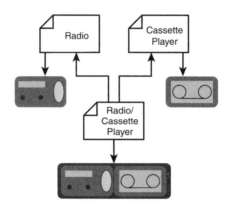

Up the Hierarchical Tree

In the first sample program, you will combine two base classes to create a derived class, called MIX, that has the properties of both of them. The process is very similar to that described in the last chapter except that you are combining class functionality rather than creating a specialized class. Our base classes have the very original names of person, which contains a person's name and age, and tele, which holds the telephone number.

The hierarchical diagram of the inheritance model used in Listing 23.1.

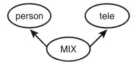

Bringing It All Together, Multiplicity Achieved

As you saw in the last chapter, professional programmers would not keep all their code in one file; they would split it into separate files and link those together. However, for clarity within this example, I will show you the whole thing and then split it up later. That way, you'll know it works and won't be able to claim that the program is faulty. It never ceases to amaze me how students and trainees always blame the computer. It's never them, always the computer.

It's the Computer's Fault

When I was an undergraduate student (and it wasn't that long ago), we had a guy in our group who claimed that he'd never managed to get a program to work. My buddies and I took pity on him and demonstrated the programs we were working on for our next assignment. We had a bit of a laugh, gave some minor criticism to our programs, and finally talked this guy through his program. His program ended up being a decent working effort, so he copied it onto his floppy disk, and off he went, contently singing and happy. The world of the programmer is a wonderful place. The next day in tutorial, he was raising hell and telling everyone what useless programmers we were. Apparently, he took his program back to his own computer and couldn't get it to work. How do programs pick up bugs when they work on one machine, are copied to a floppy disk, and then fail on another machine? Is it the program or the programmer? I'll leave that one for the jury to decide.

Step One

Here is the person class:

```
// base class 1
class person {
        protected:
            char name[20];
            int  age;
        public:
            person(char n[20], int a);
            void Show();
        };
```

Its constructor initializes the name and age member functions, as well as creating the person object, of course.

```
person::person(char n[20], int a)
{
    strcpy(name,n);
    age = a;
}
```

The Show member function just displays the contents of the data members to the screen.

```
void person::Show()
{
cout << "Person name is : " << name << endl;
        cout << "Person age is  : " << age << endl;
}
```

Step Two

Here is the tele class:

```
// base class 2
class tele{
protected:
int number;
                public:
                        tele(int x);
                        void Display();
                };
```

Its constructor just initializes the data member number:

```
                tele::tele(int x)
{
number = x;
}
```

while the member function Display shows the telephone number to the screen:

```
void tele::Display()
{
        cout << "Telephone number is : " << number << endl;
}
```

Step Three

The actual joining of the two base classes is done with the derived class definition. It is virtually the same as "normal" inheritance except that you list more than one class from which you are claiming inheritance.

You also need a constructor whose main purpose is to invoke the constructors of the base classes and pass on any relevant data.

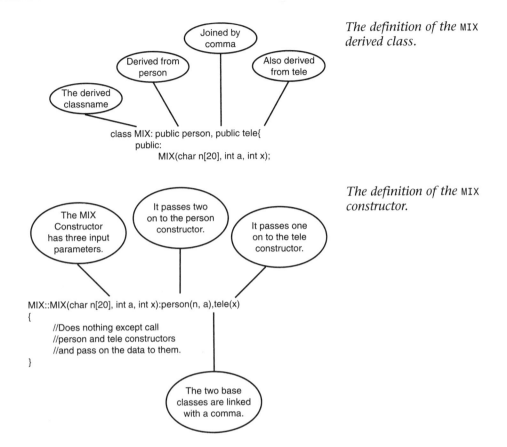

The definition of the MIX derived class.

The definition of the MIX constructor.

The Program

When you run the program, you are concerned with the lines of code in main(). Remember, this is where it is all orchestrated from.

```
main()
{
    MIX p("Paul",21,12345);
    p.Show();
    p.Display();
    return(0);
}
```

You create a MIX object called p. Behind the scenes, the MIX constructor distributes the data to the person and tele constructors where they are assigned to the appropriate data members.

Thanks to inheritance, the p object can access the member functions and data members of both person and tele and does so to output the data buried deep in the class hierarchy.

Be Original

Don't just stick with the data that I put in. Try changing the data and notice the effect. After all, I might be more than 21 when this book is actually published or I might have changed my telephone number.

Try out the program in Listing 23.1 now.

Listing 23.1   A Trivial Example of Multiple Inheritance

```
#include <iostream.h>

#include <string.h>

// base class 1
class person {
            protected:
                char name[20];
                int  age;

            public:
                person(char n[20], int a);
                void Show();
            };

person::person(char n[20], int a)
{
    strcpy(name,n);
    age = a;
}

void person::Show()
{
    cout << "Person name is : " << name << endl;
    cout << "Person age is  : " << age << endl;
}

// base class 2
```

```
class tele  {
        protected:
                int number;
        public:
                tele(int x);
                void Display();
        };

tele::tele(int x)
{
    number = x;
}

void tele::Display()
{
    cout << "Telephone number is : " << number << endl;
}

// Multiple inheritance
// Inherits from both person and tele base classes
class MIX : public person, public tele{
                public:
                        MIX(char n[20], int a, int x);
                ;

MIX::MIX(char n[20], int a, int x):person(n, a),tele(x)
{
    //Does nothing except call
    //person and tele constructors
    //and pass on the data to them.
}

main()
{
  MIX p("Paul",21,12345);
  p.Show();
  p.Display();
  return(0);
}
```

Ambiguity

What I am going to tell you now is widely regarded as bad teaching practice. I am going to tell you what not to do. I am emphasizing the no-can-do instead of the can-do, so be warned. I feel I must tell you about this problem in case you fall (and you will) into the ambiguity trap.

It is quite possible that two programmers writing separate classes could use the same name for a public member function. If you inherit both these classes and call one of those member functions from the derived class, you have a problem. The compiler doesn't know which one you are calling and grinds to a halt. The problem is shown in the next diagram.

One way around this is to write your own specification for these member functions, with the same name. You should declare it as a public member function in the derived class specification. Now when you call the member function, the one in the derived class overrides the ones in the base classes, and all is well. The ambiguity is avoided. The solution is shown in the next diagram.

The wrong way to do it.

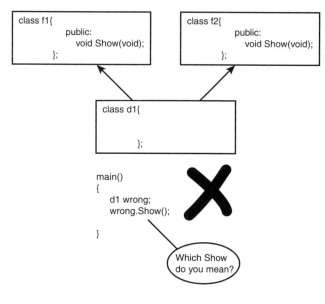

The right way to do it.

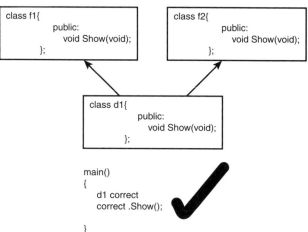

Okay, so we've covered the basic theory of multiple inheritance, and it doesn't sound too bad. In the next few sections, I'll call a time out and look at a totally unrelated subject. But don't relax—I'm not letting you off the hook yet. We shall return to inheritance later in this chapter.

Some Bitwise Wisdom

We've examined some pretty high-level concepts lately, so it's time for some fun. I'm going to introduce you to some low-level stuff known as *bitwise operations*.

Electronic Engineers, Read This!

Most modern high-level languages do not access the electronics of the machine; they shield the programmer from the workings of the computer. I have worked with electronic engineers on many occasions, and they think that high-level computer programmers are wimps. To them, the only language worth using is assembly language or even machine code. Urgh, sends shivers down the spine!

However, C++ actually lets the programmer play with binary numbers, and for this very reason, I've heard these electronic people admit that C++ is possibly okay. If you are interested in electronic input/output for data acquisition, several companies provide cards that plug into the expansion slots of your PC. Along with the cards come additional libraries to include commands in your C++ program. You just plug them in, use the library, and bingo, your PC can make lights flash or a robot do robotic things.

Ultimately, all modern-day digital computers work on a low-level machine code language that is made up of electrical pulses of two relative states, high or low. The high state is referred to as *logic 1* and the low state as *logic 0*. These voltage combinations of 0s and 1s can be modeled by a branch of mathematics based on binary numbers, which also have only two states, namely 0s and 1s. It is beyond the scope of this book to delve into binary number systems (some excellent books are already available). However, I will explain the relevant items without any form of mathematical proof normally associated with this topic. I bet you are pleased about that.

To get us started, I will give you the set of binary codes that a computer would use to represent numbers that we humans would recognize. I will also introduce you to a number system known as *hexadecimal* or *hex*, as it is more often known.

A *Bit* at a Time

The first thing to remember is that a single 0 or a single 1 is known as a *bit*. Remember this fact!

DENARY	BINARY	HEX
0	0000	0
1	0001	1
2	0010	2
3	0011	3
4	0100	4
5	0101	5
6	0110	6
7	0111	7
8	1000	8
9	1001	9
10	1010	A
11	1011	B
12	1100	C
13	1101	D
14	1110	E
15	1111	F

Hex to the Rescue

It is extremely difficult for us humans to deal with binary numbers, so we introduce hex as a shorthand to aid readability.

By convention, the machine code is arranged into groups of four bits, giving 16 different states. The hex shorthand enables us to represent these 16 states by a single digit. I must emphasize that the shorthand is for our benefit because the computer does not understand hex. It understands only binary voltage levels.

The C++ programming language offers a wide range of operations that enable the programmer to work at machine level, giving easy access to external machine control, and so on. It is an ideal language for engineering.

By sending a group of voltages to an output port, a program can easily control external machinery such as a robot or a lathe. The external machinery can also send voltages to an input port and tell a program the state of play outside the computer. This is known as *computer interfacing*.

Once again, some good books are available on this subject. I will discuss only how to manipulate the bits inside the machine. A form of input/output is discussed in Chapter 18, "Don't Lose Your Data: Get a Handle on File Handling," when we covered file handling and sent data to the disk drive. The basic technique is the same for any input/output device.

Get Your Teeth Around This

Four bits make a *nybble*, two nybbles make a *byte*. Are you feeling hungry yet?

Bitwise Operations

In Chapter 17, "Not to Be Outdone, Meet Overloaded Functions," I discussed logical operators and introduced the concept of truth tables. Take a look at this chapter if you are unsure about it. Logical operators take two operands, compare the truth of them, and depending on the applied function, return false or true. The bitwise operator looks at individual bits within two operands and compares the corresponding bits within them, not the operand as a whole. For the purposes of this discussion, I am going to give only nybble-size examples, but they can easily be scaled up to 8, 16, or 32 bits if you so desire.

The Bitwise AND

Supposing that you have two variables called A and B. Each is composed of 4 bits, and they have the following binary values:

A = 1111

B = 0011

You look down the columns where they line up, and you apply the rules of the bitwise AND truth table. The rule is that Q is 1 only if both A and B are 1. If either or both A and B are 0, then Q is 0. In the right column, A = 1 and B = 1. Therefore, the result for that column is 1. Repeat this process until all bits have been considered; the result is shown in the figure.

The bitwise AND operator.

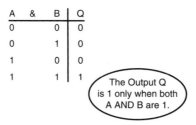

A	&	B	Q
0		0	0
0		1	0
1		0	0
1		1	1

The Output Q is 1 only when both A AND B are 1.

Evaluating a 4-bit AND operation.

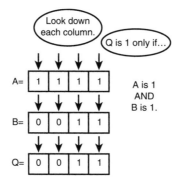

Look down each column.

Q is 1 only if...

A= 1 1 1 1

A is 1 AND B is 1.

B= 0 0 1 1

Q= 0 0 1 1

The Bitwise OR

Suppose that A and B have the same values as in the AND example; the following figure is true.

The bitwise OR operator.

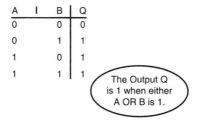

A	I	B	Q
0		0	0
0		1	1
1		0	1
1		1	1

The Output Q is 1 when either A OR B is 1.

Once again, looking down the columns, you compare the values and read off the bitwise OR truth table to establish the result.

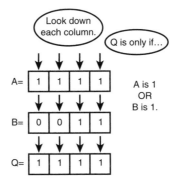

Evaluating a 4-bit OR operation.

A Binary Display

Okay, so the electronic eggheads have had their day. Let's move on to tangible things like computer programs, OOP, and classes. Until now, we have displayed the "normal" numbers onscreen. Now it's time to show those eggheads a thing or two about real computing. We shall display binary numbers onscreen and write an OOP program at the same time. I shall describe this program in a little detail because the rest of the chapter relies on these binary numbers.

Classes in Binary

You create a class called BINARY. You've seen this process many times before. Do you remember what *protected* means? Yes, you've guessed it, inheritance is likely to creep in later on. On the same issue, you will probably spot a new keyword creeping in. This word is virtual and also has to do with inheritance. I shall defer discussion of this topic until later in the chapter, so for the moment, just use it. It doesn't make any difference whatsoever to the early programs.

So I Am a Mathematician After All!

An *algorithm* is a rule for solving a mathematical problem in a finite number of steps. All pieces of computer code that solve a problem are actually algorithms.

The actual ShowBinary member function is complex and is based on a factorization algorithm. It is used to convert an unsigned integer value into binary and display it to the screen. Go on, give it a try. Listing 23.2 uses the value of 9 as a piece of test data, so the screen output is

```
1001
```

If you don't believe me, look at the conversion table earlier in this chapter.

Listing 23.2   This Program Proves the Technology

```cpp
// Display a binary number to the screen
#include <iostream.h>

class BINARY    {
                    protected:
                        unsigned int result;
                    public:
                        void GetData(unsigned int r);
                        virtual void ShowBinary();
                };

void BINARY::GetData(unsigned int r)
{
    result = r;
}


// We are testing just 4-bit numbers here
void BINARY::ShowBinary(void)
{
    int index;
    unsigned int factor;
    unsigned int n;

    n = result;
    factor = 8;                     // VALUE OF MSB
    for (index = 0; index < 4; index++)
    {
        if (n < factor)            // IS n LESS THAN MSB
        {
            cout << "0";           // BIT MUST BE ZERO
        }
        else
        {
            cout << "1";           // BIT MUST BE ONE
            n = n-factor;          // DISCARD THAT AMOUNT
        }
        factor = factor/2;         // TEST NEXT WEIGHTING
    }
    cout << endl;
}

main()
{
    BINARY test;
    test.GetData(9);
    test.ShowBinary();
    return(0);
}
```

Did you notice anything special about Listing 23.2? No?! Okay, here's a clue. Take a look at the constructor definition. What?! It hasn't got one? Oh yes it has. Don't forget that the compiler always creates a default constructor if none is specified. I haven't been lazy here. The program didn't require one, and apart from that, I am planning ahead for later in the chapter.

How to Join the 32-Bit Club

The `ShowBinary` code that displays four-bit binary numbers is for demonstration purposes only, and I will stick with it in the next few programs. However, if you want to make it really useful and display a full 32-bit unsigned integer value, you can make the following changes:

1. Change

```
factor = 8;
```

to

```
factor = 2,147,483,648
```

2. Change

```
for (index = 0; index < 4; index++)
```

to

```
for (index = 0; index < 32; index++)
```

Now you are a fully functional 32-bit binary programmer. If you run the program with the test data of 10, you will get a full 32-bit output:

```
00000000000000000000000000001010
```

Now that you have proved the concept and know that the BINARY program works, you are going to be professional. You are going to separate the useful BINARY class from the test program and create a `binary.h` header file that you can use in the rest of the programs in this chapter. Listing 23.3 shows the code required to create the header file. Here are the steps involved:

1. Open a new edit window.
2. Cut and paste the code from Listing 23.2.
3. Save the file as `binary.h`

Listing 23.3   The Binary Header File Containing the Binary Base Class

```
// Display a binary number to the screen
#include <iostream.h>

class BINARY   {
                protected:
                    unsigned int result;
                public:
                    void GetData(unsigned int r);
                    virtual void ShowBinary();
            };

void BINARY::GetData(unsigned int r)
{
    result = r;
}

// We are testing just 4-bit numbers here
void BINARY::ShowBinary(void)
{
    int index;
    unsigned int factor;
    unsigned int n;

    n = result;
    factor = 8;                     // VALUE OF MSB
    for (index = 0; index < 4; index++)
    {
        if (n < factor)         // IS n LESS THAN MSB
        {
            cout << "0";        // BIT MUST BE ZERO
        }
        else
        {
            cout << "1";        // BIT MUST BE ONE
            n = n-factor;       // DISCARD THAT AMOUNT
        }
        factor = factor/2;      // TEST NEXT WEIGHTING
    }
    cout << endl;
}
```

Don't Lose Your Head

The file `binary.h` that you have created is just text. Remember that you cannot run it on its own. It must be linked into a C++ program that has a `main()`, by the use of the `#include "binary.h"` directive. In addition, the `binary.h` file must be in the same directory as the program that uses it. This is one of the most common mistakes made. The compiler will issue an error saying something like `cannot open binary.h` if it cannot find the file in the correct location. Please take great care when dealing with separate header files.

OR Your Bits

Now you are in a position to write a program that can perform the OR function. You have already done the hard work and created the `binary.h` header with the nasty long algorithm that displays the bits. The header file is included in the program with the line `#include "binary.h"`, so don't forget to ensure that it's in the same directory as this program. Take a look at this code fragment; you should recognize inheritance taking place. Here is the inheritance model you are working with.

The inheritance model of Listing 23.4.

A Classy Operator

Don't confuse the OR class with the OR operator; they are not the same thing. The bitwise OR operator has the symbol ¦ and is part of the C++ programming language. You are writing your very own OR class, which contains data members and member functions that will use the bitwise OR operation to find the result of ORing two binary numbers.

The OR class inherits from BINARY; it adds two new data members, a new member function, and its own constructor.

```
class OR: public BINARY  {
            protected:
                  unsigned int p;
                  unsigned int q;
            public:
                  OR(unsigned int a, unsigned int b);
                  void CalcOR(void);
            };
```

The constructor takes two values (the operands) from the outside world and assigns them to its data members.

```
OR::OR(unsigned int a, unsigned int b)
{
      p = a;
      q = b;
}
```

What's in a Bar?

The bitwise OR has only a single bar (on the keyboard, it's down in the bottom-left corner). The bitwise OR looks at individual bits within an operand. The logical OR has two bars and is used to establish the combined truth of two operands. A subtle but important distinction.

The actual OR function is a single liner that takes the two operands, ORs them, and places the outcome in result.

```
void OR::CalcOR(void)
{
      result = p | q;
}
```

Okay, let's try it out. My example, in Listing 23.4, uses the values 8 and 1, which gives a screen output like this ("Why?!" I hear you cry at line one):

```
1001

8 = 1000
1 = 0001

Q = 1001
```

OR is that magic?

When you run the program, try it with several variations of inputs and verify that the truth table is correct.

Listing 23.4   The Bitwise *OR* Function

```
#include <iostream.h>
#include "binary.h"

class OR: public BINARY  {
                protected:
                        unsigned int p;
                        unsigned int q;
                public:
                        OR(unsigned int a, unsigned int b);
                        void CalcOR(void);
                };

OR::OR(unsigned int a, unsigned int b)
{
     p = a;
     q = b;
}

void OR::CalcOR(void)
{
     result = p ¦ q;
}

main()
{
     OR test(8,1);
     test.CalcOR();
     test.ShowBinary();
     return(0);
}
```

AND Your Bits

The process for AND is virtually identical to OR. You inherit from BINARY to create the AND class, and you include the binary.h header in your program. The diagram of the inheritance model shows the similarity.

Listing 23.5 shows the program, so try it now and then take a break. You are about to enter some heavy multiple inheritance concepts after this point. And you thought it was all nice and simple, didn't you.

HELP, I Can't Get the Program to Work!

Okay, it might be that you are doing something fundamentally wrong and I'm not physically there to help you. It might be that you are using an obscure compiler that doesn't allow the inclusion of user-defined header files. I don't know the answer, but I have a solution.

First, DON'T PANIC! Separating the code is a theme that continues throughout the rest of the book, and I can't lose you now. The true professional method is to separate the code just as I have shown you. However, for sound academic reasons, it's good to see all the code in a single program. I have written Appendix B with this in mind. So if you had problems using the binary.h header file, try out Listing B.1 in Appendix B. It's the same program with all the separate bits combined in a single source code, just as you have done in previous chapters.

The inheritance model of Listing 23.5.

The Educational Reason

You can find the full listing that doesn't use separate code in Appendix B, Listing B.2. But remember your alibi: You're using it for sound academic reasons.

Listing 23.5 The Bitwise AND Function

```
#include <iostream.h>
#include "binary.h"

// AND inherits from BINARY
class AND: public BINARY{
                   protected:
                          unsigned int m;
                          unsigned int n;
                   public:
                          AND(int a, int b);
                          void CalcAND(void);
                   };

AND::AND(int a, int b)
{
    m = a;
    n = b;
}


void AND::CalcAND(void)
{
    result = m & n;
}

main()
{
    AND test(9,3);
    test.CalcAND();
    test.ShowBinary();
    return(0);
}
```

Another Classy Operator

Once again, don't confuse the AND class with the AND operator; they are not the same thing. The bitwise AND operator has the symbol & and is part of the C++ programming language. You are writing your very own AND class. It contains data members and member functions that will use the bitwise AND operation to find the result of ANDing two binary numbers.

Multiple Inheritance Rides Again

We are about to embark on a discussion that raises some very interesting dilemmas. I hope that by the end of the discussion you will be saying, "Dead easy, I'm not scared of this multiple inheritance." I said that once.

The Family Tree: Children, Parents, and Grandparent

For an overall picture of where you are going, take a look at the next inheritance model diagram. This is what you shall be working with for the remainder of the chapter.

The inheritance model of the ANDOR *class.*

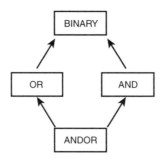

You know that BINARY can be inherited by OR. You know that BINARY can be inherited by AND. How do you know? Because you've done it, and the best way to prove a technology is to make it work in practice. However, when you move into the world of multiple inheritance, you encounter problems. I will guide you through them one at a time with small sections of code. Finally, you will put it all together to produce a full working program.

The Middle Man

The problems associated with multiple inheritance occur in the middle tier of the model. To be consistent with the design strategy, you must create a header file containing the OR class and its definitions. You must also create a header file containing the AND class and its definitions.

Listing 23.6 is the code fragment of OR. Type it in and save it as or.h.

Listing 23.6   The Bitwise OR Header File

```
#include <iostream.h>

#if !defined (BINARY_H)
    #define BINARY_H
    #include "binary.h"
#endif

class OR: virtual public BINARY    {
            protected:
                unsigned int p;
```

```
                    unsigned int q;
            public:
                    OR(unsigned int a, unsigned int b);
                    void CalcOR(void);
            };

OR::OR(unsigned int a, unsigned int b)
{
     p = a;
     q = b;
}

void OR::CalcOR(void)
{
     result = p ¦ q;
}
```

You can do the same for AND in Listing 23.7. Save it as and.h.

Listing 23.7   The Bitwise AND Header File

```
#include <iostream.h>

#if !defined (BINARY_H)
     #define BINARY_H
     #include "binary.h"
#endif

// AND inherits from BINARY
class AND: virtual public BINARY{
            protected:
                    unsigned int m;
                    unsigned int n;
            public:
                    AND(int a, int b);
                    void CalcAND(void);
            };

AND::AND(int a, int b)
{
     m = a;
     n = b;
}

void AND::CalcAND(void)
{
     result = m & n;
}
```

After all that typing, some explanation is in order. Referring back to the inheritance model, you can see that both OR and AND inherit from BINARY and, in doing so, attempt to create a copy of it when you compile the program. This is not allowed and would cause a compilation error. The way to avoid this problem is to use a conditional directive. Here is the code fragment. It checks whether binary.h is defined, and if not, it goes ahead and defines binary.h with #include. If binary.h is defined, it ignores the #include statement. This means that only one copy of binary.h is included, and the compiler is happy.

```
#if !defined (BINARY_H)
     #define BINARY_H
     #include "binary.h"
#endif
```

More Conditions

The #if !defined that you use in Listings 23.6 and 23.7 is called a *preprocessor directive*. A whole family of these directives are used to make source programs easy to change and easy to compile in different execution environments. Directives in the source file tell the compiler to perform specific actions, such as insert the contents of other files into the source file or suppress compilation of a file if it is already defined.

The preprocessor recognizes that the following preprocessor directives are available:

#define	#error	#import	#undef	#elif	#if
#include	#else	#ifdef	#line	#endif	#ifndef
#pragma					

All This Work for Nothing?

In my experience, multiple inheritance is not a widely used tool. However, it is extremely powerful and, in the right context, extremely useful. Both Microsoft and Borland use it in their class libraries. It is worth noting that other OOP languages such as Java do not support multiple inheritance. In fact, it's rumored that Java is C++ with the difficult bits removed.

Preprocessor directives can appear anywhere in your source code, but they apply only to the remainder of the file. Use your C++ help files or manual to learn more about these directives.

The next problem comes when you create the ANDOR class. We have avoided a potential problem by the use of the word virtual. In a nonvirtual model, you inherit BINARY twice, which would cause ambiguities. The potential (and wrong) model would have the following signature and look like this:

```
class OR: public BINARY
class AND: public BINARY
```

The correct way to do it is to declare the inheritance class as virtual, which has the effect of pointing any reference back to the base class rather than making a copy of the base class. This way, ambiguity is avoided because only one instance of the base class actually exists. The virtual inheritance signature and model are shown next.

```
class OR: virtual public BINARY
class AND: virtual public BINARY
```

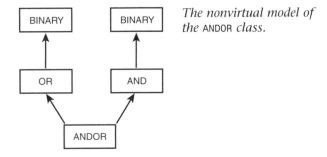

The nonvirtual model of the ANDOR *class.*

Virtually There

Only one small point remains to be discussed before you actually use inheritance. Early on in the bitwise story, I told you to just accept the virtual member function ShowBinary. The reason had to do with, once again, inheritance and ambiguity. The inheritance model shows that the function can live in all four classes, thus causing ambiguity. Like the virtual classes just discussed, declaring a member function virtual avoids these ambiguities and points any reference to it back to the base class.

Now it's program time. Here is Listing 23.8, for the ANDOR class and program.

Children, Parents, and Grandparent, All in One Place

Don't forget to ensure that the following files are all in the same directory. Failure to do so will mean that a compilation error will occur.

Listing23_11

binary.h

and.h

or.h

The Educational Reason Again

You can find the full listing that doesn't use separate code in Appendix B, Listing B.3. But remember our alibi—we're using it for sound academic reasons. This alibi might begin to wear thin, so try to come to terms with separating the code.

Listing 23.8   The Bitwise ANDOR Class

```
// Multiple inheritance
// from several base classes

#include <iostream.h>
#include "or.h"
#include "and.h"

class ANDOR: public OR, public AND{
    public:
          ANDOR(unsigned int a, unsigned int b);
    };

ANDOR::ANDOR(unsigned int a,
unsigned int b):AND(a,b),OR(a,b)
{

}

main()
{
    unsigned int one = 9;
    unsigned int two = 3;

    ANDOR test1(one,two);
    test1.CalcOR();
    test1.ShowBinary();
    ANDOR test2(one,two);
    test2.CalcAND();
    test2.ShowBinary();
    return(0);
}
```

Hexadecimal: Sixteen Steps to Wisdom

I've worked you very hard in this chapter, and I'm sure you realize it. You will be pleased to hear that it doesn't get much harder than this because you've been working with some very complicated concepts. I have tried to use simple examples, but even those were quite a job. Nonetheless, well done, I'm proud of you for getting this far. As a reward, I'm going to show you how to display hexadecimal numbers to the screen, and this really is easy, I promise. Listing 23.9 shows how to do it and looks trivial compared to what you have been doing. Only one line is new to you, and its purpose in life is to set the computer to hexadecimal mode.

Test to Destruction

I've used values of 9 and 3 in my program, but you should try lots of different values to see the effect. Have you upgraded ShowBinary to 32 bits yet? Go on, I dare you!

```
cout.setf(ios::hex);
```

And that's it! Try the program, relax, and see the numbers 0 1 2 3 4 5 6 7 8 9 a b c d e f appear onscreen.

Listing 23.9   The Hex Display

```
#include <iostream.h>

main()
{
    unsigned int index;

    cout.setf(ios::hex);
    for (index = 0; index < 16; index++)
        cout << index << endl;
    return(0);
}
```

The Least You Need to Know

➤ Multiple inheritance is the art of bringing two or more classes into a single class and thus combining their properties.

➤ If two or more member functions that exist in different base classes have the same signature, an ambiguity will occur when they are inherited into a single class through multiple inheritance.

➤ Where inheritance is likely, member functions should be declared as virtual.

➤ The `virtual` avoids ambiguity by referencing back to the base class where the member function is defined, rather than making a copy of the member function into the derived class.

➤ Preprocessor directives in the source file tell the compiler to perform specific actions such as inserting the contents of other files into the source file or suppressing compilation of a file if it is already defined.

➤ The bitwise operators OR and AND look at individual bits within a variable.

➤ Hexadecimal numbers can be displayed to the screen by using `cout.setf(ios::hex)`.

Index

B

G-H

I

J-L

M

U-V

W-Z

Hey, you've got enough worries.

Don't let IT training be one of them.

Get on the fast track to IT training at InformIT,
your total Information Technology training network.

 | **www.informit.com** |

■ Hundreds of timely articles on dozens of topics ■ Discounts on IT books from all our publishing partners, including Que Publishing ■ Free, unabridged books from the InformIT Free Library ■ "Expert Q&A"—our live, online chat with IT experts ■ Faster, easier certification and training from our Web- or classroom-based training programs ■ Current IT news ■ Software downloads ■ Career-enhancing resources

Using C++

—Rob McGregor

This book provides the essential pieces of C++ programming information needed by beginning to intermediate programmers to execute the most frequently used tasks and functions. Each chapter is a task-oriented module covering a group of related features or tasks full of real-world, practical examples. Get up to speed fast on ANSI/ISO standard C++ without having to learn C first and learn the essential information. This book is jam packed with relevant hands-on examples, rules of thumb, jump tables, and enrichment pointers that teach you C++ concepts and procedures in a fast, compact, and concise manner. Because this book does not focus on any one compiler, you can learn to program in C++ using the compiler of you choice, such as Microsoft Visual C++, Borland C++, or UNIX.

$29.99 USA/$42.95 CDN   *User Level: Beginner–Intermediate*
ISBN: 0-7897-1667-4   *750 pages*

C++ Unleashed

—Jesse Liberty

A comprehensive book to assist a current Visual C++ programmer to the next level. Covers the topics that are most important to developers, including the Visual C++ development system, ActiveX, MAPI, TAPI, ODBC, and more! *C++ Unleashed* also includes information on the Windows architecture and the Win32 API, Microsoft Foundation Classes, memory management, DAO, TCP/IP programming with Winsock, Open GL Graphics Library, Game SDK and the DirectX API, the Registry, and writing international (localized) applications.

$39.99 US/$57.95 CDN   *User Level: Intermediate–Advanced*
ISBN: 0-672-31239-5   *800 pages*

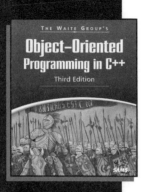

The Waite Group's Object-Oriented Programming in C++, Third Edition

—Robert Lafore

The Waite Group's Object-Oriented Programming in C++, Third Edition continues to build on the successful past performance of previous editions. It gets intermediate programmers up to speed quickly on the latest ANSI/ISO C++ standard and the emerging disciplines of object-oriented design, CRC modeling, Universal Modeling Language (UML), and high-level concepts such as design patterns. Go from simple programming examples straight up to full-fledged object-oriented applications with quick real-world examples, conceptual illustrations, questions and exercises.

$34.99 USA/$32.49 CDN   *User Level: Intermediate*
ISBN: 1-57169-160-X   *850 pages*

The Waite Group's C++ How-To

—Poney Carpenter

The all-new definitive C++ problem-solving resource! *The Waite Group's C++ How-To* presents a rich diversity of examples and techniques for pushing C++ to its limits and beyond. You can quickly and efficiently find specific solutions to real-world problems—simply locate information by task or function and then walk through a series of How-To's to find the solution. Each How-To is graded by complexity level, with information on additional uses and enhancements to fit your needs exactly.

$39.99 USA/36.84 CDN   *User Level: Intermediate–Advanced*
ISBN: 1-57169-159-6   *800 pages*

Add to Your C++ Library Today with the Best Books for Programming, Operating Systems, and New Technologies

To order, visit our Web site at www.mcp.com or fax us at

1-800-835-3202

ISBN	Quantity	Description of Item	Unit Cost	Total Cost
0-7897-1667-4		Using C++	$29.99	
0-672-31239-5		C++ Unleashed	$39.99	
1-57169-160-X		The Waite Group's Object-Oriented Programming in C++, 3E	$34.99	
1-57169-159-6		The Waite Group's C++ How-To	$39.99	
		Shipping and Handling: See information below.		
		TOTAL		

Shipping and Handling

Standard	$5.00
2nd Day	$10.00
Next Day	$17.50
International	$40.00

201 W. 103rd Street, Indianapolis, Indiana 46290   1-800-835-3202 — FAX

What's on the Disc

The companion CD-ROM contains many useful third-party software, plus all the source code from the book.

Windows 95 Installation Instructions

1. Insert the CD-ROM disc into your CD-ROM drive.

2. From the Windows 95 desktop, double-click the My Computer icon.

3. Double-click the icon representing your CD-ROM drive.

4. Double-click the icon titled SETUP.EXE to run the installation program.

5. Installation creates a program group named "Complete Idiot's Guide to C++." This group will contain icons to browse the CD-ROM.

Note

If Windows 95 is installed on your computer and you have the AutoPlay feature enabled, the SETUP.EXE program starts automatically whenever you insert the disc into your CD-ROM drive.

Windows NT Installation Instructions

1. Insert the CD-ROM disc into your CD-ROM drive.

2. From File Manager or Program Manager, choose Run from the File menu.

3. Type <drive>\SETUP.EXE and press Enter, where <drive> corresponds to the drive letter of your CD-ROM. For example, if your CD-ROM is drive D:, type D:\SETUP.EXE and press Enter.

4. Installation creates a program group named "Complete Idiot's Guide to C++." This group will contain icons to browse the CD-ROM.